POVERTY AND SOCIAL EXCLUSION
IN INDIA

POVERTY AND SOCIAL EXCLUSION
IN INDIA

THE WORLD BANK
Washington, D.C.

ISBN: 978-0-8213-8690-3
eISBN: 978-0-8213-8733-7
DOI: 10.1596/978-0-8213-8690-3

Library of Congress Cataloging-in-Publication Data has been requested.

Cover design: Naylor Design

Contents

Tables

Preface and Acknowledgments

This report has been prepared by a team led by Maitreyi Bordia Das (SDV, World Bank), under the guidance of Mansoora Rashid (Sector Manager, SASSP, World Bank) and N. Roberto Zagha (Country Director, India, World Bank).

Core team members are Soumya Kapoor (Independent Consultant), Rinku Murgai (SASEP, World Bank), and Denis Nikitin (SASSP, World Bank). John Prakash Badda (SASSD, World Bank), Gertrude Cooper (SASHD, World Bank), Sujata Pradhan (SASSD, World Bank), and Tanusree Talukdar (SASHD, World Bank) have provided administrative and document layout support.

This report draws on background papers written by the core team members with Gillette Hall (Georgetown Public Policy Institute) and with Puja Vasudeva Dutta (SASSP, World Bank). Individual papers were prepared by Neera Burra (Independent Consultant); Sonalde Desai, James Noon, and Reeve Vanneman (University of Maryland); Amaresh Dubey, Vegard Iversen, Adriaan Kalwij, Bereket Kebede, and Arjan Verschoor (respectively, Jawaharlal Nehru University, University of Manchester, Indian Statistical Institute, University of Utrecht, and University of East Anglia); Iffath Sharif (SASSP, World Bank) and Jeffrey Witsoe (University of Pennsylvania). Early work also drew on data analysis by Kiersten Johnson (ICF Macro) and Pinaki Joddar (Independent Consultant). Fieldwork commissioned for this report resulted in two papers on Dalits by Surinder Jodhka (Jawaharlal Nehru University), and the Dalit chapter heavily draws on these. In addition, the report takes qualitative evidence from the World Bank study, *Moving out of Poverty*. This report has been prepared alongside a parallel World Bank India Poverty Assessment led by Peter Lanjouw (DECRG, World Bank) and Rinku Murgai. The two reports have a few common team members and often draw on common material. Background work for this report also features in the World Bank's *Indigenous Peoples, Poverty, and Development*. The generous financial contributions of the U.K. Department for International Development–India and the Swedish International Development Cooperation Agency are gratefully acknowledged.

Valuable comments during the preparation of the report were provided by Junaid Ahmad (AFTUW, World Bank), Tara Datt (IAS, Joint Secretary, Cabinet Secretariat), A. K. Shiva Kumar (United Nations Children's Fund), Martin Macwan (Navsarjan), Aasha Kapur Mehta (Indian Institute of Public Administration), Dev Nathan (Indian Institute for Human Development), Harry Patrinos (HDNED, World Bank), Kumar Amarendra Narayan Singh (SASSD, World Bank), Shekhar Singh (Centre for Equity Studies), Varun Singh (SASSD, World Bank), and Sukhadeo Thorat (University Grants Commission).

Initial discussions on framing the issues have benefited from the views of an informal advisory group meeting held at the Planning Commission in July 2008 and comprising Drs. B. L. Mungekar (ex-Member, Planning Commission), Surinder Jodhka, Mary John (Centre for Women's Development Studies), and Virginius Xaxa (University of Delhi). The report also benefited from comments received from Mr. Amitabha Bhattacharya (Planning Commission) and Dr. T. K. Oommen (Jawaharlal Nehru University) during the presentation of draft findings to the Planning Commission in April 2010 and from representatives of various ministries and agencies of the government of India at a seminar organized by the Department of Economic Affairs, Ministry of Finance.

The team thanks peer reviewers Alaka Malwade Basu (Cornell University and Jawaharlal Nehru University), Alexandre Marc (SDV, World Bank), and Lant Pritchett (Harvard University) for their comments on a draft of this report and for participating in the Review Meeting. The team also thanks all other participants of the Review Meeting who provided comments. Finally, the team gratefully acknowledges the support and guidance received from Dr. Narendra Jadhav (Member, Planning Commission and National Advisory Council) during the preparation of the report.

The Report has been discussed with the Government of India, but does not necessarily bear their approval for all its contents, especially where the Bank has stated its judgment, opinion, or policy recommendations.

Abbreviations

DHS	Demographic and Health Survey
MGNREGS	Mahatma Gandhi National Rural Employment Guarantee Scheme
NFHS	National Family Health Survey
NSS	National Sample Survey
NTFP	nontimber forest product
OBC	Other Backward Class
PESA	Panchayats Extension to the Scheduled Areas Act
RCH II	Reproductive Child Health Survey II
SC	Scheduled Caste
SHG	self-help group
ST	Scheduled Tribe

1

Overview

In India . . . we must aim at equality. That does not mean and cannot mean that everybody is physically or intellectually or spiritually equal or can be made so. But it does mean equal opportunities for all, and no political, economic or social barrier. . . . It means a faith in humanity and a belief that there is no race or group that cannot advance and make good in its own way, given the chance to do so. It means a realization of the fact that the backwardness or degradation of any group is not due to inherent failings in it, but principally to lack of opportunities and long suppression by other groups.

Jawaharlal Nehru, *The Discovery of India* (1946)

Nehru would have been proud of India's stellar performance in the creation of a new economic system and its self-confidence relative to other nations, though not necessarily of the acquisitive society that goes against the collectivist spirit he espoused (Nehru 1946). There are other developments to be proud of as well. Poverty has declined among all groups; enrollments in schools have increased; health outcomes have improved; and fertility rates in many Indian states now resemble those of developed countries. Moreover, the 73rd and 74th amendments to the Indian Constitution that mandate the devolution of powers and responsibilities to rural *panchayats* (local governments) and urban local municipalities have set the agenda for local ownership of and participation in governance.

In parallel to these positive developments, rising inequality in India has been a subject of concern among policy makers, academics, and activists alike. The recent India poverty assessment of the World Bank (2011) shows that, when inequality is based on income rather than consumption measures, India is not so different relative to the inequality levels recorded in countries such as Brazil and South Africa, countries commonly singled out as global outliers. In other words, if inequality in India is measured on the basis of per capita income, it stands among those countries with the highest recorded inequality rates. The report also decomposes inequality according to differences within and across states, according to urban-rural status, and according to levels of educational attainment.

In our report, we focus on social exclusion, which has its roots in historical divisions along lines of caste, tribe, and the excluded sex, that is, women. These inequalities are more structural in nature and have kept entire groups trapped, unable to take advantage of opportunities that economic growth offers. Culturally rooted systems perpetuate inequality, and, rather than a *culture of poverty* that afflicts disadvantaged groups, it is, in fact, these inequality traps that prevent these groups from breaking out.[1] Therefore,

> cultural factors can play a role in sustaining inter-group *differences* in wealth, status and power. Where the mechanisms involved are self-enforcing this can be considered to be an "inequality trap." Where such an inequality trap exists, it implies that subordinate groups are maintained at least in relative poverty, and that these are associated, in part, with culturally shaped behaviors, including endogenous preferences that can limit the prospects of poorer, or subordinate, groups. (Walton 2007, 2)

So, the question we ask in this report is: who has gained and who has not from India's growth surge?

Well, then, why "social exclusion" and why not "inequality"? This is a question often asked by those who have read early chapters of this report. India is not alone in having social groups that have been traditionally excluded; yet, the structure of the caste system and its ramifications on employment, education, and the rules of social and economic exchange are distinctive and shared only with Nepal. Both caste and gender inequalities are rooted in a philosophical tradition that justifies these through religious texts that provide systematic rules for exclusion. This is what makes these inequalities particularly durable (Tilly 1999). And, for this reason, our report focuses not on inequality, but on exclusion.

The relevance of social exclusion has been incorporated into the development lexicon in a number of ways. The term "social exclusion" was first used in France in the 1970s to distinguish the excluded, who then comprised a wide variety of people: the disabled, suicidal and elderly persons, and abused children, among others (Silver 1994).

Since then, it has been used in the social science literature to distinguish from and add to the concept of poverty and to denote rules of exchange and practices that keep groups out; the term can also sometimes mean different things to different people. Globally, excluded groups tend to be ethnic or religious minorities that, by virtue of their distinct cultural practices, are considered the "other." Social exclusion as a concept perceives the individual as an entity embedded in society and groups. The focus is thus not on outcomes such as increased consumption or income or education alone, but on relations that constrain individuals from achieving these outcomes (de Haan 1997). Nobel Laureate Amartya Sen (1998) calls these the "relational roots of deprivation," whereby membership in a particular group (women, lower castes, indigenous people, or persons with disabilities) limits the "functionings" of individuals to acquire or use their capabilities.

Social exclusion is therefore not about outcomes alone, but about the processes that lead to these outcomes. De Haan (1997), for instance, calls income poverty only one element of social exclusion and refers to its eradication as a part of the broader agenda of social integration. This is because poverty focuses only on an absolute measure of individual well-being: income, consumption, or human development. In contrast, social exclusion focuses on processes or noneconomic means that exclude certain groups from equal access to basic goods and services that, in turn, determine their well-being. As a result, these groups have unequal access to labor markets and social protection mechanisms through formal and informal institutions. Even for people with equal levels of human capital and skills, there appears to be an important element of discrimination that is part of what one would define as social exclusion beyond purely economic considerations. Finally, exclusion involves unequal access to the full exercise and protection of rights and liberties, including, sometimes, the denial of basic human rights.

India is not alone in grappling with issues of social exclusion. While many other countries include similarly excluded minorities, the most relevant empirical evidence and conceptual clarity come from Latin America and the Caribbean and from Eastern Europe. Recently, the flagship report of the Inter-American Development Bank, as part of its annual series, Economic and Social Progress, focused on social exclusion. The report, *Outsiders? The Changing Patterns of Exclusion in Latin America and the Caribbean,* is a regional analysis of ways in which different groups have been excluded during a period of macroeconomic transformation (see Márquez et al. 2007). It documents the economic and welfare costs of exclusion, suggesting that inclusion policies be viewed as an investment rather than as a handout to the least well off in society. Inclusion policies are more than new programs or new institutions to redress past injustices; they imply fundamental changes in the way decisions are made, resources are allocated, and policies are implemented in democratic societies.

In Eastern Europe and Central Asia, the focus on the Roma, for instance, distinguishes between poverty and exclusion (see box 1.1).

Box 1.1 Roma in Europe: A Large Ethnic Minority Excluded at High Cost

The Roma (Gypsies) number about 10 million–12 million people in Europe and represent the largest transnational minority in the region. The most significant representation of Roma is in Central and Eastern European countries, where, overall, the Roma account for the main poverty risk group, suffering from low educational attainment, high unemployment, and poor human development outcomes. One of the most frequent sites of Roma discrimination is the labor market, where even qualified Roma are discriminated against in favor of non-Romani applicants. In general, however, Roma lack sufficient education to participate in the labor market. A recent study across four Central and Eastern European countries—Bulgaria, the Czech Republic, Romania, and Serbia—suggests that as little as 12.5 percent of working-age Roma in Bulgaria, Romania, and Serbia are educated at or above the secondary level (World Bank 2010). The low educational levels are reflected in employment rates of 60 percent, on average, relative to the majority population and, not surprisingly, much lower earnings. The study estimates an annual economic loss of €5.7 billion and a fiscal loss of €2 billion to the four countries as a result of reduced productivity and additional costs incurred to finance the social security of unemployed Roma. In fact, it warns that these losses will only increase over time as younger Roma join the working-age population.

The annual fiscal gains from investing in the education of Roma are significantly higher than the costs incurred even if all Roma people were to be educated (World Bank 2010). The Roma Education Fund is one such initiative, funding specific efforts that can make formal schools more responsive to the needs of Roma children (see Roma Education Fund, at http://www.romaeducationfund.hu/). The emphasis is on giving Romani children a good educational start by focusing on access to preschool and successful transitions into and through primary education. While the impact of the fund is yet to be assessed, funded projects reached about 30,000 Roma students in 2008, among whom 800 graduated.

Source: Roma Education Fund website, http://www.romaeducationfund.hu/.

A 2005 report on multiple deprivations in Serbia and in Montenegro found a strong ethnic dimension to exclusion (World Bank 2005). It found that the Roma population, particularly those Roma residing in settlements, was among the most deprived. A detailed analysis of Nepal has, to a large extent, influenced the manner in which the government collects data and designs policies for people who have been historically and ritually excluded (World Bank 2006). Other important analyses of social exclusion have also influenced multilateral agencies and national governments and have, in turn, been influenced by national debates on the issue (see Baker 2002 on Uruguay, for example). In Brazil, Gacitúa-Marió and Woolcock (2008) find that the poor, especially Brazilians of African descent, have been systematically excluded from the economic growth process, despite laudable improvements in education levels and broad reductions in poverty. This exclusion has persisted (even intensified) over decades.

Addressing social exclusion for its intrinsic value is sufficient reason. Many studies have shown the instrumental value of addressing social exclusion (see Akerlof 1976; Scoville 1991). This report argues, however, that addressing social exclusion because exclusion is morally and socially unjust is reason enough. Moreover, mere ethnic or linguistic heterogeneity is not the same as exclusion. However, if such heterogeneity succeeds in keeping groups out, its exclusionary role plays out in the overall development outcomes of a country or a region. In India, as this report shows, substantially higher mortality among Adivasi children in the 1–4 age-group is affecting India's overall advances in lowering child mortality.

This report does not explore or adhere to any of the myriad formulations of social exclusion, which, by themselves, are conceptually challenging. In some sense, the focus is quite simple. It is based on the established existence of three axes of exclusion in India: caste, tribe, and gender. These axes, particularly caste and gender, have a normative foundation in historically grounded processes and are responsible for a number of unequal outcomes and processes. For instance, norms of son preference, derived from the value of sons in supporting their parents and in undertaking the rituals around parental death, are the foundation for a consistent neglect of female children and women in their reproductive years. Similarly, the occupational logic of caste has meant that the traditionally lower castes remain typed into traditional trades and jobs, making mobility difficult. The geographical and cultural isolation of tribal groups has meant that they are still difficult to reach and that their traditional patterns of landownership are at variance with new developments.

The overarching themes in this report revolve around three inter-related aspects: services, markets, and political spaces. In most countries, excluded groups face discrimination, lower access to health and education, and lower returns to education and assets. They are also more likely to be poor, and this likelihood is passed down through the generations. This is true in India as well, but there are some unique aspects of the Indian trinity of caste, tribe, and gender that lead to different processes and, hence, different outcomes. For instance, unlike countries in Latin America, where excluded groups face higher unemployment rates, open unemployment in India has been historically low, and the real labor market consequence of exclusion is allocation to low-level occupations and lower mobility. Excluded groups are less likely to participate in political processes in other countries as well, but, in India, this is a more nuanced process. Social movements representing excluded groups are much more potent, and affirmative action, which is fairly new in many Latin American countries, has been constitutionally mandated in India since the country's independence. Finally, the representation of excluded groups in political spaces has also been secured, although the chapters in this report show that the impacts of this representation on group welfare have been mixed.

Organization of the Report

The focus. Exclusion operates along multiple and interrelated dimensions. Because addressing them all would be an insurmountable task, this report does not attempt to do so. It does not, for instance, focus on exclusion because of religion or disability, though there is extensive research to show that these are important axes along which people face deprivation. Even in the case of caste, tribe, and gender, the literature is vast, multidisciplinary, and so prolific that it appears to grow every day. The evidence contained in this report builds on this vast academic and activist literature, but the report is by no means an attempt to provide a comprehensive survey of the evidence or even a review of all the issues involved. The fact that each of these groups is highly heterogeneous and that outcomes and processes differ by state and district and by type of caste or tribe makes the task even more challenging and generalizations that much more difficult.

The report focuses on three select groups that face exclusion in India. In addition to Scheduled Tribes (STs) and women, the report discusses outcomes among Scheduled Castes (SCs), even though recent data suggest that Other Backward Classes (OBCs) also fare poorly on some indicators.[2] There are three reasons for this. First, as we show in the report, SCs face structural inequalities that have a ritual backing in historical processes such as untouchability. In contrast, OBCs do not face such historical deprivation. Instead, they comprise— and are defined so by the Constitution of India—as castes that are not SCs, but that are backward in most respects. Second, the issues related to OBCs, who were traditionally peasant cultivators, are different from those affecting outcomes among SCs and merit a separate analysis. Finally, National Sample Survey (NSS) data on OBC outcomes is available only after 1999–2000, meaning that it is difficult to monitor the performance of OBCs along a range of development indicators over time (for example, since 1983, as the report does for other groups). For all these reasons and because of the fact that this report deals with more deeply rooted structural inequalities, the focus is primarily on the outcomes among SCs. However, this should not suggest that caste can be conflated with SCs or that other caste-based issues are not important. Outcomes among OBCs are discussed wherever data are available. Similarly, even though exclusion by religion is significant, the issues affecting Muslims merit an entire analysis, and religion is discussed here only partially (in the context of the labor market).

For each group, too, the focus is on a subset of issues that offer some new insights. For SCs, the report focuses on poor labor market outcomes despite the expansion in education. For STs, it focuses on a distinct disadvantage in survival and on the correlates, which go beyond the health sector and include geographical isolation and the removal of tribals from their traditional lands and assets. For women, it focuses on poor health and survival outcomes, but also the disadvantage of women in the labor market and the vulnerability of women to violence within the family and insecurity in public spaces. Thus, even though there are missing variables in the analysis, it is our hope that, by deeply probing one or two of the kinds of exclusion faced by each category, we provide tools that can be applied to study other forms of exclusion or issues not covered in this report. The format of our analysis is such that we compare outcomes among one subgroup with outcomes among other subgroups. However, since the report also tracks changes in outcomes over time, the finer aspects of development reality are sometimes lost.

Objectives and data. The report is organized around three chapters, in addition to this overview, each one dealing with an excluded group: STs, SCs, and women. The objective is to provide a *diagnostic* of how the three excluded groups under analysis have fared along various development indicators during a period of rapid economic growth in the national economy. In seeking this objective, the report also addresses correlates and the processes that explain how and why these groups have fared the way they have over a period of time.

The report is not intended as a policy document, although some of the empirical findings lend themselves to policy conclusions.

Data for the report come primarily from multiple rounds of national-level household survey data (the NSS, the National Family Health Survey [NFHS], the Reproductive Child Health Survey, and the India Human Development Survey), as well as international surveys (Demographic and Health Surveys and the database of the Population Reference Bureau). Large national data sets, while allowing for national-level and, to some extent, state-level generalizations, do not allow analysis of outcomes below the state level or within group differences and processes. It is well known, for instance, that there is substantial diversity among SCs and STs even within states. This heterogeneity is widely known because of microstudies and ethnographic, anthropological, and journalistic accounts. While there is a rich body of such qualitative work in India, the results provide contextual specificity, but cannot be added up to paint an aggregate picture. Moreover, such studies or accounts generate results that are limited to one tribe, village, or state and cannot be generalized. Nonetheless, we do draw upon such studies, in particular, qualitative work commissioned for this report, to capture underlying processes and triangulate with the quantitative analysis.

A word on usage: the terms "Scheduled Caste (SC)" and "Scheduled Tribe (ST)" come from the Constitution Order passed in 1950, which contains the names of castes and tribes that are earmarked for special treatment, such as reservations in legislation, public sector employment, and government-run educational institutions. However, SCs and STs have taken names that signify both political assertion and a rejection of the previously accepted idioms that reduced them to "reserved categories." For the purposes of the tables and graphs presented in this report, we use the terms "SC" and "ST" because these are standard administrative and survey categories. In the text, we use the terms *Dalits* and *Adivasis* (or tribals) interchangeably with SCs and STs, respectively.

Main Findings

During the period of rapid economic growth, what happened to entrenched group inequalities? Were there ways in which traditionally excluded groups such as SCs, STs, and women broke out of the traps or did the traps trump the opportunities? The report emphasizes that the changes wrought in the 20 years beginning in 1983 were complex, and social groups transformed themselves in different ways in response to new opportunities. For instance, far from being the immutable frame that Weber (1958) seemed to suggest, "caste," in fact, has evolved and mutated. Nonetheless, by no means are we seeing the annihilation of caste, as Ambedkar (1936) exhorted Indians to achieve.

> I still think that after a long and convoluted path, after many a stumble and wrong turn, a different kind of moment seems to be upon us . . . there is a sense of hope across the country, which I believe is universal. There is a momentum for change.
>
> Nandan Nilekani (2008, 484)

Adivasis

The self-preferred term "Adivasi" is commonly translated as "original inhabitants," and literally means *Adi*, beginning or earliest time, and *vasi*, resident of. There is active discussion around the question of "original inhabitant," but this is not directly relevant to our report. According to the 2001 Census, the population of India includes 84.3 million STs, comprising 8.1 percent of the total population of the country. However, the proportion of STs has been increasing over census periods partly because more tribes are being included in the ST category and partly because of higher fertility rates in this category (Maharatna 2005). While the Constitutional Order declared that 212 tribes located in 14 states are STs, the Government of India today identifies 533 tribes as STs, of which 62 are located in the state of Orissa.[3]

Chapter 2 in this report focuses on the Adivasis or STs. In most analyses, this topic is addressed after the Dalits, but we have placed it first for analytical and organizational purposes. There are two reasons for this: tribal groups are not strictly within the caste system, and the bonds of rituals do not affect their relations with the world in general. Also the report shows that outcomes among Adivasis are among the worst, despite considerable variation across places of residence and tribal groupings.

Tribal groups in India are often conflated with castes, and "Scheduled Caste" and "Scheduled Tribe" are sometimes said in the same breath, although they are actually distinct social categories. As André Béteille writes (1998, 187): "Even the best ethnographers [in India] habitually confused tribe with caste, which, on any reasonable assumption, is a different kind of social category." The major difference between SCs and STs is that, while the former were subject to historical, ritualistic discrimination, STs were excluded from the national context because of their physical isolation. Inhabiting topographically inaccessible areas, STs still face difficulties in accessing services such as health care and education. Even though they own more land than SCs, a complex set of contravening forest laws means they are confronted by barriers in selling their produce from the land, perhaps explaining the high poverty rates among STs in rural areas. Most tribals therefore end up migrating, leaving their forest lands to work as casual laborers in urban centers.

The report focuses on two major markers of tribal deprivation: poverty levels, which are higher than the national average and in comparison with other groups (including SCs), and child mortality. We argue that the roots of Adivasi deprivation lie in two main factors. One, their physical segregation renders problematic the delivery to them of services such as health care and education. Two, their traditional dependence on land and forests and their widespread displacement from these areas have changed the nature of the relationship tribals share with their land. This, in part, may help explain rising poverty among STs in some states.

ADIVASIS: MAIN FINDINGS

Despite a decline in poverty rates, Adivasis in 2004–05 were 20 years behind the average. Poverty among STs (Adivasis) has fallen, but the gap between them and the average Indian is large and growing. The poverty headcount index for STs fell by 31 percent between 1983 and 2004–05, compared with a more rapid decline of 35 percent among SCs and an average overall decline in India of 40 percent (table 1.1). In 2004–05, a little less than half the ST population remained in poverty (44 percent), while, nationwide, the poverty rate had been reduced to almost one-quarter of the population (27.5 percent). STs in urban areas fared better than those in rural areas, with a lower poverty rate and steeper reductions since 1983. However, given the low share of tribal population in urban centers, ST poverty rates as a whole remained closer to the rural average. The relatively slower declines in poverty among STs also meant that they were increasingly concentrated in the poorest deciles of the population; their poverty levels in 2004–05 resembled poverty levels experienced by the average population 20 years earlier. More worryingly, in states with high tribal populations (more than 10 percent of total population), ST households exhibited poverty rates that were higher than the rates across the nation as a whole in 2004–05. In Orissa, almost 75 percent of ST households fell below the poverty line.

One should read these numbers while keeping heterogeneity in mind. STs are a highly diverse category, and the heterogeneity within the category is so striking that often the same surname may belong to different tribes in different states. Outcomes among tribals have also been shaped by the region in which they live. Development outcomes among tribals in the northeastern states, for instance,

Table 1.1 Poverty Rates: STs Are 20 Years behind the Average Population

population below the poverty line, %

Location, social group	A. 1983	1993–94	B. 2004–05	% change (A, B)
Rural				
ST	63.9	50.2	44.7	–30
SC	59.0	48.2	37.1	–37
Others	40.8	31.2	22.7	–44
All	46.5	36.8	28.1	–40
Urban				
ST	55.3	43.0	34.3	–38
SC	55.8	50.9	40.9	–27
Others	39.9	29.4	22.7	–43
All	42.3	32.8	25.8	–39
Total				
ST	63.3	49.6	43.8	–31
SC	58.4	48.7	37.9	–35
Others	40.5	30.7	22.7	–44
All	45.6	35.8	27.5	–40

Source: Staff estimates based on Schedule 1.0 of the respective NSS rounds and official poverty lines.

appear quite different relative to the outcomes among tribals in central India. We therefore keep the former out of the purview of this diagnostic and draw upon microstudies, where relevant, to explain processes that lead to deprivation among STs.

High child mortality is the starkest marker of tribal deprivation. Every monsoon season, the Indian media are rife with stories of child deaths in tribal areas, which are frequently reported as malnutrition deaths. Kalahandi District in Orissa, for instance, became a metaphor for starvation because of press reports dating back to the 1980s. Under-5 mortality remains a stark marker of tribal deprivation in India: nearly 96 tribal children die for every 1,000 live births, compared with an under-5 mortality of 74 per 1,000 for all India. ST children make up 12 percent of all children under 5 in rural areas, but account for almost 23 percent of deaths in the 1–4 age-group (table 1.2). For all other social groups, the representation of deaths is proportionate to the representation of the group in the population.

Previous analyses of the correlates of under-5 mortality did not find any difference with respect to what we already know: the effect of ST status is insignificant once we control for poverty; that is, poverty is the primary cause of excess child mortality among tribals. However, most analyses lump all under-5 mortality together. Our

Table 1.2 Adivasi Child Mortality Exceeds the Relative Population Share in Rural Areas

percent

Social group	Share of all children under 5	Share of child deaths age 1–4	Share of under-5 deaths
SC	21.6	28.1	24.6
ST	11.7	23.0	13.9
OBC	41.8	35.5	39.6
Other	24.9	13.4	21.9
Total	100	100	100

Source: Das, Kapoor, and Nikitin (2010), based on 2005 NFHS data.

Note: The table refers to children born during the five years prior to the survey in rural areas only.

Figure 1.1 Rural Adivasi Children: Lower Risk of Dying at Birth, but Greater Risk by Age 5

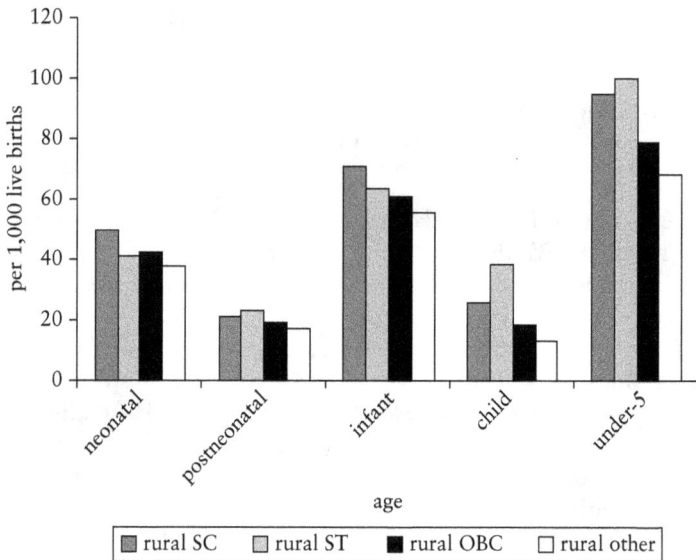

Source: Staff calculations based on 2005 NFHS data.

analysis finds that, *even after we control for wealth*, tribal children show a higher likelihood of dying between ages 1 and 4 than their nontribal peers. This comes through because we disaggregate under-5 mortality into its age-specific constituent parts. We find that the gap in mortality between rural Adivasi children and others appears after the age of 1 (figure 1.1). In fact, before the age of 1, Adivasi children face more or less similar odds of dying as other children; odds that significantly reverse later. This finding has important policy relevance for two reasons. First, because it calls for a shift in attention from infant mortality or overall under-5 mortality to factors that cause a wedge between tribal children and the rest between the ages of 1 and 5. Second, because it means that, more than socioeconomic status, the problem of high child mortality is explained by tribal group status. Addressing poverty alone therefore may not help. Unless interventions reach these groups, India may not be able to meet its goal of reducing child mortality by two-thirds by 2015.

Demographic literature in India and elsewhere is quite consistent on the correlates of child mortality. Among the more proximate reasons are child malnutrition, the lack of immunization, and the poor health of tribal mothers. While immunization coverage has expanded significantly in tribal areas, tribal children remain at much greater risk of malnutrition; nearly 55 percent are underweight, compared with 42 percent among children in the nontribal population. The appearance of ST children starts becoming different within the first 10 months of birth with respect to the appearance of other children in terms of height and weight (figure 1.2). Mothers of tribal children are also much less likely to obtain health care. For instance, ST women are much less likely to receive antenatal or prenatal care from doctors. Only 40 percent received antenatal care in 2005, compared with 63 percent in the general population category. The reason this does not show up in differences in infant mortality is because of the traditional practices of birth spacing, feeding, and weaning that tribal mothers follow. More instructive, however, are the disparities in the treatment of illness among tribal children 3 years of age and below relative to other children. All-India data of the NFHS indicate that tribal babies are not more likely to become sick with diarrhea or respiratory disease, but are much less likely to be treated relative to other children.

Behind the proximate correlates are deeper institutional and historical processes that are responsible for Adivasi deprivation. At the core of these processes is the large-scale alienation of Adivasis from their traditional sources of livelihood: land and forests. The remoteness of tribal habitations creates added problems for service delivery and monitoring. Even where health centers exist, absenteeism is high, and health surveillance is difficult because of the frequent migration of tribal families. Unlike SCs, who have been effective in claiming some form of political representation, including nationally known political parties and leaders, the tribals exercise little voice over their own development, and their leadership usually consists of non-Adivasi elite. Finally, while the Indian government's response to vulnerability among STs has been proactive and has included a mix of

Figure 1.2 More ST Children Are Severely Stunted and Wasted within the First 10 Months of Birth, 2005–06

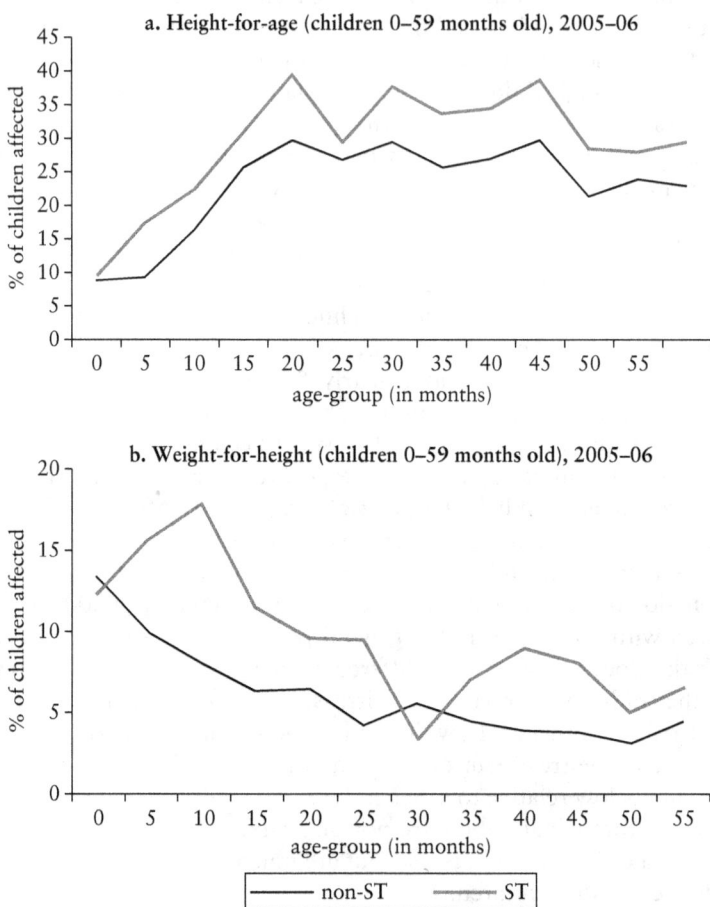

a. Height-for-age (children 0–59 months old), 2005–06

b. Weight-for-height (children 0–59 months old), 2005–06

Source: Das, Kapoor, and Nikitin (2010) based on NFHS data.

constitutional measures, legislative enactments, programs supported by earmarked funds, and quotas in public employment and publicly funded education, the major problem has been implementation. We concur with a Planning Commission report arguing that Adivasi alienation and lack of voice are at the fulcrum of the tribal angst that India is witnessing today (see Government of India 2008).

IN SUMMARY

• During a period of relative prosperity for India as a whole, poverty rates have declined much more slowly among STs than among other groups and particularly slowly in states that have large proportions of tribals.

- Health outcomes among STs, while showing more rapid progress in some respects than the rest of the population, are still poor. Convergence with other groups has occurred in only a small number of areas, notably in immunization coverage.
- Excess mortality among tribal children continues to be the starkest marker of tribal disadvantage and has its roots in a number of complex processes that involve the exclusion of STs.
- While laws and programs are in place to address the special disadvantages of STs, implementation is poor.
- The low participation of tribals in decision making and their alienation from land and forests are central to the continued exclusion of tribals from progress and development.

Dalits

The caste system has been the most predominant axis of ritually ordered exclusion in India, and Dalits fall at the lowest end of the caste hierarchy. The rules of the game in the caste system—to borrow a formulation of North (1990)—are rooted in a religiously sanctioned ordering of occupations described in ancient Hindu texts such as the *Manusmriti*.[4] While drawing their origins from such texts, cultural and social attitudes toward SCs solidified over time, and the caste system was sustained more because of these deeply rooted practices than because of adherence per se to religious principles contained in the scriptures. Caste, however, is not the immutable frame that the Weberian stereotype suggests, but an institution that has been malleable to policy and changing opportunities. Recognizing the unfair disadvantage that certain castes have had through history, the Indian Constitution explicitly recognized those castes at the bottom of the hierarchy (the untouchables) as SCs. A comprehensive listing of SCs was drawn up for the purpose of targeting development programs, and a set of laws was implemented that mandated punitive action for acts of discrimination on the one hand and affirmative action in public employment and publicly funded education on the other. Chapter 3 focuses on Dalits, a term that has united the SCs in a process that is more empowering than the process of identification by individual names, which have been and continue to be associated with ritually impure occupations.

Several features of caste make the system exclusionary. The most important among these features is the hereditary passing down of occupations, making it especially difficult for SCs to break the cycle of exclusion and move up (Thorat 2007). Other features of the system include norms of purity and pollution, the spatial segregation of residence, rules that prevent intermarriage and interdining, subordination though market transactions, and reliance on caste-based networks for coping. Such features reinforce exclusion as does the fear of being ostracized socially if one moves away from established practices. Processes of ritual discrimination and cultural devaluation are usually passed from one generation to the next, which then end up internalizing the processes (see Hoff and Pandey 2004).

Our report focuses on the exclusion of Dalits from two arenas: education and the labor market. It maps some of the changes over the last two decades and finds that Dalit men, in particular, have had the greatest convergence in educational outcomes with their upper caste counterparts. In employment, too, there are signs of change, and Dalits, who were always casual laborers, are now moving out of casual labor. However, the transformations are small, and they are more visible through localized evidence.

Dalits: Main Findings

Over time, there has been a transformation in the situation of Dalits. The report shows that there has been a huge expansion of education among Dalit men. This is correlated with some labor market changes as well. However, perhaps the most visible transformations have been in the political arena, where Dalit parties have won state elections. Microlevel evidence also shows that there is much greater group confidence and ability to assert oneself in public spaces. In fieldwork conducted for this report, Surinder Jodhka, professor at Jawaharlal Nehru University, returned to two Haryana villages after nearly 20 years and found that, with the exception of a small number of Dalits in the scavenging community, Dalit families no longer engaged in traditional caste occupations.

"In other words, they no longer see themselves as being a part of the social order of the caste system," writes Jodhka (2008, 27). "This has also given them a sense of independence and political agency." Based on a survey of Dalits in two blocks in Uttar Pradesh, Prasad (2009) found similarly far-reaching changes. Anecdotal evidence also confirms the transformation that has occurred among Dalits. However, despite this, the national data that aggregate the broad outcomes show only small changes. The changes have been more significant among Dalit men than among Dalit women, and the latter have continued to show extremely poor education and labor market outcomes.

There has been an impressive expansion of education among Dalit men, but belief systems still militate against the success of Dalit students. Education has historically had a ritual significance in that

Figure 1.3 Change in Postprimary Education, by Caste and Gender, 1983–2005

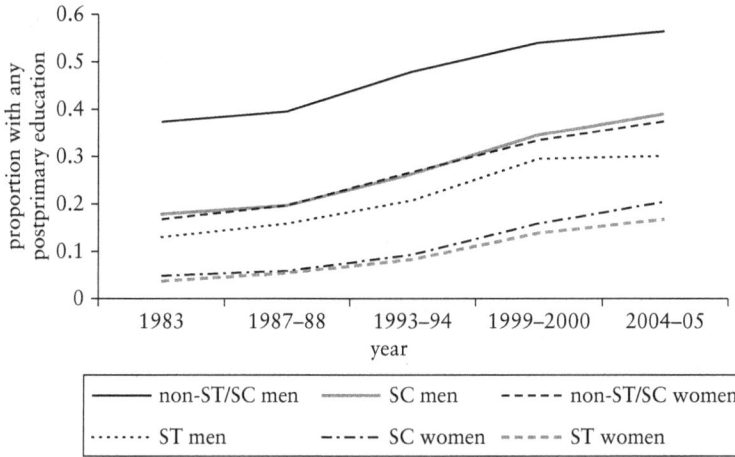

Source: Calculations based on five-year NSS rounds on the population aged 15–59.

it was the preserve of the upper castes and reflected an elaborate ideology that excluded Dalits from its pale. This has begun to change, especially among SC men, whose educational attainment above postprimary has grown at a pace similar to that of non-SC/ST women (figure 1.3). Nonetheless, even today, upper caste parents may not allow Dalit students to sit with their own children or to eat together, and other such issues are common in some parts of the country (Nambissan 2007). Historical stereotyping also affects the performance of Dalit students. Some years ago, Hoff and Pandey (2004), using controlled experiments with Dalit junior high school students in a village in Uttar Pradesh, found that beliefs shaped by a history of prejudicial treatment can have a significant impact on children's responses when opportunities are presented to them.

Dalits are slightly more likely to participate in the labor force compared with non-SCs/STs, but these effects are stronger among rural women than among other groups. The analysis in this report looks at labor force participation rates separately for rural and urban areas and men and women. Among men, there is little variation; most men, regardless of caste status, report themselves employed. However, Dalit and Adivasi women in rural areas show much higher labor force participation rates than other rural women. The ethnographic evidence also points to the lower mobility restrictions on Dalit and Adivasi women, which, if combined with higher poverty rates, makes it more likely that these women work outside the home.

For the most part, Dalits do not own land and have historically been workers in the fields of landed castes. In 2004–05, according to NSS data on usual principal status, over 41 percent of Dalit men and 20 percent of Dalit women were engaged in casual labor compared with, respectively, 19 percent of non-SC/ST men and 8 percent of non-SC/ST women. Their landless status also excludes the Dalits from the large employment category of farm-based self-employment, and, within casual labor, the Dalits mostly remain farmworkers. At the multivariate level, too, the main Dalit effect is in the assignment to casual wage work. Predicted probabilities calculated from multinomial regression models that estimate the assignment of Dalit men to various employment groups show that Dalit men do not look so different from other men except that they are much more likely to be casual laborers.

While many have received the benefits of public sector employment, Dalits still lag behind non-Dalit/Adivasi/OBCs in regular salaried work and in nonfarm self-employment. The difference between Dalits and non-Dalits in regular salaried work is not huge, because, overall, salaried work forms a small proportion of all employment. At the univariate level, against about 17 percent non-SC/STs/OBCs, a little over 13 percent of Dalits are regular salaried workers. However, as the report shows, the real differences are not in the proportions of Dalits and non-Dalits in regular salaried work, but in the kinds of jobs the Dalits land even within salaried work. The assignment to low-end jobs in the salaried market leads to wage differentials as a result mainly of occupational segregation.

Despite the changes, aggregate data indicate that Dalit men continued to be in casual labor over the 20 years beginning in 1983. Shifts in labor force activity among Dalits show, overall, a slight decline in casual labor and a slight increase in both nonfarm self-employment and opting out of the labor force. Over the 20 years or so beginning in 1983, while the proportion of Dalit men in casual labor declined slightly (from 44.6 to 41.7 percent) and in nonfarm self-employment increased slightly (from 11.0 to 15.6 percent), these changes were small (figure 1.4). Dalit men are restricted to menial, low-paying, and often socially stigmatized occupations, while upper caste groups are concentrated in preferred occupations. Among women, the major change is the fact that they have moved out of casual labor, but are also withdrawing from the labor market.

In general, while SCs were represented proportionately to their population overall at each employment level within central government services, they were vastly overrepresented in the least skilled

Figure 1.4 A Small Labor Market Transition among Dalit Men: Out of Casual Labor into Self-Employment

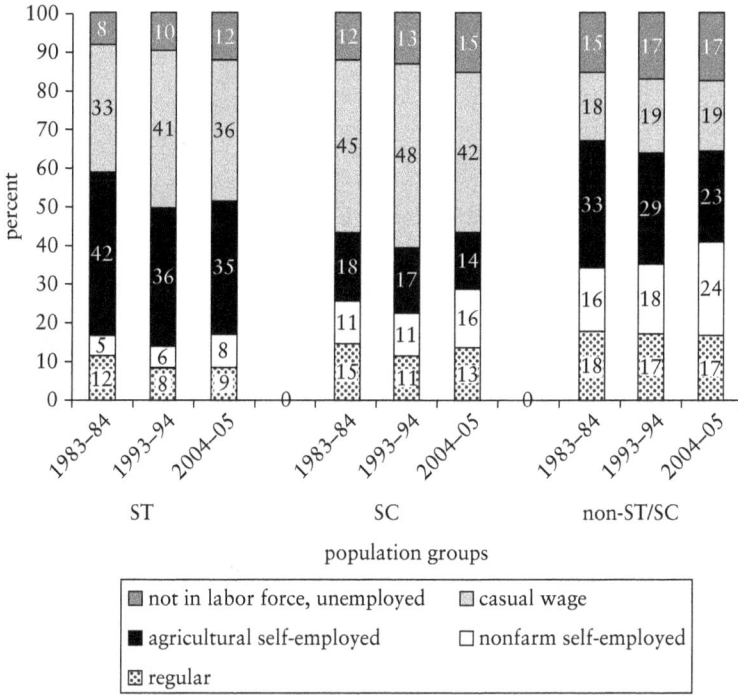

Source: Staff calculations based on 2004–05 employment-unemployment schedule NSS data.
Note: Statistics pertain to men between 20 and 65 years of age.

occupational categories at the lowest employment level. In 2006, almost 60 percent of the sweepers in central government ministries were SCs (table 1.3), indicating that SCs are more likely to undertake ritually unclean, manual work, although qualitative and small-area studies indicate that this is changing in many places. Recent work suggests that there is also subtle stereotyping along caste lines in private sector hiring. New research establishes empirically that SC applicants face particular difficulty in passing through the screening questions (such as those on family background) set up by prospective employers (Thorat and Attewell 2007; Jodhka and Newman 2007).

Dalits also seem to have lower returns to education. Our report suggests that, while all men benefit from education, Dalit men in rural areas who have completed primary education or postprimary education are less likely to be employed. This may perhaps reflect,

Table 1.3 The Representation of Dalits in Government Jobs, 2006

percent

Group	SCs
A	13.0
B	14.5
C	16.4
D (excluding sweepers)	18.3
Sweepers	59.4
Average across groups A–D, excluding sweepers	24.3
Average across groups A–D, including sweepers	15.6

Source: Calculated from data of Ministry of Personnel, Public Grievances, and Pensions (2009).

Note: Data pertain to central government services as of January 1, 2006 and exclude two ministries. Group A indicates the highest level, and Group D, the lowest.

first, that all men with education in rural areas are penalized, second, that Dalit men feel these effects especially if they have postprimary education, and, third, that the growth of jobs in rural areas does not keep pace with the increase in the supply of educated Dalit men. In urban areas, while all men show a much higher likelihood of participating in the labor force if they have education, the effects among Dalit men are not statistically significant.

The wage differentials between Dalits and others are a testimony to the continued disadvantage of Dalits in the labor market. The influence of caste affiliation on wages is a much noted feature of the Indian labor market (see, for example, Banerjee and Knight 1985; Das 2006; Unni 2001). Kernel density plots of wages by social group in 2004–05 largely bear out the expectation that SC workers in regular jobs are less likely to hold the more well paying jobs. The distribution of regular wages for general caste workers lies to the right of the distribution for SC and OBC workers (figure 1.5). Oaxaca-Blinder decompositions of wage differentials indicate that nearly 60 percent of the wage gap between SC and general caste workers is caused by unobserved factors or cannot be explained by human capital endowments.

Glass walls? Occupational segregation can explain much of the Dalit disadvantage in the labor market. The concentration of Dalits in casual work or in low-pay occupations compared with other groups is linked to relative differences in educational level, but this is only part of the story. Das and Dutta (2008) propose the notion of glass walls, whereby occupationally slotted castes cannot leave their traditional trades or jobs. Castes are clustered around occupations, whether by choice or compulsion. Microlevel studies, for

Figure 1.5 Wage Differentials between Dalits and Others Are Higher in Salaried Work than in Casual Work

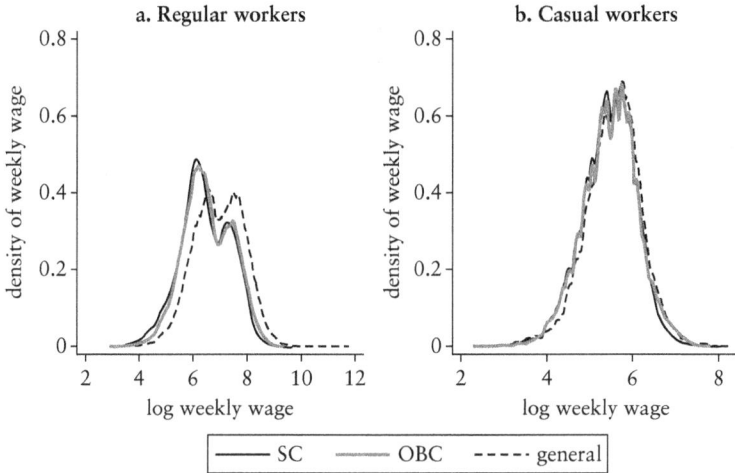

a. Regular workers   b. Casual workers

Source: Das and Dutta (2008), based on NSS data, 61st round, 2004–05.

instance, point to the possibility that small-scale Dalit entrepreneurs, especially in rural areas, are being prevented from moving out of caste-based occupations into self-employed ventures through social pressures and ostracism (Thorat 2007). There is also a possibility that people may not want to leave their caste networks because they may be advantageous in responding to new opportunities (Munshi and Rosenzweig 2005; Kishwar 2002).

The issue of Dalit entrepreneurship has been in the national discourse for some time. Despite impressive microlevel studies of Dalit entrepreneurship, the national data do not seem to capture a shift into self-employment. It is also likely that the national data of the NSS date back to 2004, while changes that we are unable to capture may have taken place in the last six or seven years. Using the 61st round of the NSS, we find that Dalit men seem, overall, less likely to have their own enterprises, but self-employment is rare among most men in India, and the hurdles for small (often household) enterprises are well documented, most recently by Kishwar (2002) and Nilekani (2008). It seems that, in rural areas, Dalit men have a huge disadvantage in self-employment. This could be caused as much by the fact that self-employment is rare in rural areas and that, where it exists, it may be ancillary to agriculture, and Dalits typically do not own land. Equally, however, rural Dalit men have fewer social networks and less access to credit, markets, and raw materials than their urban counterparts. In a study on Dalit entrepreneurship commissioned for this report, Jodhka and Gautam (2008) find that, while those who venture into nonfarm activities are able to circumvent caste norms, significant barriers exist in accessing networks, particularly social networks that would enable access to credit. Poor access to networks reflects in national data as well. Only 12 percent of SC households had access to three contacts in the formal sector in 2005 compared with 26 percent among forward caste households (see chapter 3, figure 3.6).

There are cracks in the glass walls, but relative disadvantages remain. In sum, we find evidence of subtle changes in education outcomes and the labor market among the Dalits, particularly Dalit men. However, these changes appear to be mostly cracks in the glass wall. Mobility among the Dalits is constrained largely because of the poor initial conditions Dalits face (for instance, lack of assets and poor access to markets).

IN SUMMARY

- There has been some convergence in education outcomes, particularly in postprimary education, between Dalit and non-SC/ ST men. However, while the advance has been impressive, Dalits still lag behind because of their low starting points. Dalit women, in particular, do worse, faring only marginally better than Adivasi women.
- Dalits are slightly more likely to participate in the labor market. However, they remain largely in casual jobs. Over time, there has been only a slight shift away from casual labor into nonfarm employment among men. More Dalit women, however, seem to be withdrawing from the labor force, perhaps on account of more education or social mobility.
- The picture that emerges in the employment options for educated Dalit men is more complex. In rural areas, education mostly hampers the employment opportunities for Dalits, mainly because there are few regular salaried jobs available. In urban areas, too, the combined effects of caste and education indicate that SC men have fewer chances (relative to other groups) of exiting casual labor and moving into regular salaried jobs if they have postprimary education. This may be a corollary of an increasing supply of educated SC men over time, thereby creating a system of job rationing among SCs, who cannot compete in the nonreserved salaried job market.
- The wage differentials between Dalits and others are a testimony to the continued disadvantage of Dalits in the labor market. Differences in access to occupations—or glass walls—are

an important determinant of the wage gap. Recent research suggests that there is subtle caste-based stereotyping in private hiring.
- In addition to new economic opportunities, Dalit solidarity movements and affirmative action policies have helped the Dalits claim political space. In this, they have been more successful than other excluded groups.

Women

While gender per se is a relational category, and men are arguably disadvantaged along some indicators in some areas (for example, health and mortality), our report focuses on women—who, in India, are an excluded category—in major development outcomes and processes.[5] Female disadvantage is well documented and finds its rationale, as does the caste system, in Hindu law books (Deshpande 2002). It plays out in several spheres of economic and social life: women's lower labor force participation and wages relative to men, poorer health and education outcomes, less voice in the political or general public arena, and less access to markets. In an infamously Indian pattern, we find that, in terms of sex ratios, India lags behind many countries at the same income level. This represents stark testimony of female disadvantage and the disincentive for parents to have daughters, although there may be evidence of an incipient turnaround in some parts of India (Das Gupta, Chung, and Shuzhuo 2009). Yet, when girls and women do survive, they do better today than did the girls and women of the generation of their mothers, which is another way of saying that key indicators of gender equality are improving if one discounts the "missing women" (Sen 1992). The absolute levels of the indicators, however, continue to be poor, especially for Dalit and Adivasi women, who suffer from multiple disadvantages.

Chapter 4 focuses on select outcomes among women. In particular, it addresses women's survival disadvantage both in childhood and in their reproductive years, as well as some of the processes, such as marriage, that mediate women's access to markets, services, and spaces. In addressing women's voice and agency, the chapter also looks at an oft-omitted variable: women's vulnerability to violence or threats of physical harm in the home and outside the home. It correlates the likelihood of experiencing violence with a number of human development outcomes among women and their children.

WOMEN: MAIN FINDINGS

India has made substantial investments in human development, and the changes are evident. Today, most Indian families would not be able to identify with the anachronistic *Laws of Manu*, which laid down the lower status of women. Indian women are now much more visible in public spaces and in positions of authority; fertility rates in several states are now below replacement levels and are similar to levels in developed countries; contraceptive prevalence is much higher than even a decade ago; and maternal mortality, while at stubbornly high levels across South Asia except in Sri Lanka, is showing a decline that is greater in India than in other countries. Also, there seems to be evidence of an incipient turnaround in reported son preference at least in some parts of India.

Yet, the roots of gender inequality are still strong and affect a range of outcomes among women. Despite the strides in education and health, many outcomes are worse in India than in neighboring Bangladesh and relative to some other countries at a similar income level. The Human Development Index brings this to public attention annually. Female disadvantage is most starkly apparent in the lower survival chances of infant girls compared with infant boys. India and, to a lesser extent, Nepal are the only two countries in which the survival rate among infant girls is lower than the rate among boys (figure 1.6). Declines in mortality rates overall have occurred more slowly in India than in Bangladesh and Nepal. Finally, the rate of progression of girls through to secondary school is much lower in India than in Bangladesh, although the latter spends a smaller proportion of gross domestic product on education (Das 2008). But, as in other areas, in gender inequality, too, India is highly heterogeneous and Adivasi, Dalit, and Muslim women tend to show much poorer outcomes than other women. There are also large regional variations in most of these indicators.

Adverse child sex ratios in many Indian states have received considerable attention, but is there evidence of an incipient turnaround? The strong preference for sons among Indian families plays out in the neglect of daughters and, over the last few decades, in the selective abortion of female fetuses. This has led to massive outrage; Amartya Sen (1992) famously drew attention to the missing women in China and India. Das Gupta, Chung, and Shuzhuo (2009) draw comparative evidence from the Republic of Korea to show that the fertility preference for sons is declining and that this may well be followed by better childhood sex ratios in some parts of India, which could be on the cusp of a turnaround. Similar evidence is provided by John et al. (2008), who have carried out research in some of the districts with the poorest childhood sex ratios in India.

At the core of this preference for sons seems to be a number of cultural practices, including the taboo against receiving financial help from daughters or considering daughters as old age insurance.

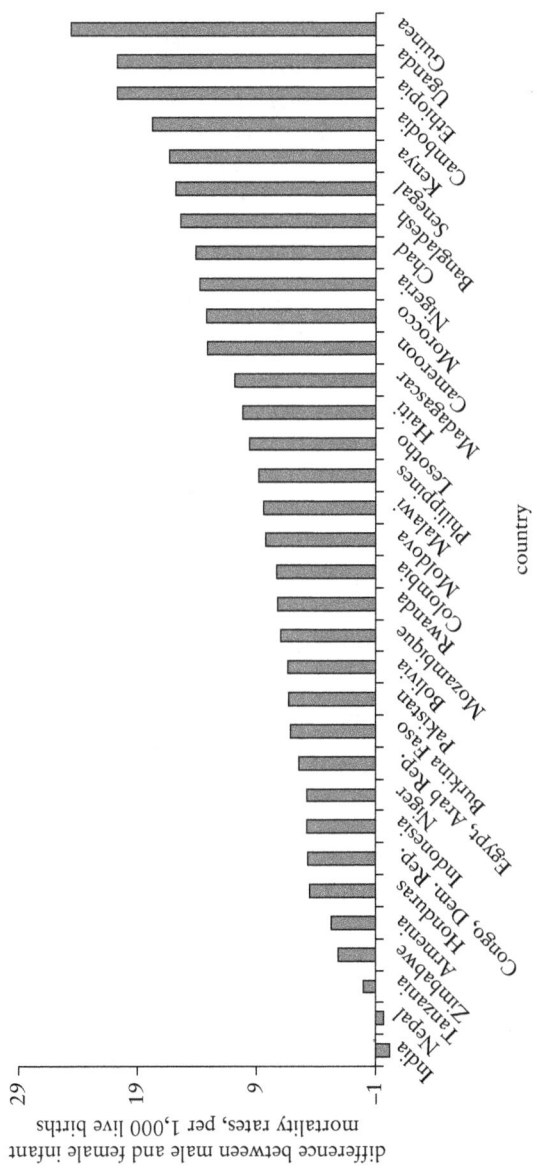

Figure 1.6 Only in India and Nepal Is Infant Mortality Higher among Girls than among Boys

difference between male and female infant mortality rates, per 1,000 live births

country

Guinea
Uganda
Ethiopia
Cambodia
Kenya
Senegal
Bangladesh
Chad
Nigeria
Morocco
Cameroon
Madagascar
Haiti
Lesotho
Philippines
Malawi
Moldova
Colombia
Rwanda
Mozambique
Bolivia
Pakistan
Burkina Faso
Egypt, Arab Rep.
Niger
Indonesia
Congo, Dem. Rep.
Honduras
Armenia
Zimbabwe
Tanzania
Nepal
India

29   19   9   -1

Source: Selected Demographic and Health Surveys, 2003–06.

Together with high dowry rates, this implies that daughters are perceived as a net loss in economic terms. In such a scenario, the easy availability of technology that detects the sex of the child allows families to abort female fetuses. However, not all states fare so badly. Andhra Pradesh, Assam, Kerala, and West Bengal show better indicators. In Haryana and Punjab, the sex ratios are so adverse that there is now a shortage of marriageable women, and families with sons have to import daughters-in-law from across the country and across caste lines. Whether these trends will have longer-term consequences is yet to be determined (Kaur 2004).

Despite many positive demographic outcomes among women, childbearing remains a high-risk event. Indian women face a 1 in 70 risk of dying in childbirth. This falls at the high end of the global spectrum, and other comparators have much better outcomes. For instance, Chinese women face a 1 in 1,400 risk of maternal death, while the risk among Vietnamese women is 1 in 280. Within India, there is considerable variation across states, and some have done worse than others over the first few years of the new millennium. Assam, Bihar, Chhattisgarh, Jharkhand, Madhya Pradesh, Orissa, Rajasthan, Uttaranchal, and Uttar Pradesh together accounted for about 65 percent of all maternal deaths in 1997–2003 (Registrar General 2006). Childbearing is entangled with many cultural factors such as the early age of marriage, which, combined with poor access to health care, may be responsible for large numbers of maternal deaths. The government is cognizant of the slow pace of decline in maternal mortality overall, and the National Rural Health Mission has put in place several interventions to address the issue (Registrar General 2006).

Less than half of Indian women receive complete antenatal care, and 60 percent of all childbirths take place at home. A majority of the women who give birth at home feel it is not necessary to deliver in a formal medical facility. The public health system has agonized over the low demand for maternal health services; cultural and behavioral factors have been blamed (see Basu 1990). Medical practitioners often cite ignorance as the reason for the poor outcomes among women (Khandare 2004). It is true that, among the women who gave birth at home, a majority felt that to give birth in a medical facility was not necessary (see chapter 4, table 4.3). However, the low demand for health care may also be triggered by gaps in supply, the inability to reach a health center in the moment of need, and the lack of information on whether the health centers would be open.

Violence could be one of the omitted variables that explains why many women do not access reproductive health services. According to the 2005 NFHS, over one-third of Indian women reported that they had experienced spousal violence at some point, and about one-fourth had experienced violence in the previous year. Violence against women is a marker of extreme inequality in gender relations, and addressing the problem has an intrinsic value because it has important implications for human rights, but addressing it also has an instrumental value. Nearly 81 percent of the women who reported that they had never experienced violence also said that they had received antenatal care; in contrast, only 67 percent of those who had experienced violence had received antenatal care. At the multivariate level, after controlling for wealth quintile, educational levels, and other background characteristics, one finds that the experience of spousal violence increases the odds of non–live births, lack of antenatal care, lack of iron supplements and tetanus shots before delivery, stunting among children under the age of 5, and diarrhea for the last child to be born in families (figure 1.7). Our report also highlights the fact that access to land, assets, and education among both men and women and campaigns to change attitudes that condone violence could go a long way to addressing the prevalence of spousal violence.

The labor market is one of the most important sites of gender inequality. Women's visibility in the high-end urban labor market in India is much greater today than it was a decade ago, but this is far

Figure 1.7 The Experience of Violence Is Associated with Worse Outcomes among Women and Their Children

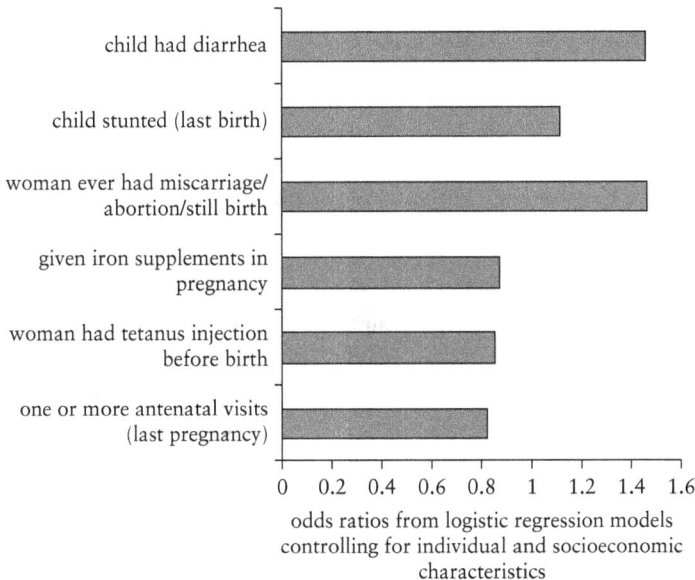

odds ratios from logistic regression models controlling for individual and socioeconomic characteristics

Source: Staff calculations based on 2005 NFHS data.

from representing a trend that may be considered general. Female labor force participation rates have remained low; only 40 percent of women are employed in full-time work (NSS 2004–05). The stagnation in female labor force participation is driven mainly by rural areas; urban areas have seen a 7 percent increase, from 20.3 percent in 1993 to 21.8 percent in 2005. There is also considerable diversity by state and by caste and tribal status. Women in the more rapidly growing regions where the norms of female mobility are more liberal, such as the south and west, are much more likely to be employed than are women in the central states. Similarly, SC and ST women participate more in the labor force out of necessity; the latter mostly take up self-employment in agriculture, while SC women undertake casual labor.

Entry into the labor market, rather than wages, is the critical marker of the employment trajectories of Indian women. This is because most Indians do not work for wages anyway, and self-employment is the default option where it is economically feasible. Casual labor is the option of last resort. In a pattern peculiar to India and much of South Asia, education lowers the likelihood that women will participate in the labor force. Two arguments have been articulated to explain the low labor force participation of Indian women. The first is a supply-side argument according to which the supply of secure well-paid jobs for educated women is low. Hence, educated women, who also belong to the higher socioeconomic strata, prefer to opt out of the labor force rather than accept low-status (manual) jobs. The second is a demand-side argument that rests on the cultural mores and values of status and seclusion in the region; this may prevent higher-status households from allowing women to work or demand jobs. Family honor in most parts of India, for instance, requires that women be restricted to the home, thus affecting the ability of women to work outside the home (Chen 1995).

Muddy waters: an income effect or a discouraged worker effect? The literature on women's labor force participation, particularly in developed countries, indicates that women's employment decisions are often contingent upon the employment status and earnings of husbands (see Cohen and Bianchi 1999). Das (2006) finds that the education and wages of husbands do lower the probability of employment among women. Moreover, after controlling for the incomes of husbands, one finds that women's postprimary education shows a positive correlation with women's labor force participation. In fact, it takes the form of a "U," with high labor force participation among uneducated women, the lowest labor force participation among women who have completed primary education, and rising labor force participation among women with postprimary education.

Thus, women with higher education may perhaps stay out of the labor force because of an income effect, but this conclusion is muddied by the lack of jobs that these women would want to take. In the absence of regular salaried jobs, the only options available to educated women, especially in rural areas, are low-status, low-paying manual work, such as work on family farms or work as petty vendors, domestic servants, or day laborers. In the face of such unsuitable employment opportunities, households decide to withdraw female labor if there are other earning members. (If women are household heads, they are more likely to be employed.) Because educated women are usually married to educated men and are likely to have some financial resources, they stay out of the labor force instead of accepting poorly paid jobs as casual wage workers.

Inequalities in wages and opportunities are an additional disincentive for women to work. While wages have risen in the aggregate for all over the last 10 years or so, lower wages among women compared with men are an added disincentive for women to work outside the home. Women's nominal weekly wages are, on average, 71 percent of men's wages in regular salaried work and 56 percent of men's wages in casual work (NSS 2004–05). Oaxaca-Blinder decompositions conducted on the wages of male and female casual workers in Bangladesh and India indicate that unobserved factors account for over 70 percent of the difference in wages (Das 2006; World Bank 2008). Of these unobserved factors, a large proportion are likely to be accounted for by discrimination. Low and unequal wages and the concentration of these in agricultural labor and in "female" occupations are added disincentives for women to work outside the home.

Counting aspirations: Indian women clearly want to work outside their homes. One of the explanations for women's low participation in the labor market is that they would prefer not to work, given the pervasive culture of seclusion, especially in states where women's employment rates are low (see Das 2006). We find quite the reverse in women's responses to the question in the NSS about why they did not work outside the home. Over 89 percent of the women are doing only domestic work say they are obliged to do so. One-third say they would accept paid work, in addition to their household duties. Clearly, their household responsibilities are paramount, but the majority say they would like regular part-time jobs in, for example, dairying or tailoring. Of these, almost 60 percent cite the lack of finance and credit as the most important constraint on finding the work they desire (table 1.4). Further analysis using 2005 NFHS data suggests that less than 40 percent know about the existence of credit facilities; of these, only 10 percent had actually applied for the credit. To a large extent, this may explain why women

Table 1.4 Three in Five Women Cite Lack of Credit as a Reason for Not Doing the Work They Want

percent

What do you need to facilitate the work you want?	Share
Nothing	4.24
Finance and credit	58.50
Raw materials	3.68
Assured markets	7.58
Training	15.63
Accommodation	0.87
Other	9.50

Source: Staff calculations based on the 61st NSS round, 2004–05.

Note: The sample consists of women who are currently doing household chores, but who say they would also like to do market work.

are so poorly represented in nonfarm employment and why they are transitioning so slowly out of agriculture.

Voice and visibility can change the outcomes among women. Data of the 2005 NFHS indicate that, at home, women do not have much voice in major decisions. For instance, they are least likely to participate in decisions about major household purchases and more likely to participate in decisions regarding their own health care or visits to their own families. Mandatory legal provisions reserving seats in legislatures for women have enabled women's participation in public spaces. However, the evidence on whether this has helped improve outcomes among a majority of women is mixed.

One of the factors that hinders women's visibility and voice is the threat of physical harm and lack of security outside the home. Threats to women's security also influence the ability of women to access markets and services and claim spaces for themselves. This is an area in which policy can have a huge effect. Making public spaces safe for women is a major step forward in enhancing women's access to these spaces.

IN SUMMARY

- Women today are doing better than their mothers' generation along a range of outcomes that include health, education, voice and visibility, and, to an extent, participation in the urban labor market.
- There are large inequalities among states in most areas of women's status and gender equity.

- Poor access to reproductive health means that too many women die unnecessarily in childbirth.
- Violence against women is a strong correlate of a number of poor outcomes among women and their children.
- Despite a period of dramatic economic growth, labor force participation rates among women virtually stagnated from 1983 to 2004–05. This is driven especially by rural areas.
- Heterogeneity across social groups is pronounced, and especially Dalit and Adivasi women are left out of nonfarm self-employment.
- Women appear to be stuck in farm-based employment; a major reason why they are not transitioning into nonfarm self-employment is their poor access to credit facilities.
- Over time, women's voice and agency both in the home and in public have increased, but the extent to which this has impacted aggregate outcomes is unclear even at the local level.

Common Themes

This report has several common themes and messages, as follows:

- First, it shows that, while growth has touched everyone, it has not done so equitably; traditional hierarchies have remained stubborn against growth. In the aggregate, STs appear to have done more poorly than other groups; they show the slowest pace of improvements in a range of areas.
- Second, although caste seems to be reinventing itself in response to economic opportunities and is far from a static stereotype, we find that SCs are still held back by, among other factors, their initial disadvantage and lack of social networks.
- Third, female disadvantage in India persists despite high rates of economic growth. Women are dying unnecessarily both in infancy and in motherhood; the outcomes are poorer among Dalits and Adivasis.

At its root, exclusion can be explained by inequality in opportunities, inequality in access to markets (for example, labor and credit), and inequality in voice and agency. Voice and agency have played out in different ways among all three groups (Adivasis, Dalits, and women), but are particularly salient drivers of exclusion. For instance, violence against women is not merely a variable that explains some of the poor outcomes; it is also a mechanism of control. Among the Adivasis and, in the past, the Dalits, militancy has represented a form of voice and assertion.

India is not alone in grappling with serious challenges in reaching its most excluded populations. In other countries as well, this challenge is a formidable one. An Inter-American Development Bank report on Latin America states that "inclusion is not just about changing outcomes, but crucially about changing the processes that produce and reproduce exclusionary outcomes" and that "in order to make normative changes effective, institutions must change the ways in which they operate, hire employees, and enforce laws and regulations. This in turn materializes as changes in the implementation of programs and policies" (Márquez et al. 2007, 14).

The Indian Constitution has set the stage for almost unparalleled affirmative action and other forms of positive actions. These have been translated into laws, programs, and procedures. Yet, the combination of identity politics, the inflexibility of the systems that seek to promote inclusion, and the attendant poor implementation have resulted in patchy impact, affecting some groups more than others. To describe the real challenge is to state a truism: the implementation of policies and the reform of institutions are the key to ensuring that economic growth becomes more equitable.

Notes

1. Coined by anthropologist Oscar Lewis, the term 'culture of poverty' refers to a unique value system of the poor. It was Lewis's belief that the poor are socialized into believing they deserve to be poor, leading to low aspirations, low effort and inability to escape poverty.

2. For instance, improvements in antenatal care have been particularly slow among OBC women.

3. See http://www.tribal.nic.in/index.asp.

4. The Hindu hierarchy is said to have evolved from different parts of the body of Brahma, the creator of the universe. Thus, the Brahmans, who originated from the mouth of Brahma, undertake the most prestigious priestly and teaching occupations. The Kshatriyas (from the arms) are the rulers and warriors; the Vaishyas (from the thighs) are traders and merchants; and the Shudras (from the feet) are manual workers and servants of other castes. Below the Shudras and outside the caste system, the lowest in the order, the untouchables, engage in the most demeaning and stigmatized occupations (scavenging, for instance, and dealing in bodily waste).

5. It is acknowledged, however, that male-female differences along a range of indicators need to be considered, and more so if one is thinking of designing interventions to *lessen* the gender gap.

References

Akerlof, G. 1976. "The Economics of Caste and of the Rat Race and Other Woeful Tales." *Quarterly Journal of Economics* 90 (4): 599–617.

Ambedkar, B. R. 1936. *Annihilation of Caste*, 2nd ed. Mumbai: Government of Maharashtra.

Baker, J. L. 2002. "Social Exclusion in Urban Uruguay." *En Breve* 2 (April). World Bank, Washington, DC.

Banerjee, B., and J. B. Knight. 1985. "Caste Discrimination in the Indian Urban Labour Market." *Journal of Development Economics* 17 (3): 277–307.

Basu, A. M. 1990. "Cultural Influences on Health Care Use: Two Regional Groups in India." *Studies in Family Planning* 21 (5): 275–86.

Béteille, A. 1998. "The Idea of Indigenous People." *Current Anthropology* 39 (2): 187–191.

Chen, M. 1995. "A Matter of Survival: Women's Right to Employment in India and Bangladesh." In *Women, Culture and Development: A Study of Human Capabilities*, ed. M. C. Nussbaum and J. Glover, 37–58. Oxford: Clarendon Press.

Cohen, P. N., and S. M. Bianchi. 1999. "Marriage, Children and Women's Employment: What Do We Know?" *Monthly Labor Review* 122 (12): 22–31.

Das, M. B. 2006. "Do Traditional Axes of Exclusion Affect Labor Market Outcomes in India?" South Asia Social Development Discussion Paper 3, World Bank, Washington, DC.

———. 2008. "What Money Can't Buy: Getting Implementation Right for MDG3 in South Asia." In *Equality for Women: Where Do We Stand on Millennium Development Goal 3?*, ed. M. Buvini, A. R. Morrison, A. W. Ofosu-Amaah, and M. Sjöblom, 261–92. Washington, DC: World Bank.

Das, M. B., and P. Dutta. 2008. "Does Caste Matter for Wages in the Indian Labor Market? Caste Pay Gaps in India." Paper presented at the Third Institute for the Study of Labor–World Bank Conference on Employment and Development, Rabat, Morocco, May 5–6.

Das, M. B., S. Kapoor, and D. Nikitin. 2010. "A Closer Look at Child Mortality among Adivasis in India." Policy Research Working Paper 5321, World Bank, Washington, DC.

Das Gupta, M., W. Chung, and L. Shuzhuo. 2009. "Is There an Incipient Turnaround in Asia's 'Missing Girls' Phenomenon?" Policy Research Working Paper 4846, World Bank, Washington, DC.

de Haan, A. 1997. "Poverty and Social Exclusion: A Comparison of Debates." PRUS Working Paper 2, Poverty Research Unit, University of Sussex, Brighton, United Kingdom.

Deshpande, A. 2002. "Assets Versus Autonomy? The Changing Face of the Gender-Caste Overlap in India." *Feminist Economics* 8 (2): 19–35.

Gacitúa-Marió, E., and M. Woolcock, eds. 2008. *Social Exclusion and Mobility in Brazil.* Washington, DC: World Bank.

Government of India. 2008. "Development Challenges in Extremist Affected Areas: Report of an Expert Group to Planning Commission." Report, April, Planning Commission, New Delhi. http://planningcommission .gov.in/reports/publications/rep_dce.pdf.

Hoff, K., and P. Pandey. 2004. "Belief Systems and Durable Inequalities: An Experimental Investigation of Indian Caste." Policy Research Working Paper 3351, World Bank, Washington, DC.

Jodhka, S. 2008. "A Forgotten 'Revolution': Revisiting Agrarian Change in Haryana." Paper prepared for the study, Poverty and Social Exclusion in India, Indian Institute of Dalit Studies, New Delhi.

Jodhka, S., and S. Gautam. 2008. "In Search of a Dalit Entrepreneur: Barriers and Supports in the Life of Self-Employed Scheduled Castes." Paper prepared for the study, Poverty and Social Exclusion in India, Indian Institute of Dalit Studies, New Delhi.

Jodhka, S., and K. S. Newman. 2007. "In the Name of Globalisation: Meritocracy, Productivity and the Hidden Language of Caste." *Economic and Political Weekly* 42 (41): 4125–32.

John, M. E., R. Kaur, R. Palriwala, S. Raju, and A. Sagar. 2008. *Planning Families, Planning Gender: The Adverse Child Sex Ratio in Selected Districts of Madhya Pradesh, Rajasthan, Himachal Pradesh, Haryana, and Punjab.* New Delhi: ActionAid and International Development Research Centre.

Kaur, R. 2004. "Across-Region Marriages: Poverty, Female Migration and the Sex Ratio." *Economic and Political Weekly* 39 (25): 2595–2603.

Khandare, L. 2004. "Korku Adivasis in Melghat Region of Maharashtra: A Socio-economic Study; a Course Seminar." Department of Humanities and Social Sciences, Indian Institute of Technology, Mumbai. http:// lalitreports.blogspot.com/2004/12/korku-adivasis-in-melghat-region-of .html.

Kishwar, M. 2002. "Working under Constant Threat: Some Setbacks and Some Steps Forward in Sewa Nagar." *Manushi* 130 (May–June).

Maharatna, A. 2005. *Demographic Perspectives on India's Tribes.* New Delhi: Oxford University Press.

Márquez, G., A. Chong, S. Duryea, J. Mazza, and H. Ñopo, eds. 2007. *Outsiders: The Changing Patterns of Exclusion in Latin America and the Caribbean.* Economic and Social Progress in Latin America 2008. Washington, DC: Inter-American Development Bank.

Ministry of Personnel, Public Grievances, and Pensions. 2009. *Annual Report 2008–2009.* New Delhi: Ministry of Personnel, Public Grievances, and Pensions.

Munshi, K., and M. Rosenzweig. 2005. "Why Is Mobility in India So Low? Social Insurance, Inequality, and Growth." Draft working paper, Center for International Development, Harvard University, Cambridge, MA.

Nambissan, G. B. 2007. "Exclusion, Inclusion and Education: Perspectives and Experiences of Dalit Children." Paper prepared for the Indian Institute of Dalit Studies, New Delhi.

Nehru, J. 1946. *The Discovery of India*. Calcutta: The Signet Press.

Nilekani, N. 2008. *Imagining India: Ideas for the New Century*. New Delhi: Penguin Books India.

North, D. 1990. *Institutions, Institutional Change and Economic Performance*. Cambridge: Cambridge University Press.

Prasad, C. B. 2009. "Sir, the World Turned Upside Down: Radical Changes in Dalits' Occupations, Food Habits and Lifestyle Observed in Two Blocks of UP." Paper presented at the Planning Commission of India, New Delhi, November 5.

Registrar General. 2006. "Sample Registration System; Maternal Mortality in India, 1997–2003: Trends, Causes and Risk Factors." Working Paper 753, Registrar General, New Delhi.

Scoville, J. G., ed. 1991. *Status Influences in Third World Labor Markets: Caste, Gender, Custom*. New York: Walter de Gruyter.

Sen, A. 1992. "Missing Women: Social Inequality Outweighs Women's Survival Advantage in Asia and North Africa." *British Medical Journal* 304 (6827): 586–87.

———. 1998. "Social Exclusion: A Critical Assessment of the Concept and Its Relevance." Paper prepared for the Asian Development Bank, Manila.

Silver, H. 1994. "Social Exclusion and Social Solidarity: Three Paradigms." IILS Discussion Papers 69, International Labour Office, Geneva.

Thorat, S. 2007. "Economic Exclusion and Poverty: Indian Experience of Remedies against Exclusion." Paper presented at the International Food Policy Research Institute and Asian Development Bank policy forum, "Agricultural and Rural Development for Reducing Poverty and Hunger in Asia: In Pursuit of Inclusive and Sustainable Growth," Manila, August 9–10.

Thorat, S., and P. Attewell. 2007. "The Legacy of Social Exclusion: A Correspondence Study of Job Discrimination in India." *Economic and Political Weekly* 42 (41): 4141–45.

Tilly, C. 1999. *Durable Inequality*. Berkeley, CA: University of California Press.

Unni, J. 2001. "Earnings and Education among Ethnic Groups in Rural India." NCAER Working Paper 79, National Council of Applied Economic Research, New Delhi.

Walton, M. 2007. "Culture Matters for Poverty, but Not Because of a Culture of Poverty: Notes on Analytics and Policy." Unpublished paper,

Centre for Policy Research, New Delhi; John. F. Kennedy School of Government, Harvard University, Cambridge, MA. http://www.afd.fr/jahia/webdav/users/administrateur/public/eudn2007/walton.pdf.

Weber, M. 1958. *The Religion of India: The Sociology of Hinduism and Buddhism.* New York: The Free Press.

World Bank. 2005. *Poverty, Social Exclusion, and Ethnicity in Serbia and Montenegro: The Case of the Roma.* Washington, DC: World Bank.

———. 2006. "Unequal Citizens: Gender, Caste and Ethnic Exclusion in Nepal." National Planning Commission (Nepal), Department for International Development (United Kingdom), World Bank, Kathmandu.

———. 2008. *Whispers to Voices: Gender and Social Transformation in Bangladesh.* Washington, DC: World Bank.

———. 2010. "Economic Costs of Roma Exclusion." Note, April, Europe and Central Asia, Human Development Department, World Bank, Washington, DC.

———. 2011. *Perspectives on Poverty in India: Stylized Facts from Survey Data.* India Poverty Assessment. New Delhi: Poverty Reduction and Economic Management Network, World Bank.

2

Adivasis

There has been a systemic failure in giving the tribals a stake
in the modern economic processes that inexorably intrude into
their living spaces. The alienation built over decades is now
taking a dangerous turn in some parts of our country.

Prime Minister Manmohan Singh
Chief Ministers' Conference on Implementation
of the Forest Rights Act
November 4, 2009[1]

Adivasi deprivation surfaces in many stark forms. In recent years,
the government and civil society have been preoccupied with the
militancy in Adivasi areas, but the prior literature in India on Adivasis is rich and has been of two kinds. The first is a body of anthropological and historical writings the authorship of which goes back
to the British era. These writings capture the immense diversity of
Adivasi life and the exchanges of Adivasis within their communities
and with the outside world. The second is a body of activist writings
that focus on the manner in which Adivasis have been excluded,
particularly the large-scale displacement of Adivasis from their traditional lands and forests, as infrastructure development, mining,
and industry have proceeded apace. There is also a body of administrative reports that bring out the challenges of working in Adivasi
areas. Quantitative empirical work that focuses specifically on Adivasis is more difficult to find. For the most part, Adivasis are bunched
with Dalits in the omnibus term "SC/ST" (that is, Scheduled Castes/
Scheduled Tribes). In other empirical work, the "ST variable" is
often a control and rarely discussed in much depth.

How are Adivasis excluded? This is a question often asked by
those who conceptualize exclusion in India in terms of ritual purity

and pollution and tribals [Adivasis] do not face ritual exclusion, at least not universally, in the same way as Dalits do. However, if exclusion is defined more broadly in terms of being "prevent[ed] . . . from entering or participating" or "being considered or accepted," Adivasis fit squarely within the conception of excluded people.[2] They are not alone in this because, elsewhere in the world, too, tribal peoples have been similarly excluded.

"Caught in a vastly enlarged and increasingly violent competition for choice natural resources, Native Americans struggled to adapt," writes Cornell (1988, 64). "But indigenous economies were coming to pieces and the alternatives were few: the process of dispossession was also the process of exclusion." There is a similar story among indigenous communities globally (see Hall and Patrinos, forthcoming).

The processes of dispossession of Native Americans or of indigenous communities in Latin America were different: these were processes of colonization. Yet, if we consider the words of Jaipal Singh Munda, this distinction may also be moot. Ramachandra Guha (2010), in an essay on the occasion of India's 60th Republic Day, points to the widespread neglect of Adivasis and quotes Jaipal Singh Munda, a spokesman for tribal interests and himself a tribal. In a moving speech to the Constituent Assembly of India, which had met to proclaim India a democratic republic, Munda stated the following:

> Sir, if there is any group of Indian people that has been shabbily treated, it is my people. They have been disgracefully treated, neglected for the last 6,000 years. This history of the Indus Valley civilization, a child of which I am, shows quite clearly that it is the newcomers—most of you here are intruders as far as I am concerned—it is the newcomers who have driven away my people from the Indus Valley to the jungle fastness. . . . The whole history of my people is one of continuous exploitation and dispossession by the nonaboriginals of India punctuated by rebellions and disorder, and yet I take Pandit Jawaharlal Nehru at his word. I take you all at your word that now we are going to start a new chapter, a new chapter of independent India where there is equality of opportunity, where no one would be neglected. (Guha 2010)

The major difference between the SCs and the STs is that, while the former have lived among, but socially segregated from the mainstream through an elaborate ritually based ideology, the latter have been isolated physically and, hence, socially (Béteille 1991). In a global assessment of indigenous peoples, Hall and Patrinos (forthcoming) find spatial (or geographical) isolation to be the predominant explanatory factor for the exclusion of indigenous communities in both China and India. However, the degree of isolation remains in question. Adivasis have distinct cultural and linguistic characteristics, but the cultural distance between them and the mainstream has sometimes been overplayed by the development literature and in some administrative writings (Bunsha 2002). This distance, along with their spatial isolation, is often cited as the reason for Adivasi deprivation.

One of the starkest portrayals, full of symbols of tension between Adivasis and non-Adivasis, is Mahasweta Devi's Draupadi, a tribal woman tortured by servants of the state, emerging strong and defiant from the oppression. Draupadi is more well known as Dopdi either because, as a tribal, she cannot pronounce her own Sanskritized name or because the origin of the word Draupadi itself is tribal (Spivak 1981). The theme of tribal or pre-Aryan influence on the Hindu tradition is a recurrent one in historical writings, too (see, for instance, Thapar 1977). The cultural relationship between tribals and the mainstream is, again, not the direct subject of this chapter, although the developmental distance between the two is. As Ratnagar (2003, 18) writes, "Tribes are characterized not by this or that race, habitat or religious practice, but (in my understanding) by the bonding fabric of kinship and joint ownership of the natural resources from which they make their living."

This chapter analyzes Adivasi deprivation through two outcomes, as follows:

- Poverty levels analyzed along three dimensions: absolute levels, changes over time, and comparison with other groups, notably Dalits
- Child mortality: trends and correlates

The primary analysis contained in this chapter is based on the National Sample Survey (NSS). The NSS allows trends in socioeconomic indicators to be examined over three rounds conducted in 1983, 1994–95, and 2004–05 and is considered one of the most reliable data sources for socioeconomic indicators in India. In addition, we report evidence on health indicators from two rounds of the National Family Health Survey (NFHS), 1998–99 and 2005–06; we also reference a World Bank (2005) report that used the Reproductive Child Health Survey (RCH II, 2005) for Orissa. Background papers for this chapter have found their way into a global volume on indigenous peoples and the 2010 World Bank India poverty assessment (see Das et al. in Hall and Patrinos, forthcoming; World Bank 2011). The chapter also draws heavily on background papers prepared for this report by Burra (2008) and Das, Kapoor, and Nikitin (2010).

However, national-level data such as the NSS or the NFHS do not permit the analysis of tribal outcomes below the state level. In the case of STs, in states where they are a majority (such as in the northeast) and where they have gained from education, their status is different from the status of STs living as marginalized minorities in the interior reaches of the central or western states. Therefore, region becomes an important factor in determining the status of STs. Similarly, there is substantial internal diversity among STs even within states, and culture, language, and food habits vary from one tribe to another. This makes it difficult to derive general conclusions (Oommen 1997).[3]

In addition, while the aggregate analysis for this chapter includes all STs, we include only Schedule V areas and not Schedule VI areas when we drill down to state-level analyses.[4] The context in the latter (the northeastern states) is different and involves a range of institutional and fiscal issues that exceed the scope of this diagnostic.[5]

Finally, the chapter discusses the possible roots of Adivasi deprivation. That land and natural resources are at the crux of Adivasi exclusion is a view well accepted in government and nongovernment debates alike (see, for instance, Government of India 2008). State control over forests during the colonial period meant that the traditional sources of livelihoods for STs became the property of the state. Having been communal owners of the forests, they became tenants, trespassers, and poachers (Baviskar 2004). Displacement has continued through India's recent industrial boom, and the 10th Five-Year Plan notes that, between 1951 and 1990, 21.3 million people were displaced, of which 40 percent, or 8.5 million, were tribal people (Burra 2008; Government of India 2001). Only a little under one-fourth of those displaced were resettled (Government of India 2002).

Poverty and the Gap between Adivasis and Non-Adivasis

We have noted India's acclaimed success in terms of poverty reduction elsewhere in this report. In only two decades, the national poverty rate was almost halved, from 46 percent in 1983 to 27 percent in 2004–05. Yet, to what degree did the STs benefit from this general climate of improving living standards? This section presents detailed results on poverty among STs and the extent to which the welfare status of STs declined relative to that of other groups. The findings are sobering. They tell us that, while poverty has fallen for everyone, the decline has been slower among STs than among other groups. This has led to an increasing concentration of STs in the poorest wealth deciles.

While poverty rates have declined among STs since 1983, they have done so at a slower rate relative to the rest of the population. While less than half of all Indians (46 percent) and over half of SCs (58 percent) were below the official poverty line in 1983, almost two-thirds of the ST population (63 percent) fell below the poverty line in 1983 (table 2.1). Over the period spanning approximately two decades to 2004–05, the STs recorded considerable progress in absolute terms: a higher proportion of the ST population (19.5 percent) moved out of poverty compared with population groups in the general category (17.8 percent). However, because such large numbers of STs were poor to begin with (that is, the base was higher), the rate of poverty decline among STs was lower. The poverty rate among STs fell by 31 percent between 1983 and 2005, while SCs registered a decline of 35 percent. and the average decline for India was 40 percent. Thus, in 2004–05, almost half the ST population remained in poverty (44 percent), the level at which the average population had been 20 years previously. STs fared better in urban

Table 2.1 In Terms of Poverty, STs Are 20 Years behind the Average Population

percent

Social group	1983	1993–94	2004–05	% change, 1983–2005
Rural				
ST	63.9	50.2	44.7	–30
SC	59.0	48.2	37.1	–37
Others	40.8	31.2	22.7	–44
All	46.5	36.8	28.1	–40
Urban				
ST	55.3	43.0	34.3	–38
SC	55.8	50.9	40.9	–27
Others	39.9	29.4	22.7	–43
All	42.3	32.8	25.8	–39
Total				
ST	63.3	49.6	43.8	–31
SC	58.4	48.7	37.9	–35
Others	40.5	30.7	22.7	–44
All	45.6	35.8	27.5	–40

Source: Staff estimates based on Schedule 1.0 of the respective NSS rounds and official poverty lines.

areas than in rural areas, showing a lower poverty rate and steeper reductions after 1983.

If a relatively impoverished group registers slow progress in poverty reduction, exploring changes in other poverty measures can be useful, particularly those measures that examine the poverty gap (the depth of poverty) and the severity of poverty.[6] The depth and severity of poverty fell more rapidly than the poverty headcount rate (table 2.2), indicating that improvements were not confined only to those in the vicinity of the poverty line and that the extremely poor were also positively affected. However, as with the poverty headcount rate, the depth and severity of poverty are greater among STs, and these indicators have declined more slowly among STs than among other social groups.

Relatively slower declines in poverty among the STs have meant an increase in the concentration of STs in the poorest deciles of the population. Table 2.3 draws from NFHS data and gives the distribution of STs across population deciles using a wealth index.[7] The index is constructed

> using household asset data and housing characteristics. Each household asset is assigned a weight (factor score) generated through principal components analysis, and the resulting asset scores are standardized in relation to a normal distribution with a mean of zero and standard deviation of one. . . . Each household is then assigned a score for each asset, and the scores are summed for each household; individuals are ranked according to the score of the household in which they reside. (IIPS and ICF Macro 2007, 43)

Table 2.3 shows that STs in 1993 made up 22 percent of the total population in the poorest decile and only 1.7 percent of the population in the wealthiest decile. By 2005, their share in the poorest decile had risen to 25 percent, signifying a widening wealth gap between STs and the rest of the population (table 2.3, first three columns). Looking within the ST population, we find that, in 1993, 25 percent fell in the poorest wealth decile. By 2005, 30 percent were in the poorest decile (table 2.3, last three columns).

In sum, it is clear that not only are the STs poorer than any other group, they are also among the poorest. Their initial consumption levels are so far below the poverty line and they have such limited assets that gains made by them over the two decades to 2005 have not been sufficiently substantial to allow them to catch up with the general population or even the SCs. Dubey and Verschoor (2007) arrive at similar findings using income instead of consumption as a measure of welfare.[8]

Table 2.2 The Depth and Severity of Poverty Have Declined More Slowly among STs than among Other Social Groups

Social group	Trends in the depth of poverty				Trends in the severity of poverty			
	1983	1993–94	2004–05	% change, 1983–2005	1983	1993–94	2004–05	% change, 1983–2005
Rural								
ST	21.2	12.2	10.7	−50	9.5	4.3	3.7	−61
SC	18.7	11.7	7.5	−60	8.2	4.1	2.2	−73
Others	11.1	6.7	4.1	−63	4.6	2.1	1.1	−76
All	13.6	8.4	5.5	−59	5.8	2.8	1.6	−72
Urban								
ST	17.4	12.4	10.9	−37	7.2	5.0	4.7	−35
SC	16.8	14.1	10.4	−38	7.1	5.6	3.8	−46
Others	11.0	7.2	5.2	−52	4.5	2.6	1.8	−61
All	11.9	8.3	6.2	−48	4.9	3.0	2.2	−56
Total								
ST	20.9	12.2	10.7	−49	9.4	4.3	3.8	−60
SC	18.4	12.2	8.1	−56	8.0	4.3	2.5	−68
Others	11.1	6.8	4.4	−60	4.6	2.3	1.3	−72
All	13.2	8.4	5.7	−57	5.6	2.8	1.8	−68

Source: Staff estimates based on Schedule 1.0 of the respective NSS rounds and official poverty lines.

Table 2.3 The Increasing Concentration of STs in the
Poorest Wealth Deciles, 1993–2005

index

	Share of STs in population by deciles			Distribution of ST population across deciles		
Deciles	1993	1998	2005	1993	1998	2005
Poorest decile	0.223	0.217	0.251	0.253	0.245	0.297
2	0.132	0.148	0.167	0.149	0.167	0.198
3	0.106	0.118	0.120	0.120	0.134	0.142
4	0.108	0.123	0.081	0.122	0.139	0.096
5	0.099	0.091	0.065	0.113	0.102	0.077
6	0.081	0.061	0.048	0.091	0.069	0.057
7	0.052	0.052	0.037	0.059	0.059	0.044
8	0.035	0.035	0.031	0.040	0.039	0.037
9	0.030	0.031	0.027	0.034	0.035	0.031
Richest decile	0.017	0.015	0.017	0.020	0.017	0.021

Source: NFHS data.
Note: The wealth index is a factor score based on the ownership of assets.

These findings need to be nuanced considering the highly unequal results across states. What is important and worrying is that, in states with significant tribal populations (about 10 percent or more of the state's total population), ST households exhibited poverty rates that were higher than the rates across the nation as a whole in 2004–05 (with the exception of Assam; see table 2.4). The highest poverty rates recorded for tribal groups were in Orissa, where the tribal population registered a poverty headcount of 75 percent in 2004–05, an *increase* of about 6 percent over 1993–94 levels. Tribals in rural areas in Orissa were particularly affected; among this group, poverty levels declined by only 13 percent compared with a decline of 44 percent among other groups (non-SCs/STs) in 1983–2005. Tribals in rural areas in Chhattisgarh, Jharkhand, Madhya Pradesh, Maharashtra, and Rajasthan, too, recorded far lower declines in poverty relative to other groups.

The high correlation between poverty and tribal concentration plays out at the district level as well. A World Bank report (2008a) on lagging regions in India finds that poor infrastructure, which is otherwise a significant explanatory variable of district-level poverty in lagging states, cannot explain poverty in rich states such as Gujarat. In the rich states, pockets of poverty largely overlap with

Table 2.4 Trends in Poverty Incidence in States with a High Proportion of Adivasis

percent

State	1983		1993–94		2004–05	
	STs	All	STs	All	STs	All
Assam	48.5	41.5	40.9	41.4	12.3	20.5
Gujarat	58.5	33.0	30.9	24.1	33.1	17.0
Madhya Pradesh	71.6	50.4	60.4	41.7	57.5	38.2
Maharashtra	63.1	44.3	53.1	36.8	54.2	30.6
Orissa	86.2	66.3	70.9	48.7	75.2	46.6
Rajasthan	63.0	38.6	44.5	27.5	32.2	21.4
Jharkhand	73.5	59.6	67.7	55.4	53.4	42.1
Chhattisgarh	58.7	50.5	53.1	44.4	53.8	41.0
All India	63.3	45.6	49.6	35.8	43.8	27.5

Source: Staff estimates based on Schedule 1.0 of the respective section of NSS rounds and official poverty lines.

Note: The states shown had an Adivasi population of 10 percent or more in 1983, excluding the northeastern states.

significant tribal presence, that is, the poorest districts in the rich states have a much higher proportion of STs (10 percent compared with a state average of 3 percent).

Results also vary by place of residence; on average, Adivasis in urban areas did better than those in rural areas. Figure 2.1 shows growth incidence curves for STs in rural and urban areas, indicating the growth rate in expenditures between 1993–94 and 2004–05 at each percentile of the expenditure distribution. In urban areas, in a pattern similar to that of other social groups, richer STs registered higher expenditure growth than poorer STs. This may perhaps reflect a situation in which a few elite among the STs had access to and benefited from reserved jobs, while a significant proportion served as manual labor in construction projects (see box 2.3 elsewhere below). Table 3.4 in chapter 3 shows that, among Adivasi men who are self-employed in nonfarm jobs, an overwhelming 60 percent are in professional or managerial occupations. It is important to note that only a little over 8 percent of Adivasi men are in nonfarm jobs to start with and that these are clearly people who may have acquired upward mobility over several generations of education and movement out of rural areas. In public employment, too, while it is often not possible to find qualified ST candidates even to fill the reserved quotas, some tribes tend to dominate in higher-level public sector jobs. There is anecdotal evidence that the Meena tribe holds a large

Figure 2.1 Consumption Growth among Urban STs Was Highly Skewed with Bigger Gains Near the Top of the Distribution

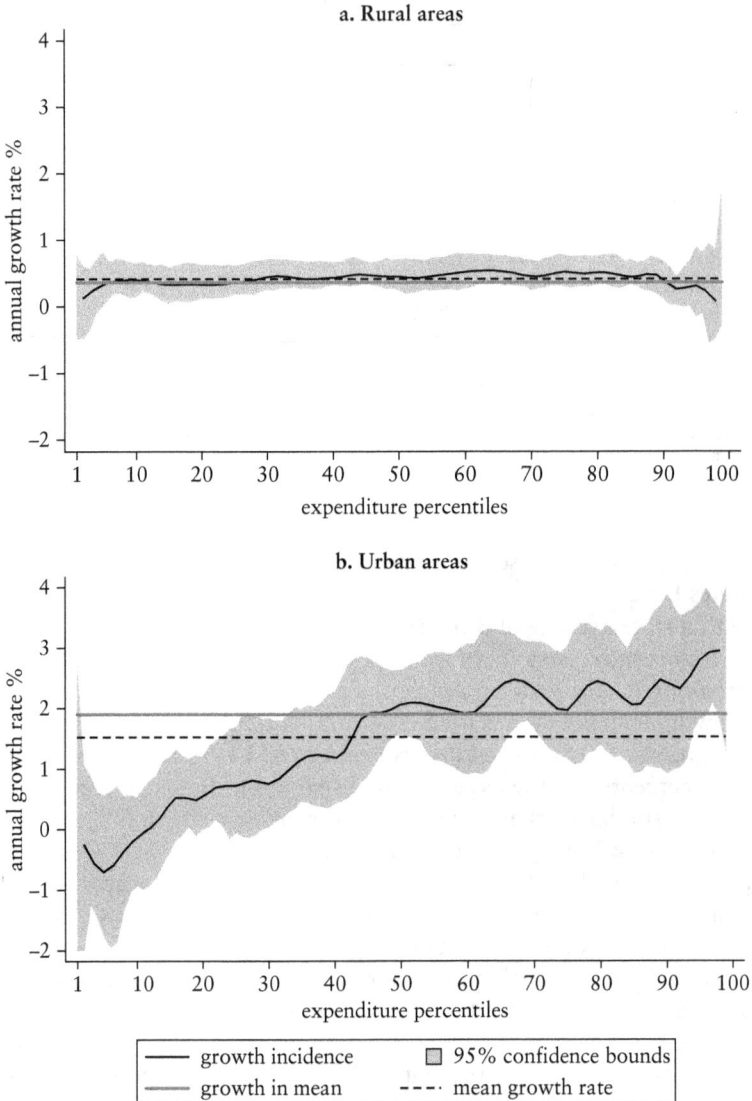

a. Rural areas

b. Urban areas

Source: Staff estimates based on Schedule 1.0 of the respective NSS rounds.
Note: The growth incidence curves show growth in per capita consumption between 1993–94 and 2004–05 at each percentile of the expenditure distribution.

share of these higher-level public sector jobs in Rajasthan, where many of them live, but also at the all-India level.

The Survival Disadvantage: Mortality among Adivasi Children

> Yes, how many deaths will it take till we know
> That too many children have died?
>   Adapted from Bob Dylan, "Blowin' in the Wind," 1962[9]

Every monsoon season, the Indian media are rife with stories of child deaths in tribal areas, which are frequently reported as malnutrition deaths. Kalahandi District in Orissa, for instance, has been a metaphor for starvation because of press reports dating back to the 1980s. The Melghat area in Maharashtra has similarly surfaced in the press, especially during the monsoon when migrant Adivasis return to the villages to find empty food stocks in their homes (box 2.1). This is followed by public outrage, sometimes by public interest litigation, and often by haggling over numbers (see Bunsha 2002). And, so, the saying in Maharashtra that sums up the apathy of the political and administrative elite at the local level goes, "nehmi yeto pavsala" ("the monsoon comes every year") (Das 2001). This section documents the stark disadvantage of tribal children compared with children in other social groups.

Child deaths in tribal areas typically cluster around periods of seasonal stress such as periods of drought, when household food supplies are low and employment dries up (as in Rajasthan), or during the monsoon (as in Maharashtra), when access to remote communities is broken (see Prabhu 1992). Public interest law suits have been filed on behalf of families that have lost their children, and state governments have been repeatedly directed by the courts to take remedial action.[10] The government's response to the excess mortality among tribal children is to state that the deaths are not due to malnutrition, but that poverty and ignorance are the causes (Khandare 2004; Bunsha 2002; Bavadam 2005). Nonetheless, state governments have undoubtedly become more vigilant on this issue, though solutions are still ad hoc and in a crisis mode. For instance, during an emergency, large numbers of medical personnel are deployed to vulnerable areas, but, normally, absenteeism among doctors is endemic in rural and, especially, tribal areas. Additionally, the poor registration of births and deaths has meant that there is frequent haggling over the real numbers of deaths and of children otherwise affected (see Bang, Reddy, and Deshmukh 2002).

Box 2.1 Melghat: Years of Reporting Malnutrition

Melghat, a forested region in Maharashtra inhabited mostly by the Korku tribe, has long been a metaphor for starvation. It consists of two *talukas* (development blocks)—Chikaldhara and Dharni—in Amravati District. Every year, there are estimates of deaths on a large scale among tribal children (Menon 2009). Any attempt at understanding tribal deprivation in Melghat is incomplete without a historical account of the region. The major part of Melghat is covered by the Tiger Reserve (a buffer zone) and a reserve forest. Conversion of the forest in 1974 into a buffer zone to protect tigers has meant an occupational shift for the Korkus, who were traditionally gatherers of forest produce. This has precipitated problems in recent years. The government has banned the collection of products such as *kendu* or *tendu* leaves (*Diospyros melanoxylon*), which are used in the production of *bidi*, an Indian cigarette. The Korkus also have limited access to hunting and fishing. The introduction of cash crops such as soybeans instead of local crops such as *kodo* (a type of millet grain) and *savarya* (a local crop used to produce a drink) has upset the balance of food security.

Some Korkus therefore migrate and then return during the monsoon to transplant rice and other crops on their subsistence plots of land. This is the time when household food stocks deplete rapidly, and cash for the purchase of food is scarce. The local administration, which is located far away in Chikaldhara and Dharni, has difficulty responding to issues in a timely manner. Moreover, most line officials perceive the Korkus as ignorant people, selling their nutritious food such as *tur* (a bean) and *gram* (mung bean) for cash. To this, tribal people respond, "Do you think we don't like to eat lentils? We sell them because we have to pay back loans from the landlord."

Source: Khandare (2004).

While STs saw significant gains in health indicators, some of which improved at rates that were more rapid than the population average, the gains were not sufficient to bridge the gap between the STs and the rest. Under-5 mortality remains a stark marker of tribal deprivation in India; nearly 96 tribal children die for every 1,000 live births, compared with an under-5 mortality of 74 per 1,000 for all India. Most child deaths among Adivasis are concentrated in rural areas and in the 1–4 age-group. These children make up about 12 percent of all children under 5, but account for 23 percent of all deaths in the 1–4 age-group in rural areas. Dalit children account for about 22 percent of all children under 5, but 28 percent of the deaths in the 1–4 age-group. Among Other Backward Classes (OBCs) and general category children, the proportion of deaths is much lower than the representation of these groups in the under-5 population (table 2.5).

Table 2.5 Child Mortality among Adivasis Far Exceeds
Their Relative Share in the Rural Population

percent

Social group	% of all children under 5	% of child (1–4) deaths	% of under-5 deaths
SC	21.6	28.1	24.6
ST	11.7	23.0	13.9
OBC	41.8	35.5	39.6
Other	24.9	13.4	21.9
Total	100	100	100

Source: Das, Kapoor, and Nikitin (2010) based on 2005 NFHS data.

Note: The table refers to children born during the five years prior to the survey in rural areas only.

Most states with larger tribal populations (excluding the north-eastern states) also have higher child mortality rates. While child mortality among STs is high (over 37 deaths per 1,000 live births for the cohort of children born in 2001–05), the numbers differ considerably across states. Table 2.6 examines the geographic distribution of mortality rates among STs in India. Considering only states where STs account for 9 percent or more of the state's population (at or above their share in the national population), we find that there is significant state-level variation in child mortality among STs (from 8 deaths per 1,000 in Sikkim to 43 in Jharkhand).[11] Four states—Jharkhand, Madhya Pradesh, Orissa, and Rajasthan—register child mortality rates greater than 39 per 1,000. However, these are also states that are inhabited by a large number of STs.[12]

These high levels of child mortality in states with larger tribal populations also bear out at the district level. Analyzing the health status of different social groups in Orissa, the World Bank (2006), for instance, found that infant mortality is directly proportional to the share of STs in the district (figure 2.2).

Tribal children are on a par with others at birth, but fall well behind by the time they are 5. Studies in other parts of the world also disaggregate mortality outcomes by race or ethnicity. Heaton and Amoateng (2007), for instance, document child mortality and child survival rates for different ethnic groups in South Africa and find white children to have clearly the highest rates of survival. Gaps in mortality between black and white South African children tend to appear at early ages and widen as the children grow older. The pattern of the mortality gap between STs and non-STs in India is curiously different in that the former are on a par with their nontribal counterparts at birth, but are rapidly disadvantaged by the time they are 5 years old. This divergence is all the more striking if compared

Table 2.6 Child Mortality Rates among STs, by State, 2005
deaths per 1,000 live births

State	Neonatal	Postneonatal	Infant	Child	Under-5	STs as % of state population
Rajasthan	24.0	19.3	43.3	40.0	83.3	12.6
Sikkim	11.7	25.3	37.0	7.7	44.7	20.6
Arunachal Pradesh	32.4	23.9	56.3	26.0	82.3	64.2
Nagaland	12.7	18.8	31.5	17.3	48.8	89.2
Manipur	33.6	22.0	55.6	9.3	64.9	32.3
Mizoram	15.6	16.7	32.3	23.8	56.1	94.5
Tripura	23.8	40.1	63.9	11.6	75.5	31.1
Meghalaya	24.9	21.5	46.4	14.6	61.0	85.9
Assam	35.6	13.0	48.6	34.5	83.1	12.4
Jharkhand	52.1	25.3	77.4	43.0	120.4	26.3
Orissa	52.2	28.0	80.2	39.2	119.4	22.1
Chhattisgarh	44.0	22.8	66.8	30.8	97.6	31.8
Madhya Pradesh	50.2	25.2	75.4	41.6	117.0	20.3
Gujarat	29.5	38.8	68.3	28.5	96.8	14.8
Maharashtra	47.0	8.8	55.8	30.7	86.5	8.9

Source: Compiled by the authors.
Note: Only states with ST populations of 9 percent or above according to the 2001 Census; calculations based on NFHS-3 for the cohort 0–4 years of age.

Figure 2.2 The District-Level Relationship between Infant
Mortality and the Concentration of STs

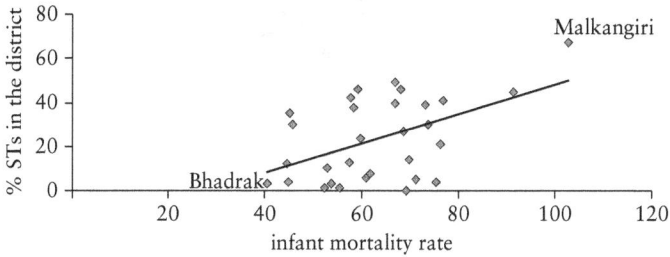

Source: Staff calculations based on the Reproductive Child Health Survey.

Figure 2.3 Adivasi Children: Lower Risk of Dying at Birth,
but Greater Risk by Age 5

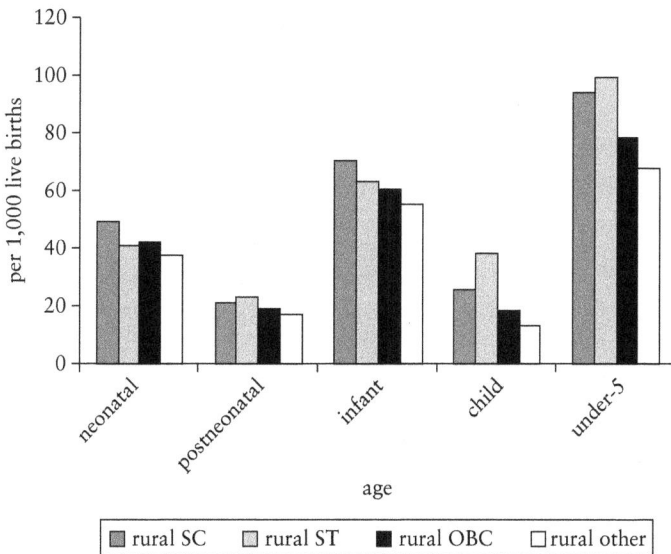

Source: Staff calculations based on 2005 NFHS data.

with SC children, who also face disadvantages. From the neonatal
to the infant period, ST children in rural areas have a lower chance
of dying than SC children. However, between the ages of 1 and 4,
they start to lag behind and register much higher mortality than SC
children (figure 2.3).

Table 2.7 shows the diverging hazard functions for STs and non-
STs. During the first year, the probabilities of survival of STs and

Table 2.7 STs and Non-STs: The Gap in the Relative
Hazard Rate

Indicator	Neonatal	Postneonatal	Infant	Child	Under-5
Relative hazard rate					
Non-STs	1.01	0.98	0.99	0.92	0.98
STs	0.96	1.17	1.06	2.25	1.26
Test of significance of difference					
Wald chi2(1)	1.69	1.85	0.78	36.77	16.44
Pr>chi2	0.194	0.174	0.378	0.000	0.000

Source: Das, Kapoor, and Nikitin (2010) based on 2005–06 NFHS data.

non-STs do not differ significantly, that is, there is no significant difference in their infant mortality rates. However, during the second year, the gap in the chances of dying between Adivasi and non-Adivasi children widens and becomes statistically significant.

The initial parity in mortality outcomes between Adivasi children and others is perhaps related to the cultural and environmental practices, including birth spacing, feeding, and weaning, that the former follow (Maharatna 1998, 2000). These sustainable practices also seem to help if access to formal medical care for children and their mothers is difficult or costly. It is as tribal children grow up and are weaned, particularly in the age range of 1–4, that they face substantially greater risk than children in other categories. This is also the age when, perhaps, formal medical care (for example, the proper and timely treatment of diarrhea and acute respiratory infections) is critical, and reliance on traditional mechanisms alone does not work. It is here that the chasm between the tribals and the rest begins to appear and widen.

Not all regions and tribes show the same patterns of diverging mortality rates between tribal and nontribal children with increasing age. Some studies report a higher infant mortality rate among tribal groups, while others show a distinct advantage among tribal groups over the nontribal population in the same location (Maharatna 2005). For instance, a survey in Panchmahals District in Gujarat, the results of which were published in 1992 (Gujral, Chohan, and Gopaldas 1992), showed inordinately high rates of infant mortality among tribals and a declining tribal-nontribal differential with increasing age. While, in the aggregate, sex ratios among tribal children are better than those among nontribals, this study found the reverse to be true in Panchmahals.

If one controls for poverty, does the tribal effect on mortality disappear? The answer is no. Our multivariate results, which are presented and discussed in Das, Kapoor, and Nikitin (2010), are in keeping with the trends described above. We find that, even in the

presence of controls, the disparity between STs and non-STs in terms
of mortality rates is robust at older ages (1–4 and under 5). During
the neonatal, postneonatal, and infant periods, ST and non-ST children have more or less similar odds of dying. *Yet, between the ages
of 1 and 4 and, overall, under age 5, mortality trends among tribal
and nontribal children diverge: ST children face much higher (more
than two times higher) odds of dying than non-ST children.*

This finding is striking for a variety of reasons. Most analyses
lump all under-5 mortality together and find that poverty status
explains most of the differential in mortality among SCs and STs (in
comparison with other social groups). A World Bank study (2007)
in Orissa, for instance, finds that, while child and infant mortality
rates are higher among the STs, this is largely a function of poverty
(lower levels of income and assets), low levels of education, and the
poor access and utilization of health services. This has been confirmed more recently by Sharma et al. (2009), whose analysis of the
NFHS data for Orissa shows significant disparity in the neonatal,
infant, and under-5 mortality rates in the state according to tribal
status, wealth, and education groups. These authors find that the
lowest and the second-lowest wealth quintiles (based on an asset
index) experience the highest under-5 mortality (119 and 97 deaths
per 1,000, respectively, compared with, respectively, 66 and 28
deaths per 1,000 among children of families belonging to the top
two quintiles). In other words, children in the poorest households
are four times as likely to die before their fifth birthday compared
with children in the richest quintile. Finally, our own multivariate
analysis using Reproductive Child Health Survey data (RCH II,
2005) also finds that the effect of tribal (and Dalit) status disap-
peared once we controlled for wealth quintile (World Bank 2006).

In sum, the conventional narrative is that the higher mortality
among tribal children is explained by the poverty status of these
children. However, our analysis finds that, *even after we control for
wealth*, tribal children show a higher likelihood of dying than their
nontribal peers between ages 1 and 4. This comes through because
we disaggregate the under-5 mortality rate into its age-specific constituent parts. This finding has significant policy relevance because
it means that, more than socioeconomic status, the problem of high
child mortality is explained by concentration in tribal groups.
Addressing poverty alone therefore may not help. Unless interventions reach these groups, India may not be able to meet its goal of
reducing child mortality by two-thirds by 2015.

*While there has been improvement among all children over the
last decade or so, the child mortality rates among tribals in rural
areas have nearly stagnated.* In table 2.8, we look at changes in

Table 2.8 Early Childhood Mortality Rates by Residence and Ethnicity among Different Cohorts, 2005
deaths per 1,000 live births

Indicator	Birth cohort 0–4			Birth cohort 10–14			Change (t2/t1–1), %		
	Overall	Rural	Urban	Overall	Rural	Urban	Overall	Rural	Urban
Neonatal mortality									
SCs	42.9	46.4	31.1	55.4	62.2	35.0	–23	–25	–11
STs	41.9	43.3	28.3	66.5	68.3	45.8	–37	–37	–38
OBCs	38.4	42.1	26.8	53.9	60.0	36.1	–29	–30	–26
Other	35.2	38.9	28.2	40.5	45.9	30.8	–13	–15	–8
Postneonatal mortality									
SCs	20.8	22.7	14.3	26.2	29.0	18.0	–21	–22	–21
STs	21.8	22.7	13.3	33.3	33.1	34.5	–35	–31	–61
OBCs	17.2	17.6	15.5	24.9	26.4	20.8	–31	–33	–25
Other	15.2	18.5	9.0	20.5	24.6	13.5	–26	–25	–33

Infant mortality									
SCs	63.7	69.1	45.4	81.6	91.2	53.0	−22	−24	−14
STs	63.7	66.0	41.6	99.8	101.4	80.3	−36	−35	−48
OBCs	55.6	59.7	42.3	78.8	86.4	56.9	−29	−31	−26
Other	50.4	57.4	37.2	61.0	70.5	44.3	−17	−19	−16
Child mortality									
SCs	23.6	24.5	20.6	33.4	37.9	19.9	−29	−35	4
STs	37.9	40.2	16.4	39.4	40.3	29.5	−4	0	−44
OBCs	15.2	18.1	6.5	23.6	26.9	14.2	−36	−33	−54
Other	9.3	10.9	6.2	18.2	22.1	11.2	−49	−51	−45
Under-5 mortality									
SCs	87.3	93.6	66.0	115.0	129.1	72.9	−24	−27	−9
STs	101.6	106.2	58.0	139.2	141.7	109.8	−27	−25	−47
OBCs	70.8	77.8	48.8	102.4	113.3	71.1	−31	−31	−31
Other	59.7	68.3	43.4	79.2	92.6	55.5	−25	−26	−22

Source: NFHS-3.

Note: The birth cohort is expressed in years preceding the NFHS-3.

childhood mortality rates for different birth cohorts (by caste or tribe status). We compare the mortality rates among children born in 2001–05 (0–4 years old at the time of the fielding of the NFHS-3 survey) with the rates among children born in 1991–95 (the 10–14 age cohort at the time of the fielding of the NFHS-3).

The table reveals several interesting stylized facts. It suggests that the neonatal, postneonatal, and infant mortality rates declined among children in all groups. In fact, STs, especially those in urban areas, experienced the most dramatic reductions (in the range of 30 to 60 percent) with respect to these mortality measures. Similarly, the neo-natal, postneonatal, and infant mortality levels among SCs dropped considerably (the reduction in rates ranging from 11 to 21 percent). Driven by improvements in children's survival to the first birthday, the under-5 mortality rates also declined among all groups.

However, among STs and SCs (particularly STs in rural areas and SCs in urban areas), the change in child mortality has not kept pace with improvements in the other four mortality indicators. In fact, child mortality *increased* among the SC children in urban areas: with respect to 1991–95, SC children in cities or towns had a higher prob-ability of dying between their first and fifth birthdays. Meanwhile, in rural areas, child mortality among SCs declined by over one-third.

Though there was no increase in child mortality among STs over-all, there was a definite stagnation in rural areas. While significant declines (44 percent) were recorded in child mortality rates among tribal children in urban areas, this needs to be qualified by the fact that only small numbers of tribals live in cities and towns. Yet, over-all, there is *stagnation in child mortality among urban SCs and rural STs* despite the government's focused attempts to reduce child mor-tality. Mortality among 1- to 4-year-olds in these groups has not responded to policy interventions, perhaps because a wider range of socioeconomic factors are affecting survival at this stage. Few stud-ies document the need to differentiate between age-specific child-hood mortality, and those that do are limited in scope to only a few specific tribes (for instance, see Kapoor and Kshatriya 2000).[13] This reemphasizes the need to shift attention from infant mortality to child mortality as an indicator of tribal deprivation and tailor policy responses accordingly.

Other Processes Related to Higher Mortality among Adivasi Children

Tribal children are at much greater risk of malnutrition. Malnutri-tion is widespread in India. Among all children, 48 percent exhibit

stunting, a deficit in height-for-age that is a sign of long-term malnutrition; 24 percent exhibit severe stunting; and 42 percent show
signs of being underweight.[14] Worse than the all-Indian figures are
the outcomes among ST children: 53 percent are stunted; 29 percent
are severely stunted; and 55 percent are underweight. The gap
between ST children and children in other groups appears within the
first 10 months after birth and persists, with some variations,
throughout early childhood. The rise in severe wasting among ST
children during the first 10 months of life is particularly alarming
(figure 2.4).

Microstudies on food insecurity among Adivasi households provide a contextual picture of the causes of chronic malnutrition. For
instance, a 2005 survey of Adivasi areas in two Indian states found

Figure 2.4 More ST Children Are Severely Stunted and
Wasted within the First 10 Months of Birth, 2005–06

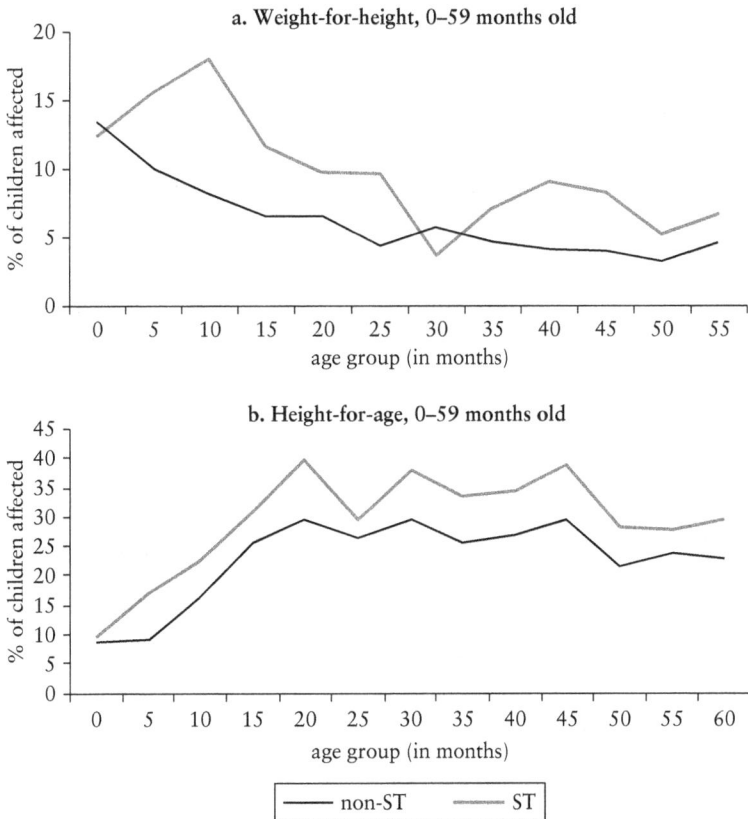

a. Weight-for-height, 0–59 months old

b. Height-for-age, 0–59 months old

non-ST   ST

Source: Das, Kapoor, and Nikitin (2010) based on NFHS data.

that 99 percent of the sample Adivasi households faced chronic hunger, one-quarter had faced semistarvation during the previous week, and not a single household had more than 4 of 10 assets from a list that included such basic items as a blanket, a pair of shoes, and a radio (CEFS 2005). Following reports of child deaths, there have been media reports of empty household food stocks, that may have led to high levels of malnutrition (see above). The least well off are the tribes that are not mentioned in the notified list of STs. These "denotified" tribes remain not only marginal, but mostly invisible in the national debate.

Are tribal children more likely to become sick as they grow older, and, so, more of them die? The answer is no. Contrary to expectations, tribal babies are not more likely to become sick because of diarrhea or respiratory disease, although they are more malnourished than other children. However, they are much less likely than other children to receive treatment. Figure 2.5 shows that disparities remained in the treatment of illnesses among tribal children 3 years of age and below, compared with other children, although the incidence of disease varied only slightly. The gap was more acute in the treatment of acute respiratory infections. Over 41 percent of ST children received no treatment for fever or cough as opposed to only 27 percent among SC children, 28 percent among OBC children, and 25 percent among children in other castes. In the case of the treatment of diarrhea, OBC and ST children were less likely to receive any treatment; yet, in this case, too, the incidence of diarrhea is

Figure 2.5 Tribal Children: Less Likely to Fall Sick with Cough or Fever, but Much Less Likely to Be Treated

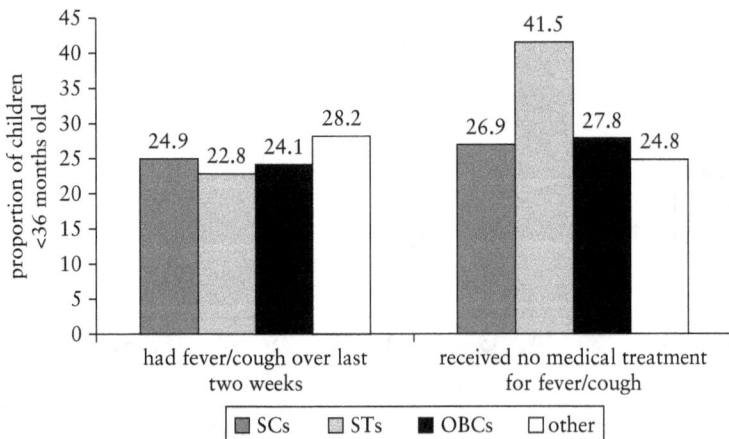

Source: Das, Kapoor, and Nikitin (2010) based on NFHS-3.

roughly the same across social groups. In sum, even though ST children experience disproportionately higher levels of malnutrition, they do not experience much higher levels of the morbidity associated with common childhood ailments.[15] This is a puzzle for it suggests that malnutrition among tribal children alone cannot explain high child mortality rates (except through severe malnutrition). Clearly, therefore, the major story in the health and mortality of tribal children is not so much that they are malnourished and weak and become sick more often, but that they receive treatment less often.[16] This finding has important policy implications for it suggests that, even as food security efforts must pick up to address malnutrition, what is needed, urgently, is much better medical care to address common childhood ailments among tribal children.

Vaccine preventable diseases are an important proximate cause of mortality among children in all groups. There has been overall improvement in immunization coverage in India, but, as we document here, while improvements have been larger in magnitude among tribals, the absolute proportions are still low, and gaps between tribal and nontribal children remain large, especially in rural areas.

We measure immunization coverage using two indicators: the *breadth* of coverage (percentage receiving any basic vaccination) and the *intensity* or *quality* of coverage (percentage receiving all basic vaccinations). Our analysis using NFHS data suggests that both indicators registered substantial improvement between 1992 and 2005, especially among STs, thus narrowing the differential between tribal and nontribal populations (table 2.9). At the all-India level, of the 12- to 23-month-olds born to non-ST women in the 15–49 age-group who have ever been married, the proportion that received any of the basic vaccines increased from 71 to 95 percent (a 34 percent increase). The corresponding increase among ST children was 53 percent, from 58 to 89 percent. The intensity of coverage expanded more slowly: 23 percent for all India and 30 percent among STs.[17] The improvement was slower in rural areas, where most of the tribal groups are concentrated. This expanded coverage of immunization is perhaps responsible for the fact that tribal children and other children are at similar risk of becoming sick from certain causes.

Mothers of tribal children are much less likely to receive health care. While improvements occurred at a more rapid pace among tribal women than among other women, the low base from which the former started has driven the more rapid progress. Moreover, the gaps between tribal and other women on a range of indicators related to access to maternal health care continue to be wide (figure 2.6). For instance, the proportion of tribal women making antenatal visits or using contraception was lower than the population average or the

Table 2.9 ST Children: The Breadth of Immunization Coverage Improved, but the Intensity Expanded More Slowly

percent

Indicator	Urban			Rural			Overall		
	ST	Other	Total	ST	Other	Total	ST	Other	Total
All basic vaccinations (intensity)[a]									
1992–93	36	51	51	24	32	31	25	37	35
1998–99	43	57	57	22	39	37	25	43	41
2005–06	52	58	58	30	40	39	32	45	44
Change									
1993–2006	45	13	13	27	25	25	30	22	23
Any basic vaccination (breadth)[b]									
1992–93	79	84	84	56	67	66	58	71	70
1998–99	85	95	95	75	86	85	76	88	87
2005–06	94	97	97	89	95	94	89	95	95
Change									
1993–2006	19	15	15	57	41	43	53	34	35

Source: NFHS.

a. Children 12 to 23 months of age born to women 15 to 49 years of age who have ever been married.

b. Basic vaccinations include three rounds of polio (1–3) vaccine, three rounds of diphtheria-pertussis-tetanus (DPT 1–3) vaccine, tuberculosis (BCG) vaccine, and measles vaccine.

Figure 2.6 Mothers of Tribal Children Are Less Likely to Receive Health Care

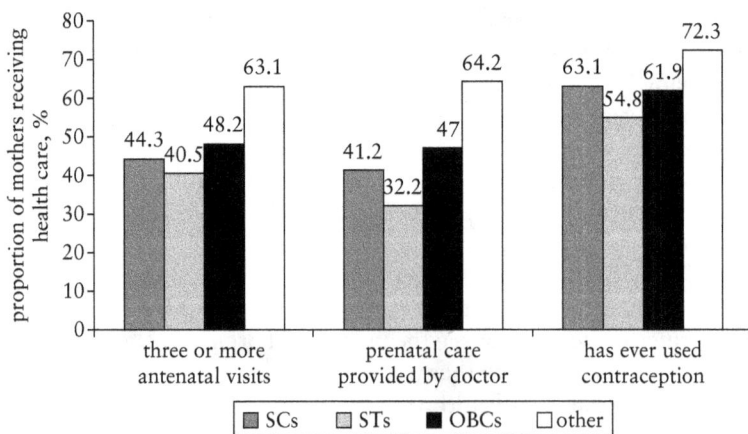

Source: NFHS-3.

average among women belonging to other social groups. Overall, almost 60 percent of all women and 80 percent of tribal women give birth at home.

The comparisons with SC and OBC women are particularly instructive. In the 2005 NFHS, 55 percent of tribal women reported that they had used contraception at some point, compared with 63 percent of SCs, 62 percent of OBCs, and 65 percent for all India (figure 2.6). In comparison with SC and OBC women, a relatively smaller proportion of ST women reported three or more antenatal visits (40 percent, compared with 44 percent among SC women and 48 percent among OBC women). ST women were also less likely to receive prenatal care from doctors. Only one-third received such care in 2005, compared with the population average of 49 percent. Worse, the proportion of ST women to receive such care actually declined marginally from 1998 levels (from 35 to 32 percent).

Medical practitioners and others often link poor health outcomes among tribals to lack of demand or ignorance. Nagda (2004) documents the reluctance of tribal women to accept modern treatment. Using his research in Rajasthan, he describes how about 86 percent of tribal births in the state occur at home, and over three-fourths are conducted by untrained *dais* (traditional midwives) or other personnel largely because antenatal care is not accepted and is not considered necessary or customary in tribal societies. The decision about the nature of the treatment is taken at the community level (mostly by traditional healers known as *bhopas*) based on traditional health care systems. However, the evidence of Adivasis not accepting modern treatment is patchy. Duggal (1990) showed that, even 20 years ago, Adivasis in Dhule did not use traditional systems of medicine and that *bhagats* (holy persons) were almost nonexistent. He also found that Adivasis had complete faith in allopathic systems of medicine. However, the rate of utilization of public health services is higher if a community health worker is present. Because the health workers are Adivasis, they tend to be used more by Adivasis. Also, where health workers are active, the rate of utilization of all levels of the public health system rises. Thus, from the study, it appears that there is mistrust of the public health delivery system rather than of the allopathic system. The migration of tribals during the lean season to cities and towns makes the task of surveillance for antenatal care, immunization, and growth monitoring among children even more difficult. It is therefore likely that low demand for health or nutrition may also be triggered by gaps in supply (Bharat, Patkar, and Thomas 2003; Pallavi 2004; Suchitra 2005; see also box 2.2).

Box 2.2 Mistrust Is a Barrier to Adivasi Access to
Health Services

"Korku women have to be taught everything about taking care of
children. . . . They don't know how to take care of or feed children.
When a child eats dogs, and cats eat with him, and the mother does
nothing. . . ."
Non-Adivasi woman, Dharni Block, Amravati District, Maharashtra

"Many times, a sick child is taken to the health center and doesn't
become better, but dies there. There is no use in taking a child to the
health center."
Korku woman, Dharni Block, Amravati District, Maharashtra

Sources: Government of Maharashtra, UNICEF, and WHO (1991).

Metaled roads penetrated only the fringe, as far as the foot of
the hills. All communication beyond that point was by earth
roads. There was no wheeled traffic, except for a few bicycles
owned by some prosperous residents.

Cited in Hunt and Harrison, *The District Officer in India,*
1930–1947 (1980)

*The remoteness of tribal habitations creates problems in service
delivery and monitoring.* The words above seem to describe many
of today's tribal hamlets, but they are actually the words of officers of British India who were based in the Agency Tracts in the
early part of the last century. (British officers in tribal areas were
known as agents and reported directly to the governor-general of
Madras.) The inability of service providers to reach tribal areas
and of tribals to reach services was a consistent theme in the development and administrative literature on India during the British
period.

Because tribals live in hamlets that are much smaller than the
typical revenue villages, connecting them by a road network has
proven extremely challenging.[18] The new rural roads program, the
Pradhan Mantri Gram Sadak Yojana, includes a large allocation to
connect those areas that have been left out. In tribal areas, it uses
relaxed criteria and permits the connection of communities or habitations that have populations of 250 or more, but it gives prece-
dence to those villages that have populations of 500 or more (unless
they fall within the 34 Naxal-affected areas).[19] However, tribal
areas are mostly sparsely populated, and many tribal hamlets have

a population below 250. In Rajasthan alone, there are 591 unconnected tribal habitations, each with a population below 250 (Government of Rajasthan 2009). In Orissa, after the implementation of the current phase of the rural roads program, 1,049 habitations with a population of 1,000 and 1,662 habitations with a population of 500 will still have to be covered. The number is even larger for unconnected habitations of 250 or more.

The issue of tribal remoteness has been underscored in a number of recent studies, which highlight that this factor accounts for a large part of the structural disparities between STs and others (see Kijima 2006). A longitudinal study in tribal-dominated Bolangir District in Orissa found, for instance, that villagers took young children to the hospital only if the condition of the children was critical, given the difficulty with transportation (poor roads) and the expenditure associated with hiring a vehicle. They also identified giving birth as a risk because mothers could not reach health centers because of inadequate road access, particularly during the rainy season (van Dillen 2006). Remoteness also affects the construction of facilities; Banerjee and Somanathan (2007) find that, between 1971 and 1991, fewer education and health facilities were available in parliamentary constituencies with ST concentrations.

W. H. Christie, an imperial civil service officer in 1928–47, wrote as follows while he was district commissioner in Chittagong Hill Tracts:

> I was compelled to become a kind of witch doctor or medicine man. These villages were several days' march from the nearest hospital or dispensary and wherever I camped, the villagers brought their sick for me to cure. (Hunt and Harrison 1980)

Even where health centers exist, absenteeism is high. There are two issues with absenteeism. The first is that vacancies in health departments are high in tribal areas. Second, even if medical personnel are assigned to these areas, they either do not appear because they take leave, or, even if they do appear, they are often not found at the health centers. Doctors and technical staff find tribal areas difficult as family stations because of the poor infrastructure, and few states have a sustainable personnel policy for placing medical personnel in these areas (Rao 1998). Placements in tribal areas are often perceived as punishment postings that are assigned to nonperformers. Several states have instructed district administrations and health departments to recruit local women as auxiliary nurse midwives and accredited social health activists. However, in the remoter tribal pockets, there are often no women with even the minimal educational qualifications necessary to serve in these positions. As a result, the positions either remain vacant or are filled by nontribal, nonresident providers. Some nongovernmental organizations, such as the Society for Education Action and Research in Community Health, have innovated by giving uneducated tribal women training in basic health care management for common ailments and for the newborn, but this is far from the norm, and the absence of adequate personnel continues to be a binding constraint on the delivery of health services in tribal areas. Perhaps in tribal areas more than anywhere else, the idea suggested by Lant Pritchett (2008)—that the Indian state has strong head, but little control over its trunk—has the greatest relevance.

There have been a number of successful initiatives in both the nongovernmental and the public sectors to improve access to services in many tribal areas.[20] Studies from around the world suggest that the adaptation of health services to the culture of the beneficiaries (for instance, by recognizing the importance of traditional medicine) leads to better outcomes. Yet, the most well-known efforts have often been small, resource-intensive ones, making scaling-up a challenge. What K. Sujatha Rao, the current secretary of the Ministry of Health and Family Welfare, expressed in writing about health services among tribals in Andhra Pradesh in 1998 holds true today, over a decade later:

> The state's inability to provide a credible and feasible health care system that is accessible and affordable is indicative of the system failure in an important area of concern. . . . Even while tribal areas are the biggest challenge and most difficult to handle, unfortunately, experimentation is most in this area. So long as policy is "building and doctor oriented" there is little hope of any substantial improvement in the health status of the tribals. But then in the kind of planning process we have in the country, how do people get onto the agenda? How does policy become people oriented and be insulated from the influences of various interest groups: contractors, physicians, pharmaceutical industry, bureaucrats, foreign donors? Till an answer is found to these questions, this bungling will continue and the tribals will have to continue to pay the price. (Rao 1998)

Land and Natural Resources: A Central Role in Explaining Tribal Deprivation

Land and forests are the mainstay of tribal livelihoods. A large proportion of ST men in rural areas (44 percent) report that they are

self-employed farmers. However, the productivity of tribal agriculture is low: it is mostly rainfed hill cultivation undertaken with
limited resources. Even where horticulture is plentiful, poor marketing and transportation make tribal agriculture an unviable income-
generating enterprise. The relationship of STs to land is not restricted
merely to subsistence cultivation. It extends to their dependence on
natural resources for livelihoods and for food security (Saxena
1999). Over time, nonetheless, the average landholding has declined
more rapidly among STs than among other groups. Table 2.10
shows that average landholdings declined among all rural households from 1983 to 2004–05, but that they declined sharply among
STs. This reflects the alienation of STs from their traditional lands.
This alienation explains, to a large extent, the poor outcomes among
tribals. Besides loss of housing and land, the loss of control over
their *jal*, *jungle*, and *zameen* (water, forest, and land) has alienated
STs from public schemes, affected their traditional food practices, and
forced them to migrate to cities to work under harsh conditions.

*The welfare of STs is also dependent on the access of STs to non-
timber forest products.* About 60 percent of India's forests lie in the
187 tribal districts covered by Schedules V and VI of the Indian
Constitution (MOEF 2003). Estimates on Orissa indicate that over
one-fifth to one-half of the annual incomes of tribal households are
derived from nontimber forest products (NTFPs). Many NTFPs have
a high value. The debate over kendu leaves, for instance, is a heated
one. Tribal rights activists allege that the state and middlemen are
working to keep the tribals' share of the profits small. Thus, Vasundhara (2006) reports that the wages of kendu leaf pickers as a proportion of the total value of sales are much lower in Orissa compared
with Andhra Pradesh and Madhya Pradesh. Orissa has devolved the
procurement and marketing of 69 NTFPs to *gram sabhas* (village
assemblies in which each village resident is a member). However,
the lack of capacity among the gram sabhas in these areas has meant
that middlemen may have benefited more than tribal people.

Table 2.10 The Average Landholding in Rural Areas

hectares

Year	STs	SCs	Non-SCs/STs
1983	2.16	0.89	1.72
1993–94	1.37	0.53	1.19
2004–05	0.99	0.37	0.86

Source: Calculations based on NSS data.

The marketing of NTFPs has been taken over by the public sector, but this has led to a reduction in prices because many buyers have opted out. The inefficient government machinery has led to delayed payments, and widespread corruption has allowed contractors to continue making profits at the expense of tribals (Burra 2008). Saxena (2004, 2) explains as follows:

> On paper the state agencies have worked with multiple objectives: to collect revenue; to protect the interests of the tribals as sellers; and to satisfy the conflicting demands by industry and other end-users. In practice, a hierarchy of objectives developed: industry and other large end-users had the first charge on the product at low and subsidized rates; revenue was maximized subject to the first objective which implied that there was no consistent policy to encourage value addition at lower levels; tribals and the interest of the poor [were] relegated to the third level.

According to the Panchayats Extension to the Scheduled Areas Act (PESA) discussed elsewhere below, the *gram panchayats* (local governments) and gram sabhas are the owners of NTFPs, but the forest departments maintain that villages do not have control over reserved forests because these are outside village boundaries, and PESA is therefore not applicable to them. This is a legal issue, and even the two relevant ministries in the government of India, the Ministry of Environment and Forests and the Ministry of Rural Development, hold different views about the applicability of PESA to reserved forests and about the inclusion of kendu (or tendu) and bamboo (high-value products) among the NTFPs to be controlled by the panchayats (Saxena 2004).

> In spite of Government's intention to bring development to the people, development interventions do at times create undesirable consequences.
> Orissa Resettlement and Rehabilitation Policy, 2006

Tribal lands have been alienated from tribals for a variety of reasons, and large infrastructure has led to large-scale displacement and discontent. With the increase in the number of large infrastructure projects, the relationship of tribals with the land has been translated into a relationship with development more generally. The issue of land alienation has spearheaded massive movements (that include both tribals and nontribals), particularly against the acquisition by the state of land for development. For example, the movement against the Sardar Sarovar Dam on the Narmada River has been a watershed of sorts: it brought environmental activists and tribal rights activists together in a strong critique of a development paradigm perceived as exploitative of tribals.[21]

While other groups have also suffered, tribals comprise a large proportion of those displaced by infrastructure projects, far in excess of their proportion in the population. Ekka (2000) notes that, in Jharkhand, nearly 90 percent of those displaced by various projects (such as dams) between 1951 and 1995 were tribals. Displacement, in turn, leads to what Shah (2007) calls a "logjam of adverse conditions" for those affected: productive assets and income sources are lost; people find themselves shifting to a new area and a new pattern of economy with which they are least acquainted; community systems and social networks are weakened; and cultural identity, traditional authority, and the potential for mutual help are diminished (Beck 2009).

Tribal land is also vulnerable to private transactions. Private transactions have contributed to tribal deprivation (see von Fürer-Haimendorf 1982). Over time, tribal lands have been "usurped" or "alienated," according to the Planning Commission, as:

> non-tribal outsiders who converge into these areas corner both land and the new economic opportunities in commerce and petty industry. The incomplete rehabilitation of the displaced tribals has further compounded their woes as they are pushed into a vortex of increasing assetlessness, unemployment, debt bondage and destitution. (Government of India 2002, 458)

Tribal indebtedness is one of the main causes of land alienation. In his research on the reasons for the displacement of tribals in Madhya Pradesh, Mander (2002) discusses how tribal people borrow at usurious rates from moneylenders to finance consumption. However, to service their high-interest debt, several of the borrowers borrow again from government banks. The cycle of indebtedness eventually ends in tribal borrowers seeking permission to transfer their land to the government to repay the government loan. Some tribals who are unable to pay their debts join the ranks of bonded labor, an extensive practice in the Mahanadi Valley (for details, see Roy 2002; see also box 2.3).[22] A major reason for borrowing from private sources is the poor network of government banks in remote tribal areas. According to the India Human Development Survey, only 10 percent of Adivasi women had individual or joint bank accounts in 2005, only about one-third the proportion among non-SC/ST/OBC women (Desai et al. 2010).

Box 2.3 Distress Migration among Adivasis

A survey in 2004 found that nearly 80 percent of Adivasis in rural Maharashtra migrated to cities for four to six months each year. A majority worked under harsh and hazardous conditions in stone quarries, brick kilns, salt pans, and excavation and construction sites and as casual laborers. One report in the salt commissioner's records in the state estimates that nearly 90 percent of all workers employed in salt pans in Raigad, Sindhudurg, and Thane districts were Adivasis. Most were distress migrants. Some were picked up by contractors from tribal villages as bonded laborers in exchange for distress loans to pay for emergencies such as sudden illnesses. Lump-sum wages were fixed through *thar* (an oral agreement) between the laborer and contractor and paid at the end of the season after advances had been deducted. Despite exploitation, the Adivasis preferred the assurance of thar to the insecurity of working as daily wage laborers. In the latter case, they assembled in fixed spots (*nakas*) in urban centers for work and were often paid less than the mandatory minimum wage. There were also instances of contractors disappearing at the time of payment. Cases were seldom filed in labor courts because this required the tribal laborer to travel back to the original site of work numerous times to pursue the case.

Source: Bulsara and Sreenivasa (2004).

Finally, tribals may also lose land to nontribals through marriage or fraudulent means or to contractors and lenders through the recovery of loans given to the tribals. In her research on the Santhal tribe in Jharkhand, Rao (2005) reports how illegal lease arrangements with local contractors have caused several Santhals to give up their land to the contractors for stone quarrying. In many states, the issue of counterfeit ST certificates has sensitive political ramifications. Despite the publicized Supreme Court case of Madhuri Patil, who fraudulently received an ST certificate that identified her as Mahadeo Koli (an ST) when, in fact, she was a Hindu Koli (OBC), there continue to be similar cases.[23] In recent years, Orissa has been rife with allegations that non-STs have obtained ST certificates and thereby usurped ST lands and obtained other advantages.

It is imperative to note that the fraudulent sale or transfer of property and forcible eviction take place although most states prohibit the sale of tribal land to nontribals (or permit it only with the consent of a competent authority). There may be several reasons for this. For instance, while the sale of land by tribals is prohibited in tribal or scheduled areas, the acquisition of land is permissible for development projects, which creates a contradictory situation, whereby smaller contractors and landowners are able to evict tribals in the garb of inconsistent policy.

Legislation prevents Adivasi land from being alienated, but this can be a double-edged sword. It may mean that tribals cannot sell their land to nontribals even if they wish to, but that landgrabbing can continue regardless. There are several ways in which this can happen: through fraud by contractors and lenders (see above) under the garb of recovering loans from tribals, through marriage and the subsequent sale or transfer of land by tribals to nontribals, through the forcible eviction of tribals by nontribals or public authorities, and through the conversion of tribal land from communal to individual ownership (Government of India 2006).

Furthermore, the law does not cover tribals living outside scheduled areas, and these people also face eviction as often (if not more often) than tribals in scheduled areas. In any case, a large majority of tribals can claim only nominal ownership of their land because there are no land records or titles to prove their ownership. This makes eviction relatively easy. Thus, while the government allots land to tribals under various schemes, substantive ownership is not given. In a study of more than 8,000 cases of land dispute following land reform in 316 villages in Madhya Pradesh, Ekta Parishad, a nongovernmental organization working in the state, found that nearly 85 percent of the disputes had arisen because of the inability of the land allottees to take control of the land or because the land had not been transferred to the rightful cultivators (Ekta Parishad 2002). About 87 percent of the cases involved Adivasis and Dalits. Moreover, litigation around land issues is heavily weighted against the tribal poor, "most of whom despair and are pauperized before the almost unending legal battle reaches its conclusion" (Mander 2002, 97). This suggests that even measures such as land reform may not help unless ownership is secured through land records and is proven for all purposes of implementation.

There are various legal safeguards for tribals, but implementation has been difficult. The government is cognizant of the issue of tribal rights over land and forests. While land reforms have been a key objective since independence, other legislation has also been in place to protect tribal land and prevent alienation. One of the most important pieces of legislation in the last decade has been PESA.[24] Applicable to Schedule V areas, PESA gives special powers to gram sabhas in a bid to enhance the voice of tribal groups in development. In particular, PESA seeks to strengthen the voice of gram sabhas on issues related to mining leases and infrastructure development in tribal areas. PESA is unique in that it is in consonance with customary laws and, rather than on revenue villages, focuses on tribal hamlets on the basis of culture. Most states have amended their gram panchayat legislation to make it compatible with PESA; attendant rules have been passed; and monitoring is under way. However, it is widely believed that PESA has not been implemented in spirit. In particular, a tension has been noted between the functions of the gram sabha and the functions of the gram panchayat (see Saxena 2004; Upadhyaya 2007).

Recently, the Scheduled Tribes and Other Traditional Forest Dwellers (Recognition of Forest Rights) Act, 2006, known variously as the Forest Rights Act or the Tribal Rights Act, recognizes the preeminent rights of tribals over forest land and guarantees them access to forests and forest produce. Associated with these rights are responsibilities whereby the tribals must ensure the sustainable use of forests and conserve biodiversity. However, many of the provisions of the law contradict the Indian Forest Act and even PESA. Moreover, published rules have diluted in many ways the spirit of the law. For instance, while the law provides that forest dwellers have rights over water resources and may undertake fishing, the published rules do not address this issue. Confusion also remains on critical aspects of implementation, for example, on who has overriding powers in case of disputes between the gram sabha and gram panchayat and various other aspects of the rights over forest lands and forest produce.

Both PESA and the Tribal Rights Act fundamentally question the power relations between Adivasi and non-Adivasi areas and purport to transfer greater power to the former. However, tribal rights activists and scholars widely believe that the stage for tribal deprivation was set during colonial rule and the state control exercised over forests and other resources at the time. The Land Acquisition Act, 1894; the Forest Act, 1927; and the Wildlife Protection Act, 1972 were all major vehicles for this approach because they established a state monopoly over any land not having an individual patta (individual property) (see Menon 2007; Baviskar 1994; Rao 2003; Sharan 2005). The institutional mechanisms set in place to implement these acts and the ethos that has passed into the postcolonial period make it difficult to implement the new legislation asserting tribal rights.

As large-scale mining has become more pervasive, the tripartite relationship among tribals, the government, and mining companies has also become more tense. A large share of valuable mineral-rich lands is in tribal areas, and, although PESA requires consultation with gram sabhas before mining leases are granted, consultation does not imply clearance. So, gram sabhas, at best, perform a safety-valve function. The large-scale protests against major mining companies by tribals in the case of Vedanta Alumina in Kalahandi and TISCO in Kalinganagar in Orissa are examples in the long history of resistance to mining. However, tribals do not have a blanket objection to all mining.[25] They usually want environmental sustainability to be ensured and to receive adequate benefits from the mining activity (see World Bank 2008b).

If benefits of development, particularly large industry or mining, are shared more equitably and if tribals are involved in the process of decision making, the solution will be more sustainable. The landmark Supreme Court judgment, *Samatha* v. *State of Andhra Pradesh,* 1997 (known as the Samatha judgment) has laid out the contours of benefit sharing in mining.[26] The judgment describes the tension between the rights of the state and the state's responsibilities to citizens, tribals in particular, in the exploitation of mineral resources. Its conclusion is clear: the state has the right to exploit mineral wealth, but the state also has the duty to safeguard the interests of tribals who reside in mineral-rich areas. It also lays out a framework for sharing the benefits of mining between private companies and citizens, with the state acting as facilitator and enforcer.

The literature on benefit sharing in the context of extractive industries focuses primarily on the manner in which revenues accruing from mining are managed and put to use in benefit-sharing arrangements. These arrangements usually involve the establishment of funds from a portion of the royalties and other revenues. The Orissa example in this context is a unique one. Because the royalties from mining in India are collected by the state government, but belong to the central government, Orissa has tried a novel experiment by setting up a periphery development fund to which mining companies contribute, in addition to taxes and royalties. International evidence suggests, however, that setting up funds from mining profits (or revenues) and using them for the development of the areas from which they accrue is by no means an easy task; many states in India have realized this. A recent review of such instruments shows the importance of the governance and accountability framework, strong local institutions, and the proactive role of the government as the key drivers of success. In particular, the involvement of citizens even before leases are granted and the continuing representation and voice of citizens in the decisions related to the funds are key to ensuring effective functioning and management of perceptions of local residents (Fischer 2005).

Adivasi Deprivation Is Tied Up with the Limited Voice of Adivasis

While SCs and STs have faced political disadvantages, the former have been more effective in coming together as a pan-India group and claiming political representation. SCs benefit from nationally well-known political parties and leaders who can represent their claims in the wider political system. In contrast, in no state of India, with the exception of the northeastern states, are Adivasis in a majority.[27] Because tribals live in isolated areas and their numbers form a small proportion of state populations, they are unable to influence the political agenda. States such as Chhattisgarh and Jharkhand, which were carved out of Bihar and Madhya Pradesh to secure tribal rights, have nontribal populations of more than 60 percent. There is little incentive for mainstream political parties to address tribal issues given the insignificant share of tribals in the populations (Guha 2007; Xaxa 2001). Tribals can influence election results in only a few isolated districts or, perhaps, a few remote villages where they form the majority. Thus, the concerns of STs remain marginal in the national context. According to Xaxa (2001), the absence of a political party to represent tribals and the absence of a charismatic leader have also contributed to the relative neglect. For all these reasons, the formal political system has not helped bring voice to the tribes. The fact that hardly any tribals occupy positions of power is itself a reflection of the situation of tribals.

Protest movements among tribal groups have a long history. Spontaneous tribal uprisings against the state occurred before the British period, and each such conflagration was an assertion of the cultural and political identity of tribals, as well as a claim on natural resources. A Planning Commission report links movements since independence and the militancy that accompanies them squarely with the underdevelopment and marginalization of STs (Government of India 2008). Two such movements have culminated recently in the creation of Chhattisgarh and Jharkhand, states based on tribal identities. However, it is not clear whether political parties based on Dalit and OBC identities have improved the welfare of their poorest supporters, and the status of the poorest tribals in the new states is also controversial.

In this chapter, we reach the following conclusions:

• During a period of relative prosperity in India, poverty rates have declined much more slowly among STs than among other groups, and they have declined particularly slowly in states that have large proportions of tribals.

• Health outcomes among STs, while indicating more rapid progress in some respects relative to the rest of the population, are still poor. Convergence with other groups has occurred in only a small number of areas, notably in immunization coverage.

• Excess mortality among tribal children continues to be the starkest marker of tribal disadvantage. It has roots in a number of complex processes involving the general exclusion of STs.

• While a number of laws and programs are in place to address the special disadvantages of STs, implementation is poor.

• The low voice of tribals in decision making and the alienation of tribals from land and forests are central to their continued exclusion from progress and development.

This chapter suggests three factors that lie at the root of Adivasi deprivation. First, Adivasis are traditionally dependent on land and forests, but many have been removed from their lands and forests. Second, the political leadership that speaks for Adivasis arises, for the most part, among non-Adivasi elites and has limited voice in effecting power sharing between the state and Adivasi areas, which, many feel, is the ultimate solution to Adivasi deprivation. Recently, de Haan and Dubey (2005) have hypothesized, in the context of Orissa, that severe caste, tribal, and regional disparities are related to the lack of voice among excluded groups and the lack of accountability by the ruling elites with respect to excluded groups. This is somewhat of a truism, but the articulation of this hypothesis is widely accepted and usually ensconced in the language of exploitation and marginalization associated with Adivasis issues (see, for instance, Government of India 2008).

Finally, while the response of the Indian government to the vulnerability among STs has been proactive and has included a mix of constitutional measures, legislative enactments, programs supported by earmarked funds, and quotas in public employment and publicly funded education, the major problem has been implementation. To enforce its far-reaching instruments, the state must simultaneously afford a measure of de facto autonomy and self-rule to Adivasis. The intent of the government seems to be to achieve this. Yet, two problems arise. The first is the broader political issue that, to hand over power to some, one must take power from others. The elites who hold power find that letting go of power is difficult. The second related point is that the state hesitates to transfer power to areas, institutions, and people who lack the capacity to implement such complex programs and laws. This is a classic conundrum in Indian

policy circles. Do you wait for capacity to be built before you transfer power, or do you gradually transfer power so that it builds capacity? The Indian states are at different points in this power-sharing
arrangement, and much seems to depend on the movements from
below that wrest power. The most extreme form of attempting to
wrest power is the widespread Maoist movement that claims to
articulate the demands of Adivasis militantly.

Unfortunately, it is not always clear what tribals themselves would
like, that is, how much they want to protect their traditional ways
versus how much they want to integrate with the mainstream and
share the fruits of material progress in the country. Tribal perspective, if at all visible, is revealed in microstudies that are not representative of all tribal groups. More discussion of tribal aspirations and
problems from the tribal point of view is needed, rather than an
examination of such issues through the lens of objective measures
developed by policy makers, the bureaucracy, or civil society.

These findings resonate with the views expressed in the Planning
Commission's expert group report on extremism in tribal areas,
which points out that the failure of governance in tribal areas can,
to a large extent, be explained as follows:

> Overwhelmingly large sections of bureaucracy/technocracy
> constituting the delivery system come from landowning domi-
> nant castes or well to do middle classes, with their attachment
> to ownership of property, cultural superiority, purity-pollution
> governed behaviour and a state of mind which rationalizes and
> asserts their existing position of dominance in relation to oth-
> ers. This influences their attitudes, behaviour and performance.
> As it happens, the politics has also been aligned with this social
> segment, which constitutes the power structure in rural and
> urban areas since colonial times. It is this coalition of interests
> and social background that deeply affect governance at all lev-
> els. (Government of India 2008, 19)

Notes

1. See http://pmindia.nic.in/speech/content4print.asp?id=842.

2. The quoted definitions of exclusion are drawn from Encarta Online
Edition.

3. Oommen (1997) argues that variation both across and within societies is important for understanding ethnicity.

4. Schedule V of the Indian Constitution identifies special privileges for
those areas where the majority of the population belongs to STs. Schedule VI

is different in that it applies special privileges to tribals who reside in the northeastern states. While tribes in the northeastern states represent less than 20 percent of the total ST population, these states have been isolated from the development process mainly because of the geographical and cultural isolation of these areas.

5. In some respects, such as education, tribes in these states do relatively better. Mizoram, for instance, has the second highest literacy rate among all states in India, after Kerala, based on 2001 Census data.

6. The poverty gap or depth of poverty is also referred to as the FGT P1 index. It measures the average distance between household consumption and the poverty line. Poverty severity or the FGT P2 index measures the severity of poverty, accounting for the fact that, under FGT P1, an income transfer from two households beneath the poverty line would register no change in the index.

7. Specifically, the "wealth index is based on the following 33 assets and housing characteristics: household electrification; type of windows; drinking water source; type of toilet facility; type of flooring; material of exterior walls; type of roofing; cooking fuel; house ownership; number of household members per sleeping room; ownership of a bank or post-office account; and ownership of a mattress, a pressure cooker, a chair, a cot/bed, a table, an electric fan, a radio/transistor, a black and white television, a color television, a sewing machine, a mobile telephone, any other telephone, a computer, a refrigerator, a watch or clock, a bicycle, a motorcycle or scooter, an animal-drawn cart, a car, a water pump, a thresher, and a tractor." (IIPS and ICF Macro 2007, 43)

8. Using a panel data set for rural India for the period 1993–94 to 2004–05, Dubey and Verschoor (2007) find that Adivasis are still substantially poorer than upper castes. They earn about half as much income as the latter, are more likely to be chronically poor, and are more likely to fall into poverty.

9. Bob Dylan, "Blowin' in the Wind." Copyright © 1962 by Warner Bros. Inc.; renewed 1990 by Special Rider Music. http://www.bobdylan .com/#/songs/blowin-in-the-wind.

10. See, for instance, Sheela Barse versus State of Maharashtra 1993.

11. While we have made every effort to match the mortality numbers in table 2.6 with published numbers, it has not always been possible because a proprietary code has been implemented in the Demographic and Health Survey (DHS) to compute the mortality rates. For these calculations, we have relied on the ltable command in Stata, using matching interval int(0,1,3,6,12,24,36,48,60), as suggested in the DHS methodology guide (Rutstein and Rojas 2006). This approach is also recommended in O'Donnell et al. (2008). Beyond deriving matching statistics, relying on the DHS methodology does not offer any additional benefits because there are a number of other reliable techniques for calculating mortality rates. In fact, moving beyond the descriptive analysis of mortality requires a shift away from the

DHS methodology altogether in favor of survival estimation based on the Kaplan-Meier method used in stcox regressions in Stata.

12. The states of Jharkhand, Madhya Pradesh, Maharashtra, Orissa, and Rajasthan together account for 58 percent of the ST population in India.

13. Kapoor and Kshatriya (2000) compute selection potential based on differential fertility and mortality rates for six tribal groups in India: Bhil, Mina, and Sahariya of Rajasthan and Lodha, Munda, and Santal of West Bengal. They find that childhood mortality constitutes the bulk of postnatal mortality among all these tribal groups.

14. Malnutrition is usually measured along three dimensions: stunting (deficit in height-for-age), wasting (deficit in weight-for-height), and underweight (deficit in weight-for-age). Stunting reflects the long-term effects of malnutrition, while wasting measures the current nutritional status of individuals, that is, their food intake immediately prior to the survey. The underweight indicator is a combination of the former two conditions; it captures both the long-term and the short-term effects of deficient food intake. A child is considered malnourished with respect to each of these measures if the indicator falls below −2 standard deviations from the median (defined for a 2006 international reference population of the World Health Organization). A fall below −3 standard deviations signals severe malnutrition.

15. There are other sources of childhood morbidity, notably malaria, which is endemic in tribal areas.

16. This is similar to the finding of Basu (1989) during her field study questioning skewed intrahousehold food distribution as a key factor explaining malnutrition and, hence, higher childhood mortality among girls in South Asia. She finds that the causal link between malnutrition and mortality is ambiguous. Other factors, such as differential utilization of modern health care (with girls clearly at a disadvantage), matter as well.

17. This is not surprising given that improvements in the intensity of coverage are considerably more difficult to bring about, insofar as they are more costly and require a more coordinated immunization policy.

18. A revenue village, a village with defined borders, is an administrative unit. A revenue village may encompass many hamlets.

19. Tara Datt, personal communication, April 2010. The Naxal-affected areas are troubled by militant communist groups. For information about the rural roads program, see http://www.orissa.gov.in/RD/ruralworks/FAQ-RW.htm.

20. In the remote tribal areas of Gadchiroli (Maharashtra), the Society for Education Action and Research in Community Health, for example, is an international success story in maternal and neonatal health.

21. The dam is estimated to have displaced between 100,000 and 200,000 people (Joseph 1995; Morse and Berger 1992). Two-thirds of the affected families have been tribals (Paranjpye 1990).

22. Documenting people's movements and protests over land in Chattisgarh and Madhya Pradesh, Roy notes how civil society demonstrations, followed by a Supreme Court order, led to the release of nearly 9,000 bonded laborers in one district of Chattisgarh alone between 1986 and 1989.

23. Kumari Madhuri Patil versus Addl. Commissioner [1994] RD-SC 445 (2 September 1994).

24. PESA came into effect on December 24, 1996. It covers the nine Schedule V states of Andhra Pradesh, Chattisgarh, Gujarat, Himachal Pradesh, Jharkhand, Madhya Pradesh, Maharashtra, Orissa, and Rajasthan.

25. Dev Nathan, correspondence dated May 25, 2009.

26. The decision in Samatha versus the State of Andhra Pradesh, 1997 was reiterated in Writ Petition (Civil) No. 202 of 1995, T. N. Godavaraman Thirumulpad versus Union of India & Others in the matter of M/S Vedanta Alumina Ltd.

27. Even in states such as Chhattisgarh and Jharkhand, which have large proportions of tribals, roughly two-thirds of the population is nontribal.

References

Banerjee, A., and R. Somanathan. 2007. "The Political Economy of Public Goods: Some Evidence from India." *Journal of Development Economics* 82 (2): 287–314.

Bang, A., M. H. Reddy, and M. D. Deshmukh. 2002. "Child Mortality in Maharashtra." *Economic and Political Weekly,* December 7: 4947–65.

Basu, A. M. 1989. "Is Discrimination in Food Really Necessary for Explaining Sex Differentials in Childhood Mortality?" *Population Studies* 43 (2): 193–210.

Bavadam, L. 2005. "Dying Young." *Frontline* 22 (19), September 10–23. http://www.flonnet.com/fl2219/stories/20050923006500400.htm.

Baviskar, A. 1994. "Fate of the Forest: Conservation and Tribal Rights." *Economic and Political Weekly* 29 (38): 2493–2501.

———. 2004. *In the Belly of the River: Adivasi Battles over "Development" in the Narmada Valley.* New Delhi: Oxford University Press.

Beck, H. 2009. "Development Induced Displacement 'A Cause of Concern.'" Paper presented at the "International Seminar on Adivasi/ST Communities in India: Development and Change," New Delhi, August 27–29.

Béteille, A. 1991. *Society and Politics in India: Essays in a Comparative Perspective.* London School of Economics Monographs on Social Anthropology. New Delhi: Oxford University Press.

Bharat, S., A. Patkar, and D. Thomas. 2003. "Mainstreaming Equity and Access into the Reproductive and Child Health Programme." Health Systems Resource Centre, Department for International Development, London.

Bulsara, S., and P. Sreenivasa. 2004. "Driven to Bondage and Starvation." *Combat Law* 2 (5). http://www.indiatogether.org/combatlaw/vol2/issue5/bondage.htm.

Bunsha, D. 2002. "The Excluded People." *Frontline* 19 (11), May 25–June 7. http://www.hinduonnet.com/fline/fl1911/19110460.htm.

Burra, N. 2008. "The Political Economy of Tribals in India in the Context of Poverty and Social Exclusion." Paper prepared for the study, Poverty and Social Exclusion in India, Indian Institute of Dalit Studies, New Delhi.

CEFS (Centre for Environment and Food Security). 2005. *Political Economy of Hunger in Adivasi Areas: A Survey Research on Hunger in Adivasi Areas of Rajasthan and Jharkhand.* New Delhi: CEFS.

Cornell, S. 1988. *The Return of the Native: American Indian Political Resurgence.* New York: Oxford University Press.

Das, M. B. 2001. "Domination and Democracy: The Political Economy of Health among Adivasis in Maharashtra." Paper presented at the American Sociological Association's Annual Conference, "Cities of the Future," Anaheim, CA, August 18–21.

Das, M., G. Hall, S. Kapoor and D. Nikitin. Forthcoming. "India: The Scheduled Tribes." In *Indigenous Peoples: Poverty and Development,* ed. G. Hall and H. Patrinos, chapter 6. Washington, DC: World Bank; New York: Cambridge University Press.

Das, M. B., S. Kapoor, and D. Nikitin. 2010. "A Closer Look at Child Mortality among Adivasis in India." Policy Research Working Paper 5321, World Bank, Washington, DC.

de Haan, A., and A. Dubey. 2005. "Poverty, Disparities, or the Development of Underdevelopment in Orissa." *Economic and Political Weekly* 40 (22–23): 2321–29.

Desai, S., A. Dubey, B. Joshi, M. Sen, A. Shariff, and R. Vanneman. 2010. *Human Development in India: Challenges for a Society in Transition.* New Delhi: Oxford University Press.

Dubey, A., and A. Verschoor. 2007. "Income Mobility and Poverty Dynamics across Social Groups in India, 1993–2005." Paper presented at the international seminar "Revisiting the Poverty Issue: Measurement, Identification and Eradication," A. N. Sinha Institute, Patna, India, July 20–22.

Duggal, R. 1990. "Health and Population in Three Tribal Villages." In *Demography of Tribal Development,* ed. A. Bose, R. P. Tyagi, and U. P. Sinha. New Delhi: BR Publishing Corporation.

Ekka, A. 2000. "Jharkhand Tribals: Are They Really a Minority?" *Economic and Political Weekly* 35 (52–53): 4610–12.

Ekta Parishad. 2002. "Towards a People's Land Policy." Ekta Parishad, New Delhi.

Fischer, C. 2005. "Review of International Experience with Benefit Sharing Instruments." Unpublished report, World Bank, Washington, DC.

Government of India. 2001. *Report of the Steering Committee on Empowering the Scheduled Tribes in the Tenth Five Year Plan (2002–2007).* New Delhi: Planning Commission. http://planningcommission.gov.in/aboutus/committee/strgrp/stg_sts.pdf.

———. 2002. *Tenth Five Year Plan, 2002–2007.* New Delhi: Planning Commission.

———. 2006. *Report of the Working Group on Land Relations for Formulation of 11th Five Year Plan.* New Delhi: Planning Commission.

———. 2008. "Development Challenges in Extremist Affected Areas: Report of an Expert Group to Planning Commission." Report, April, Planning Commission, New Delhi. http://planningcommission.gov.in/reports/publications/rep_dce.pdf.

Government of Maharashtra, UNICEF (United Nations Children's Fund), and WHO (World Health Organization). 1991. "Women and Children in Dharni: A Case Study of Villages after Fifteen Years of ICDS." Western India Office, UNICEF, Mumbai.

Government of Rajasthan. 2009. "Draft Annual Plan (2009–2010)." Planning Department, Government of Rajasthan, Jaipur, Rajasthan.

Guha, R. 2007. "Adivasis, Naxalites and Indian Democracy." *Economic and Political Weekly* 42 (32): 3305–12.

———. 2010. "Ambedkar's Desiderata." *Outlook* 50 (4), February 1. http://www.outlookindia.com/article.aspx?263878.

Gujral, S., A. Chohan, and T. Gopaldas. 1992. "Age and Sexwise Child Mortality and the Influencing Socio-Economic Factors in a Rural and Tribal Population in Western India." *Indian Journal of Maternal and Child Health* 3 (4): 113–17.

Hall, G., and H. Patrinos, eds. Forthcoming. *Indigenous Peoples, Poverty, and Development.* Washington, DC: World Bank; New York: Cambridge University Press.

Heaton, T. B., and A. Y. Amoateng. 2007. "The Family Context for Racial Differences in Child Mortality in South Africa." In *Families and Households in Post-apartheid South Africa: Socio-demographic Perspectives,* ed. A. Y. Amoateng and T. B. Heaton, 171–87. Cape Town: HSRC Press.

Hunt, R., and J. Harrison. 1980. *The District Officer in India, 1930–1947.* London: Scolar Press.

IIPS (International Institute for Population Sciences) and ICF Macro. 2007. *National Family Health Survey (NFHS-3), 2005–06: India,* Vol. 1 (September). Mumbai: IIPS.

Joseph, J. 1995. "Resettlement and Rehabilitation of Displaced Tribal Families of Sardar Sarovar Project in Maharashtra: A Successful Experiment."

Paper presented at the Refugee Studies Programme's "International Conference on Development Induced Displacement and Impoverishment," Wadham College, Oxford University, Oxford, January 3–7.

Kapoor, A. K., and G. K. Kshatriya. 2000. "Fertility and Mortality Differentials among Selected Tribal Population Groups of North-Western and Eastern India." *Journal of Biosocial Sciences* 32 (2): 253–64.

Khandare, L. 2004. "Korku Adivasis in Melghat Region of Maharashtra: A Socio-economic Study; a Course Seminar." Department of Humanities and Social Sciences, Indian Institute of Technology, Mumbai. http://lalitreports .blogspot.com/2004/12/korku-adivasis-in-melghat-region-of.html.

Kijima, Y. 2006. "Caste and Tribe Inequality: Evidence from India, 1983–1999." *Economic Development and Cultural Change* 54 (2): 369–404.

Maharatna, A. 1998. "On Tribal Fertility in Late Nineteenth and Early Twentieth Century India." Working Paper 98.01, Center for Population and Development Studies, Harvard University, Cambridge, MA.

———. 2000. "Fertility, Mortality and Gender Bias among Tribal Population: An Indian Perspective." *Social Science and Medicine* 50 (10): 1333–51.

———. 2005. *Demographic Perspectives on India's Tribes*. New Delhi: Oxford University Press.

Mander. H. 2002. "Tribal Land Alienation in Madhya Pradesh: The Problem and Legislative Remedies." In *Issues of Equity in Rural Madhya Pradesh*, ed. P. K. Jha, 82–104. Vol. 7 of *Land Reforms in India*. New Delhi: Sage Publications.

Menon, A. 2007. "Engaging with the Law on Adivasi Rights." *Economic and Political Weekly* 42 (24): 2239–42.

Menon, M. 2009. "Melghat: A Synonym for Malnutrition." *Hindu*, July 23. http://www.hindu.com/2009/07/23/stories/2009072360660900.htm.

MOEF (Ministry of Environment and Forests). 2003. *State of Forest Report 2003*. Dehradun, Uttarakhand, India: MOEF.

Morse, B., and T. Berger. 1992. *Sardar Sarovar: The Report of the Independent Review*. Ottawa: Resource Futures International.

Nagda, B. L. 2004. "Tribal Population and Health in Rajasthan." *Studies of Tribes and Tribals* 21 (1): 1–8.

O'Donnell, O., E. van Doorslaer, A. Wagstaff, and M. Lindelow. 2008. *Analyzing Health Equity Using Household Survey Data: A Guide to Techniques and Their Implementation*. WBI Learning Resources Series. Washington, DC: World Bank.

Oommen, T. K. 1997. *Citizenship, Nationality and Ethnicity: Reconciling Competing Identities*. Sociology and Cultural Studies. Cambridge: Polity Press.

Pallavi, A. 2004. "Why Their Kids Are Dying." *India Together*, September. http://www.indiatogether.org/2004/sep/adv-dyingkids.htm.

Paranjpye, V. 1990. *High Dams on the Narmada: A Holistic Analysis of the River Valley Projects*. New Delhi: Indian National Trust for Art and Cultural Heritage.

Prabhu, P. 1992. "Tribal Deaths in Thane District: The Other Side." *Economic and Political Weekly* 27 (47): 2527–30.

Pritchett, L. 2008. "Is India a Flailing State? Detours on the Four Lane Highway to Modernization." Draft working paper, John F. Kennedy School of Government, Harvard University, Cambridge, MA.

Rao, K. S. 1998. "Health Care Services in Tribal Areas of Andhra Pradesh: A Public Policy Perspective." *Economic and Political Weekly* 33 (9): 481–86.

Rao, N. 2003. "Life and Livelihood in Santal Parganas: Does the Right to a Livelihood Really Exist?" *Economic and Political Weekly* 38 (39): 4081–84.

———. 2005. "Displacement from Land: Case of Santhal Parganas." *Economic and Political Weekly* 40 (41): 4439–42.

Ratnagar, S. 2003. "Our Tribal Past." *Social Scientist* 31 (1–2): 17–36.

Roy, D. 2002. "Land Reforms, People's Movements and Protests." In *Issues of Equity in Rural Madhya Pradesh*, ed. P. K. Jha, 33–50. Vol. 7 of *Land Reforms in India*. New Delhi: Sage Publications.

Rutstein, S. O., and G. Rojas. 2006. *Guide to DHS Statistics*. Calverton, MD: ICF Macro. http://www.measuredhs.com/pubs/pdf/DHSG1/Guide_DHS_Statistics.pdf.

Saxena, N. C. 1999. "Forests in Tribal Lives." Draft report, Planning Commission, New Delhi.

———. 2004. "Policies for Tribal Development: Analysis and Suggestions." Paper prepared for the National Advisory Council, New Delhi.

Shah, A. 2007. "Patterns, Processes of Reproduction, and Policy Imperatives for Poverty in Remote Rural Areas: A Case Study of Southern Orissa in India." Working Paper 179, Gujarat Institute of Development Research, Gota, Ahmedabad, Gujarat, India.

Sharan, R. 2005. "Alienation and Restoration of Tribal Land in Jharkhand: Current Issues and Possible Strategies." *Economic and Political Weekly* 40 (41): 4443–46.

Sharma, M., B. L. Sarangi, J. Kanungo, S. Sahoo, L. Tripathy, A. Patnaik, J. Tewari, and A. D. Rath. 2009. "Accelerating Malnutrition Reduction in Orissa." *IDS Bulletin* 40 (4): 78–85.

Spivak, G. Chakravorty. 1981. "'Draupadi' by Mahasweta Devi." *Critical Inquiry* 8 (2): 381–402.

Suchitra, M. 2005. "Remote Adivasis Face Health Care Chasm." *India Together*, July 25. http://www.indiatogether.org/2005/jul/hlt-attappadi.htm.

Thapar, R., ed. 1977. *Tribe, Caste and Religion in India*. New Delhi: Macmillan.

Upadhyaya, S. 2007. "Assessment of Orissa PESA: Legal Perspective." Paper prepared for the study Poverty and Social Exclusion in India, Indian Institute of Dalit Studies, New Delhi.

van Dillen, S. 2006. "Child Health and Mortality in Western Orissa: A Report Based on a Longitudinal Household Survey in Bolangir District." Report, World Bank, Washington, DC.

Vasundhara. 2006. "Improvement of Livelihood Conditions of Kendu Leaf Pluckers Requires Policy Changes Encouraging Ploughing Back of 100% Profit." Unpublished paper, Vasundhara, Bhubaneswar, Orissa, India.

von Fürer-Haimendorf, C. 1982. *Tribes of India: The Struggle for Survival.* Berkeley, CA: University of California Press.

World Bank. 2005. "Achieving the MDGs in India's Poor States: Reducing Child Mortality in Orissa." Draft report, World Bank, Washington, DC.

———. 2006. "Exploratory Analysis of the Health Status of Social Groups from RCH II Data." Draft, work in progress, World Bank, Washington, DC.

———. 2007. "Achieving the MDGs in India's Poor States: Reducing Child Mortality in Orissa." Report, World Bank, New Delhi.

———. 2008a. "Accelerating Growth and Development in the Lagging Regions of India." Report, World Bank, New Delhi.

———. 2008b. "Sharing the Benefits of Mineral Wealth with Citizens: The Periphery Development Fund in Orissa." Unpublished report, World Bank, New Delhi.

———. 2011. *Perspectives on Poverty in India: Stylized Facts from Survey Data.* India Poverty Assessment. New Delhi: Poverty Reduction and Economic Management Network, World Bank.

Xaxa, V. 2001. "Protective Discrimination: Why Scheduled Tribes Lag behind Scheduled Castes." *Economic and Political Weekly* 36 (29): 2765–72.

3

Dalits

The legs of those born from the feet
were snapped like green buds.
Everyone says: "The safety of the pyramid is worth fifty legs.
O come on,
bear a little pain."
They paint the pyramid's pinnacle
Your name is not mentioned.

Daya Pawar, *Kondwada* (1974)

Structural inequalities in India are determined, to a large extent, by the historical caste system, which has been the predominant marker of deprivation and privilege in India. The caste hierarchy is said to have evolved from different parts of the body of Brahma, the creator of the universe. Thus, the Brahmans, who originated from the mouth of Brahma, undertook the most prestigious priestly and teaching occupations. The Kshatriyas (from the arms) were the rulers and warriors; the Vaishyas (from the thighs) were traders and merchants; and the Shudras (from the feet) were manual workers and servants of other castes. Below the Shudras and lowest in the order were the untouchables, who engaged in the most demeaning and stigmatized occupations (scavenging, for instance, and dealing in bodily waste). Stratification along caste lines solidified through a system of occupational segregation and rules of purity and pollution, which played out in strict adherence to norms of intermarriage and interdining. In practice, the caste system developed into a broad organizational framework for Hindu society wherein each caste consists of hundreds of endogamous *jatis* (subcastes), which are the operative social units.

After independence, the Indian Constitution abolished untouchability, and erstwhile untouchables came to be known in administrative and legal parlance as Scheduled Castes (SCs) through Constitution (Scheduled Castes) Order 1950. A comprehensive listing of SCs was drawn up for purposes of targeting in development programs, compensatory policies to amend for prior discrimination, and policies to prevent violence against untouchables. A recent proposal to enumerate Other Backward Classes (OBCs) in the 2011 Census has generated much controversy. While proponents of the enumeration feel it would strengthen the empirical evidence for indicators on OBCs and, hence, help target benefits for OBCs, others believe that the step would only skirt the deeper, underlying issue of the definition of backwardness. The latter feel that the ideal would be to enumerate all subcastes and then identify the truly marginalized ones among them (for instance, see Desai 2010; Yadav 2010).

Concomitant to these administrative classifications, several subcastes within the SC category, over time, chose to identify themselves under a broad umbrella term, *Dalits*, or the oppressed people. The term politically united them in a process more empowering than the identification by their individual names, which are associated with ritually impure occupations.[1] More recently, the emerging literature on Dalits suggests that there has been a shift, which, if not systemic, is at least gradual, in the way caste hierarchy influences outcomes among Dalits. This is reflected in many individual stories of hope and triumph that have a large demonstration effect and some aggregated stories based on national data that this chapter documents (for instance, see Jadhav 2003, 2005).

The *Laws of Manu*, which lay down the foundations of gender inequality, also dwell at length on the manner in which castes should be ordered and the rules governing exchanges among them. While these rules have changed and evolved, B. R. Ambedkar, the iconic Dalit leader, confronted these foundational laws head-on in his scathing critique and rejection of Hinduism, which, he believed, was the religious and cultural system that stigmatized those he represented. The principle of "graded inequality," Ambedkar (2004, page 60) argued,

> has been carried into the economic field. It does not recognize equal need, equal work or equal ability as the basis of reward for labor. Its motto is that in regard to the distribution of the good things of life, those who are reckoned as the highest must get the most and the best and those who are classed as the lowest must accept the least and the worst.

The historic public burning of the *Manusmriti* (*Laws of Manu*) by Ambedkar in 1927 is celebrated even today by Dalits across India in one of the many rites of self-assertion. Ambedkar's political and ideological legacy has been the basis for some of the most powerful political and social movements in contemporary India. As a result, the national idiom around Dalits is not only about oppression, but also about assertion.

Despite the potent Dalit assertion, there is large heterogeneity among Dalits, and a similar diversity in the extent to which Dalits and those writing about them view how Dalits have fared during a period of rapid growth. While some argue that growth has touched and will continue to touch the lives of Dalits such that opportunity will trump entrenched inequalities (Prasad 2008, 2009a), others point to the persistence of degrading rituals and a belief system that conspire to keep Dalits out of high-quality education and jobs (see Hoff and Pandey 2004; Zaidi 2006; Thorat and Newman 2010). However, caste is not today, nor has it ever been, an immutable constraint to development or progress. As an institution, it has adapted to changing opportunities and circumstances (see Thapar 1966; Srinivas 1966). In the last 20 years of rapid economic growth, too, we find that outcomes by caste have changed in complex ways, but that this comes across more strongly in microlevel evidence. Yet, the opportunities today are far different from those at any other time.

This chapter focuses on two arenas, education and the labor market, to examine the nature of change over the last two decades. Education and occupations both had ritual significance in that they were the preserve of upper castes and relied on an elaborate ideology that excluded, particularly, Dalits and relegated them to what were called impure occupations. This historical disadvantage played out in terms of lower educational status among SC/Scheduled Tribes (SC/STs) in comparison with non-SC/STs. Caste has had implications for poverty and other welfare outcomes especially because occupations are passed down through generations, which makes it difficult for lower castes to move up. Recognizing the unfair disadvantage that certain castes and tribes have had through history, the Constitution of independent India put in place a set of provisions that mandated punitive action against discrimination on the one hand and affirmative action in public employment and publicly funded education on the other. It is generally accepted that job quotas in public employment have been successful in helping historically marginalized groups find a space in the public arena. However, there are also concerns that elites within these groups have monopolized the gains in employment.

The data and other material for this chapter have been taken mainly from the National Sample Survey (NSS), qualitative studies commissioned for the report (Jodhka 2008; Jodhka and Gautam 2008; Witsoe 2008), and analyses based on the India Human Development Survey (Desai, Noon, and Vanneman 2008; Dubey et al. 2008). The chapter also draws on recent evidence from individual surveys and experimental studies that highlight the ways in which caste has mutated and the ways in which caste has remained the same.

Educational Expansion for All: Yet More for Some than for Others

One of the main ritual markers of lower caste status has been exclusion from education or matters of the mind. SCs have generally lagged behind in higher education, and, while there is evidence of some convergence with the upper castes, it takes generations to overcome the initial disadvantage. Microstudies continue to document discrimination against SC students by teachers in schools. Most Dalit students drop out by the time they reach the college level. The 11th Five-Year Plan indicates that about 74 percent of Dalit boys and 71 percent of Dalit girls drop out of school between grades 1 and 10 (Government of India 2008). For those who do manage to remain in school, there is evidence of both discrimination and lower returns to education. Dalit students are held back because of their low starting point, and, while affirmative action policies boost the possibilities, their initial disadvantage holds them back. In this section, we review evidence that points to factors beyond the demand and supply of education that influence outcomes, especially among Dalits. We also show that education has large and significant effects on labor market outcomes, although not always in the direction one might expect.

Education is expanding across India, and Dalit men and non-SC/ ST women have similar trajectories in the growth of postprimary education. Figure 3.1 shows changes in postprimary education in the two decades after 1983.[2] Despite a large gap between the educational attainment of SCs and non-SC/STs, the educational levels among SC men, in particular, have improved at a pace almost similar to the pace of the improvement recorded by non-SC/ST women. Thus, Dalit men showed a 39 percentage point improvement, which was close to the improvement among non-SC/ST women (38 percentage points). As one might expect, non-SC/ST men showed the most rapid improvement, 56 percentage points. At the bottom are

Figure 3.1 Change in Postprimary Education, by Caste and Gender, 1983–2005

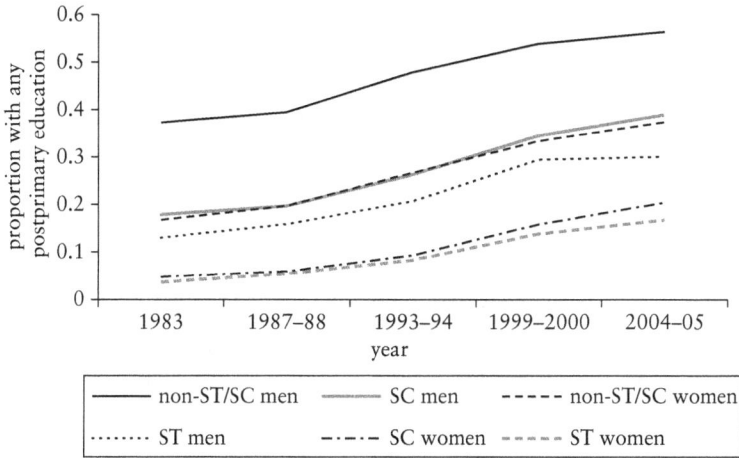

Source: Calculations based on five-year NSS rounds on the population aged 15–59.

Adivasi (ST) women, followed closely by Dalit women. The latter showed only a 21 percentage point improvement in postprimary education after 1983. More worrying is the fact that growth in postprimary education among Adivasi men and women seems to have plateaued after 1999–2000. This trend needs to be observed more carefully in the forthcoming five-year rounds of the NSS.

There may be greater convergence between Dalits and non-Dalits at higher levels of education. Desai and Kulkarni (2008) compare the probabilities of transition to the next educational level among SCs, STs, and Muslims with those of upper caste Hindus. Their results indicate that, while SC/STs continue to lag behind upper caste Hindus, the disadvantages have been diminishing over time, particularly in the 1990s. Among Muslims, meanwhile, there has been a secular improvement in educational status, but this has not matched the improvements that SC/STs have experienced in terms of convergence with Hindus. This may be because, while Muslims also suffer from educational disadvantage, they do not benefit from affirmative action policies, as do SC/STs, leading to the conclusion that the reservation policy seems to have worked favorably for SC/STs.

All things equal: Belief systems still affect outcomes. Despite improvements in postprimary education, especially among Dalit men, the gap between Dalit men and their upper caste counterparts is still wide, and success or failure still depends to a large extent on factors beyond the demand and supply of education. A strong expectation of poor outcomes, for instance, may result in poor effort on the part of those facing discrimination. Comparing the job market performance of black and white employees in the United States, Datcher-Loury and Loury (1986) found that young men's subjective attitudes and occupational aspirations had a large, significant effect *on the hours they worked* independent of variations in objective factors. This effect was much stronger among black men than among white men and, in the case of the former, was relatively constant across widely varying data samples. Rao and Walton (2004) attribute this to belief systems that are shaped by a historical legacy of discrimination. They note that culture, that is, the way groups define themselves in relation to other groups through social practices and interaction, may perpetuate inequality within a society as individuals internalize their statistical chances of success or failure and transform them into aspirations and expectations.

Experimental studies in India confirm the importance of belief systems. Hoff and Pandey (2004), using controlled experiments with SC junior high school students in a village in Uttar Pradesh, found that beliefs shaped by a history of prejudicial treatment can have a significant impact on children's responses when opportunities are presented to them. The experiment involved three maze-solving tasks. In the first task, the caste of students was not publicly revealed. In the second task, the caste of each subject was publicly announced. In the third task, students were separated into high and low caste (SC) groups, and the caste of each group was then revealed. While the authors find no statistically significant difference in performance if the caste is not known, the gap becomes significant if the caste is made salient: the announcement reduces the average number of mazes solved by SC subjects by 23 percent. Segregation into high and low caste groups only deepens the decline in the performance of the latter.

Recent ethnographic evidence also points to the isolation of Dalit students in the classroom. Despite the assertions of equality in the Constitution and in school curricula, discrimination still exists, especially in villages. Chandrashekhar Gokhale's words in Marathi, the local language among people in the state of Maharashtra, sum up the irony in a way to which the English translation fails to do justice, as follows:

Pratyek gaavabaher chhota Maharwada aahe
Chavathichya pustakat matra samanatecha dhada aahe
[Outside every village is a small Dalit hamlet.
Yet the fourth grade textbook includes a lesson on equality].
     Chandrashekhar Gokhale, quoted in Shah et al. (2006, 75)

The study by Geetha Nambissan on Dalit students in two Rajasthan sites documents the insidious form that discrimination takes in schools. Dalits are particularly excluded in situations involving the sharing of food and water and prayers.

> What emerges from the study are diverse spheres of school life where social relations and pedagogic processes fail to ensure full participation of Dalit children, and they are in fact subject to discriminatory and unequal treatment in relation to their peers. While on the one hand these experiences are detrimental to children's self-esteem and self-worth, on the other hand they are likely to have serious implications for their interest and motivation in studies. It is not surprising that the majority of Dalit children who enter and are formally "included" in schools often fail/perform poorly and discontinue their studies. (Nambissan 2010, 282)

There is also considerable anecdotal evidence indicating that students from SC communities face discrimination in hostels, scholarship grants, and so on.[3]

How Does the Labor Market Behave toward Dalits?

> We have to recognize that even in a free society there are glass windows and glass ceilings. The first step in dealing with such problems is to recognize their existence. The second step is to come up with universally acceptable policies that are not viewed as a zero sum game, but as win-win solutions through which everyone is better off and no one is worse off.
>
> Prime Minister Manmohan Singh
> Dalit-Minority International Conference
> New Delhi, December 27, 2006[4]

Because caste was, at its core, a system of occupational segregation, and occupations were inherited, the remnants of that system still mark labor market outcomes among Dalits. However, quotas in publicly funded education and public sector jobs have mediated these outcomes to an extent. This is because, while the public sector still dominates in wage employment, it represents only a small proportion of all employment. This section documents the following:

- Labor force participation and the assignment of Dalits to different types of employment
- Changes in employment during the 20 years beginning in 1983

- The relationship of education and labor market outcomes
- Wage differentials between Dalits and others in salaried employment
- Dalit entrepreneurship and the transition out of casual labor and into self-employment

Dalit Labor Force Participation and the Assignment to Various Types of Employment

Dalits are slightly more likely to participate in the labor force compared with non-SC/STs; these effects are stronger among rural women than among other groups. The analysis in this chapter looks at labor force participation rates separately for rural and urban areas and for men and women. Regardless of caste, the majority of Indian men tend to report that they participate in the labor force, and open unemployment, though rising slightly, is, for the most part, contained at less than 5 percent. Adivasi men show the highest labor force participation rates because the vast majority work on their own subsistence farms. Dalit men are only slightly more likely than non-SC/ST men to be employed, but Dalit women, who do not experience the same controls on mobility that upper caste women experience, are much more likely to be employed than their non-SC/ST counterparts. Adivasi women show even higher labor force participation rates. The ethnographic evidence does point, however, to the lower mobility restrictions on both Dalit and Adivasi women, which, combined with higher poverty rates, makes these women more likely to work outside the home (see also Das and Desai 2003). At the multivariate level, using regressions predicting the probability of participation in the labor force and controlling for a number of household and individual characteristics, one finds that Dalits are indeed more likely than others to be in the labor force (partial results are reported in table 3.1). Poverty drives the labor force participation of Dalits because they seldom have the luxury of staying out of the labor force.

For the most part, Dalits did not own land and have historically been workers in the fields of landed castes. Table 2.10 in chapter 2 shows the distribution of land across caste and tribal groups. Over 60 percent of the Indian workforce is self-employed, and agriculture is still the major source of self-employment. This is where the Dalit disadvantage plays out and explains the preponderance of Dalits in casual labor. Using usual principal status from the NSS, one finds that, in 2004–05, over 41 percent of Dalit men and 20 percent of Dalit women were engaged in casual labor as opposed to 19 percent of non-SC/ST men and 8 percent of non-SC/ST women (see table 3.2,

Table 3.1 Odds Ratios Predicting Labor Force Participation

Indicator	Rural				Urban			
	Men	Men	Women	Women	Men	Men	Women	Women
SC	1.162***	1.505***	1.169***	1.163***	1.229***	1.334	1.154***	1.156**
ST	1.117*	2.023***	3.182***	3.182***	0.98	2.306*	1.512***	2.265***
Education: below primary	1.335***	1.365***	0.686***	0.686***	1.971***	1.960***	0.695***	0.700***
Education: completed primary	0.855**	1.001	0.548***	0.561***	2.129***	2.017***	0.554***	0.550***
Education: postprimary	0.222***	0.271***	0.367***	0.362***	0.370***	0.385***	0.465***	0.481***
SC*primary completed		0.796		0.947		1.132		1.265
SC*postprimary		0.715***		1.062		0.887		0.931
ST*primary completed		0.541***		1.143		0.753		0.642
ST*postprimary		0.430***		0.896		0.345**		0.412***

Source: NSS, 61st round, 2004–05.
Note: The table shows partial results from logistic regression models.
*p ≤ .05 **p ≤ .01 ***p ≤ .001.

Table 3.2 Small Labor Market Transitions among Dalit Men, While Dalit Women Are Exiting Casual Work and the Labor Market

percent

Employment type	1983–84			1993–94			2004–05		
	1. ST	2. SC	3. Non-SC/ST	4. ST	5. SC	6. Non-SC/ST	7. ST	8. SC	9. Non-SC/ST
Men									
Regular	11.5	14.6	17.8	8.4	11.3	17.3	8.6	13.4	16.9
Nonfarm self-employed	5.3	10.9	16.4	5.5	11.2	17.8	8.5	15.6	24.0
Agricultural self-employed	42.3	18.0	32.9	35.9	17.1	28.8	34.6	14.2	23.5
Casual wage labor	33.1	44.6	17.9	40.6	47.6	19.3	36.3	41.7	18.6
Not in labor force, unemployed	7.8	11.9	15.1	9.5	12.9	16.8	12.0	15.1	17.1
Total	100.0	100.0	100.0	100.0	100.0	100.0	100.0	100.0	100.0
Women									
Regular	2.1	2.9	2.6	1.8	2.3	3.0	2.6	3.8	3.8
Nonfarm self-employed	2.6	3.7	3.3	2.5	3.0	3.7	4.5	5.2	6.8
Agricultural self-employed	30.2	8.9	13.9	23.9	6.9	11.5	26.3	7.1	10.6
Casual wage labor	27.5	27.5	10.2	26.2	25.4	9.8	24.4	20.1	8.3
Not in labor force, unemployed	37.6	57.0	70.1	45.6	62.4	71.9	42.3	63.8	70.6
Total	100.0	100.0	100.0	100.0	100.0	100.0	100.0	100.0	100.0

Source: Staff calculations based on NSS data, various rounds.

columns 8 and 9). The landless status of Dalits also excludes them from the large employment category of farm-based self-employment, and, within casual labor, they are mostly farmworkers. While a few states have implemented the land reforms envisaged immediately after independence and have redistributed land to Dalits, this has not been the norm.

At the multivariate level, too, the main Dalit effect is in assignment to casual wage work. Figure 3.2 graphs the predicted probabilities calculated from multinomial regression models that estimate the assignment of Dalit men to various employment groups. For the most part, the results for Dalit men do not look different from those for other men except that Dalit men are much more likely to be casual laborers. The Dalit effect in casual labor is much stronger in rural areas, where Dalit men have a 23 percent greater likelihood

Figure 3.2 Dalit Men: More Likelihood of Casual Labor in Rural Areas; Less Likelihood of Self-Employment in Urban Areas

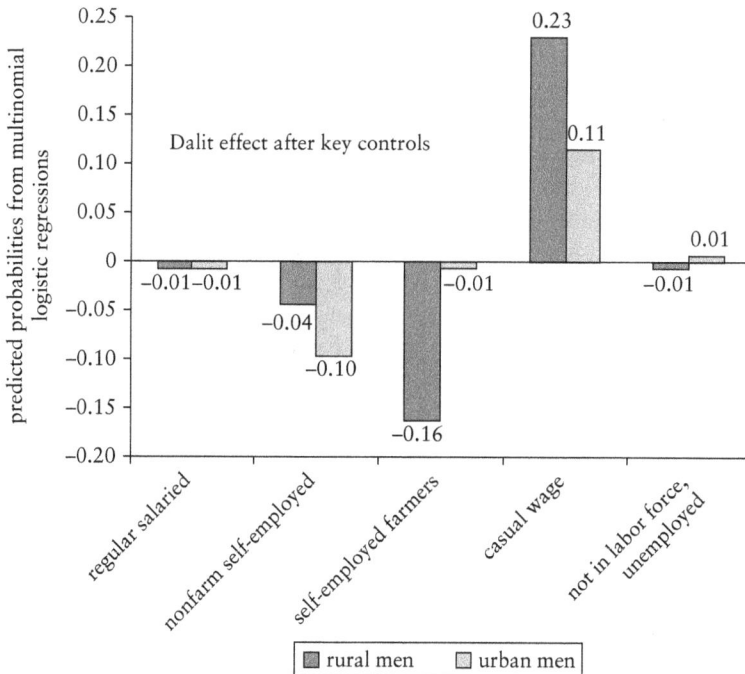

Source: Data on men aged 15–59 in the NSS 61st round, 2004–05.
Note: For the core model, see annex table 3A.1.
All effects are significant at the .001 level except *not in labor force*.

than other men to be in casual wage work. In urban areas, while the effect is not as strong, one finds, after holding other characteristics constant, that Dalit men are 11 percent more likely than other men to be casual laborers. In urban areas, where the majority of nonfarm jobs and enterprises are located, being Dalit reduces the probability that one is an entrepreneur. As noted above, the fact that Dalits are, for the most part, landless means that they are also less likely to be farmers.

While many have received the benefits of public sector employment, Dalits still lag behind non-Adivasi/Dalit/OBCs in regular salaried work and in nonfarm self-employment. The difference between Dalits and non-Dalits in regular salaried work is not huge because, overall, salaried work forms a small proportion of all employment. At the univariate level, compared with about 17 percent among non-SC/STs/OBCs, a little more than 13 percent of Dalits are regular salaried workers (table 3.2). Yet, the real differences are not in the proportions of Dalits and non-Dalits in regular salaried work, but in the kind of jobs Dalits land even in salaried work (see elsewhere below). The assignment to low-end jobs in the salaried market leads to wage differentials in favor of non-Dalits as a result mainly of occupational segregation.

We also discuss below the issue of nonfarm self-employment because the issue has been debated in public forums, and several microlevel research projects have tried to understand why Dalits have not graduated to self-employment during India's period of rapid growth and in the context of the improving educational attainment among Dalits. At the univariate level, about one-fourth of non-SC/ST men (including OBCs), but only 15.6 percent of Dalit men, report that they are self-employed in the nonfarm sector (table 3.2, columns 8 and 9). Almost half of self-employed Dalit men are working in the manual trades (see table 3.4). Figure 3.2 shows that, at the multivariate level, Dalit men have a huge disadvantage in nonfarm self-employment, especially in rural areas, where nonfarm enterprises are limited in any case and a large share of the nonfarm enterprises that do exist are likely to be ancillary to farm production. Controlling for a number of individual and family characteristics, including region of residence, one finds that Dalit men are 4 percent less likely in rural areas and 10 percent less likely in urban areas to be self-employed in the nonfarm sector. Women are generally excluded from nonfarm enterprises, and only about 5 percent of women are self-employed in the nonfarm sector. Given the small proportion, there is little scope for variation, and Dalits or Adivasi women are not significantly more disadvantaged.

Changes in Employment among Dalits

In the aggregate, despite small shifts, Dalit men continued to be found in casual labor during the 20 years beginning in 1983. Shifts in labor force activity among Dalits showed, overall, a slight decline in casual labor and a slight increase in nonfarm self-employment and in opting out of the labor force. Over the 20 years or so beginning in 1983, the proportion of Dalit men in casual labor declined slightly, from 44.6 to 41.7 percent, while the proportion in nonfarm self-employment increased slightly, from 11.0 to 15.6 percent. These changes were small, however. Dalit men are still mainly restricted to menial, low-paying, and, often, socially stigmatized occupations, while upper caste groups are concentrated in preferred occupations.[5]

Recent small-area studies in north India suggest that changes are taking place, but that these cannot be aggregated into a consistent national picture. When Jodhka returned to the Haryana villages where he had done fieldwork in the 1980s, he found profound changes in the relationship of Dalits with the land, as follows:

> Nearly all of the Dalits have been landless and they no longer like working as labourers in the farms. Working with farmers implies accepting their domination and power. By refusing to work on land Dalits express their dissent against the traditional structure of patron-client ties. Even if it means cycling to the town for casual labour and no higher wage or secure income, a Dalit would refuse to work on land. Some of them also told me that work on farm was much more demanding and number of working hours invariably exceeded eight. Though their numbers had declined, two villages still had a number of attached labourers working with big farmers. . . . 20 years back most of them were from local Dalit castes. Today not even one of them is a Dalit in any of the two villages. (Jodhka 2008, 21)

Prasad (2009b) also finds similar changes (highlighted elsewhere below) based on a survey in two blocks of Uttar Pradesh.

Over time, Dalit women, while moving out of casual labor at a more rapid pace than men, are also withdrawing from the labor force. Rather than transitioning from casual wage work to other forms of employment, Dalit women are opting out of the labor force more rapidly than any other group. In 1983, 57 percent of Dalit women were out of the labor force. By 2004–05, this had increased to 64 percent. While Adivasi women were also withdrawing from the labor force during the same period, the magnitude of the withdrawal was much larger among Dalit women. Non-SC/ST women have always been the least likely to be employed; this has not changed over time; and 70 percent of these women were out of the labor force in 1983, as well as in 2004–05.

The withdrawal of Dalit women from the labor force may be a replication of the pattern that non-SC/ST women have historically shown. This is on account of both cultural and structural factors. As their educational attainment has increased, Dalit women, like others, are perhaps seeking more suitable employment opportunities. The chances are that the job quotas in the public sector have been cornered by their male counterparts, and, if they live with earning members in the same households, they may opt out of the labor force in the absence of suitable alternatives. It is also likely that, as Dalits become socially mobile, they replicate upper caste norms of female seclusion, and, for them, it likewise becomes a matter of family honor that women do not work outside the home (see Das and Desai 2003). The issue of the withdrawal of Dalit women from the labor force needs to be examined in the next five-year round of the NSS to determine the factors that drive it and whether policy can make a difference.

Educational Attainment and Labor Market Outcomes

Comparing racial and ethnic minorities in the United Kingdom and the United States, Loury, Modood, and Teles (2005, 5) make a general statement that holds true for caste and tribe in India as well, as follows:

> Racial and ethnic groups are not just fictive categories that exist only in the minds of outsiders. They are also real social groupings, through which mobility-relevant skills, habits, and attitudes are produced. And, in some cases they harbor real institutions through which resources are hoarded and distributed. Decisions to invest in education, to defer consumption, to accept or resist superiors in the workforce, and to delay or accelerate childbearing come down, in part, to questions of what "people like me do." That is, they are affected by the meaning embedded in racial and ethnic identity, meanings that are produced by some combination of group insiders and outsiders.

That education across the board improves labor market outcomes is well documented. However, there is also evidence showing that returns to education vary by ethnicity. For instance, in Brazil, the evidence suggests that whites are much more efficient at converting their experiences and educational investments into monetary returns, while nonwhites experience increasing disadvantages in climbing the social ladder (Gacitúa-Marió and Woolcock 2008). In India, education increases the likelihood of labor force participation among all men, but not among women (see chapter 4). The positive effects of education on male labor force participation are stronger in urban areas, where the bulk of the preferred jobs are located. The discussion above shows that the major transitions among Dalit women are out of casual labor, but also out of the labor force. Moreover, education has not expanded at the same pace among Dalit women as among Dalit men, and, in absolute terms, Dalit women lag far behind both their non-SC/ST women peers and their Dalit men peers. Those Dalit women who are employed therefore tend to be even more concentrated in casual labor than are their male counterparts. Because of the small variation in employment outcomes among Dalit women, much of our analysis is therefore based on the situation among Dalit men.

Returns to education seem to be lower among Dalit men than among others. Returns to education are conventionally measured in terms of earnings, but, if the labor market weighs heavily in self-employment, on which there are no earnings data, we can construct returns in terms of assignment to preferred employment types (see Das 2006). Figures 3.3 and 3.4 are based on cross-tabulations between the educational status of men and the assignment to employment type among different social groups in rural and urban areas. Across the board, higher educational attainment is associated with withdrawal from casual labor and entry into salaried employment. At the multivariate level, however, the multiplied effect of Dalit status and postprimary education actually appears to disadvantage Dalit men in rural areas (also see annex table 3A.1).

Bertrand, Hanna, and Mullainathan (2008) estimate the impact of reservations on lower caste groups in engineering colleges in India. They find that, while marginal lower caste entrants do benefit from the policy, the gains in their earnings deriving from admission are half the gains accruing to marginal upper caste entrants. This is mostly because few lower caste graduates end up being employed in high-skilled jobs. The findings of Bertrand, Hanna, and Mullainathan corroborate the findings of the research of Deshpande and Newman (2007) on Dalit and non-Dalit graduates at three major universities. The latter find that, despite being equally qualified, Dalit students are far less likely to find a job in the private sector. Kijima (2006) also documents lower returns to education among Dalits.

Figure 3.3 Where Does Education Take Rural Men in the Labor Market?

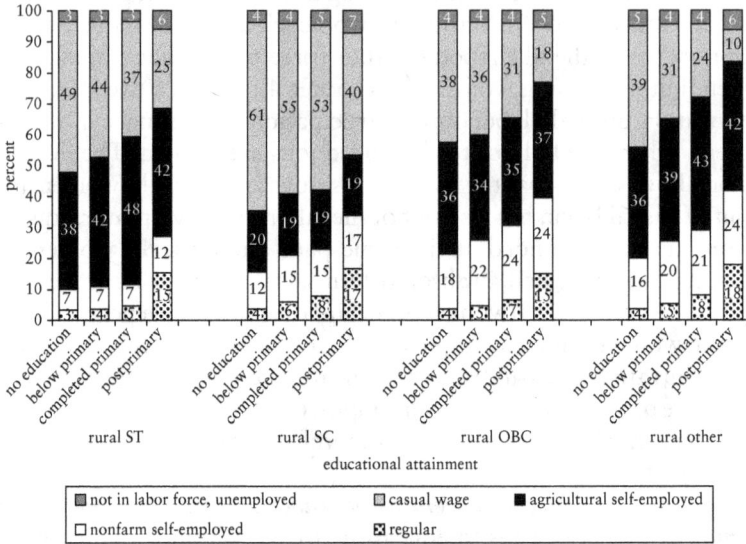

Source: Simple weighted cross-tabulations based on NSS 2004–05.

Annex table 3A.1 shows the multiplied effects of Dalit status and education on labor force participation. It suggests that Dalits with both primary and postprimary education in rural areas are less likely to be employed. This perhaps reflects, first, that all men with education in rural areas are penalized; second, that Dalit men feel these effects more if they have postprimary education; and, third, that the growth of jobs in rural areas has not kept pace with the increase in the supply of educated Dalit men. In urban areas, while all men show a much higher likelihood of participating in the labor force if they have education, the effects among Dalit men are not statistically significant. These results are reinforced by a study in Bijnor in Uttar Pradesh by Jeffrey, Jeffery, and Jeffery (2004), who find that increased formal education has given young Dalit men a sense of dignity and confidence at the village level, but that this cultural capital does not seem to translate into secure employment. They argue that this is leading to an emerging culture of "masculine Dalit resentment." In response, Dalit parents are beginning to withdraw from investing money in young men's higher secondary and tertiary education.

The exit from casual labor associated with higher levels of education is most pronounced among non-SC/ST men and least pronounced among Dalit men. For instance, in urban areas, where the bulk of preferred jobs are located, all men benefit from education, but the effects on Dalit men are muted in comparison with the effects on other men (figure 3.4). While 22 percent of urban Dalit men without any education are in salaried work, this is true of 47 percent of urban non-Dalit men with postprimary education. The increase in educational attainment is also marked by an exit from casual labor. While 35 percent of uneducated Dalit men in urban areas are casual laborers, only 16 percent of Dalit men with postprimary education do casual labor. In contrast, urban ST men seem to benefit far more from education, and the exit from casual labor is more marked at higher levels of educational attainment. In chapter 2, we indicate that STs in urban areas generally do better in most respects and that this may be associated with ST elites who have established themselves in urban areas over generations. The effect of education is even more pronounced in the improvement in the chances among non-SC/ST men of exiting casual work.

Figure 3.4 Where Does Education Take Urban Men in the Labor Market?

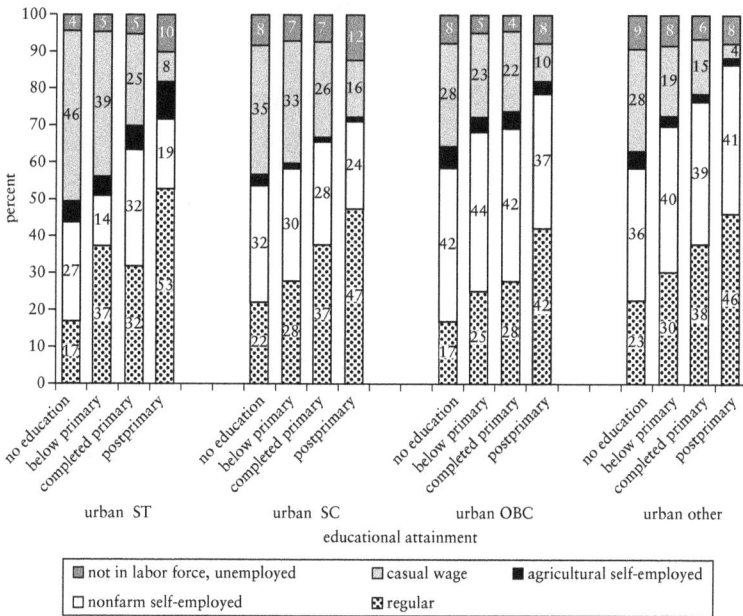

Source: Simple weighted cross-tabulations based on NSS 2004–05.

Is it Enough to Get a Salaried Job? What About Wage Differentials and Occupational Segregation?

The salaried market for most workers in India is remarkably tight, but, because most salaried jobs are still in the public sector, Dalits have the advantage of their reserved positions. Nonetheless, wage differentials between Dalit men and general category men are evident in almost all occupational categories. This finding on inequality in earnings concurs with other studies showing that caste is an important determinant of the wages received (Banerjee and Knight 1985; Das 2006; Unni 2001). The wage distribution among Dalit workers may be similar to that of general caste workers at the bottom and middle quantiles, but differences appear at the top quantiles. The kernel density plots reproduced in figure 3.5 bear out this expectation, particularly for regular workers, where the distribution is shifted farther out to the right for general caste workers relative to the other groups (SCs and OBCs). If one controls for selection, the gap is increased. In contrast, casual workers are, in large part, a homogenous pool of low-skilled workers. Thus, the kernel density plots do not reflect significant differences across casual workers in different social groups.

Oaxaca-Blinder decompositions of wage differentials show that 59 percent of the earnings gap between SC workers and regular

Figure 3.5 Salaried Work: Wage Differentials between Dalits and Others Are Higher

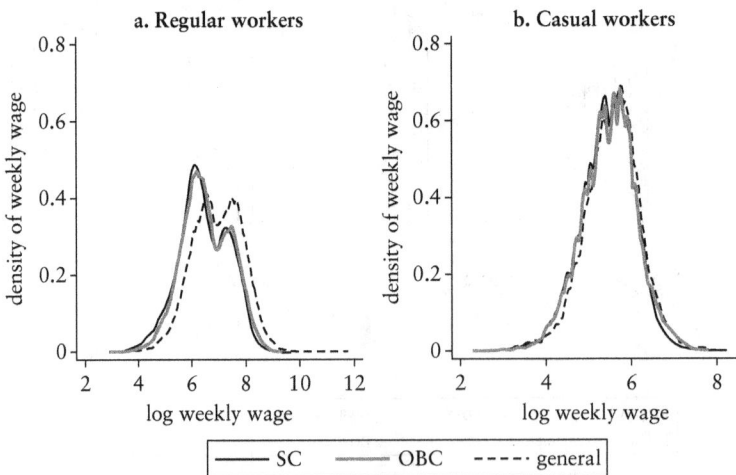

Source: Das and Dutta (2008), based on NSS 61st round, 2004–05.

general category workers is accounted for by differences in treatment or the return to characteristics rather than endowments. This does not imply that the entire treatment effect is attributable to discrimination. At least part of the effect may be caused by omitted variables such as ability or family background, and a large part may be caused by type of occupation. However, it may be argued that unequal earnings have their roots in historical discrimination that indirectly results in lower investments in schooling or the poor quality thereof, poorer health, or lower social capital and, hence, lower earnings (Das and Dutta 2008). Similarly, what may appear discrimination in private hiring may actually be a discount factor applied to SC candidates because they had gained preferential admission. In this sense, private employers may not be acting irrationally or inefficiently, and the magnitude of pure discrimination is difficult to judge.

The occupational typecasting of Dalits means they are stuck in low-paying jobs. This is the context in which the notion of Das and Dutta (2007) of glass walls plays out. Rather than stone walls, these are walls through which Dalits can see opportunities, yet not gain access to the opportunities. There are also glass ceilings, and Dalit workers find obtaining high-paying jobs difficult. This indicates that there is both horizontal segregation (workers are restricted to certain occupations) and vertical segregation (workers from different social groups may be represented differently in the hierarchy of positions within the same employment type). In each case, the movement of Dalit workers through occupational categories and social hierarchies may be hampered by institutional barriers and negative social attitudes. Analysis indicates that educated Dalit men have an advantage in low-end formal public sector jobs, ones that require primary education. However, a system of rationing seems to deter the entry of these men into higher-level jobs. Perhaps, once reserved quotas are filled up (especially for groups A, B, and C in the categorization of government jobs), SC candidates have few options or other avenues such as self-employment. Thus, job quotas may be leading to the rationing of regular salaried (public sector) jobs among SC men, thereby adding a cap on their access to regular jobs, since these men cannot penetrate nonreserved public sector jobs. A corollary of this outcome is the creation of an entrenched elite among SC men that benefits from reservations across generations (Das 2006).

Some of the results on wage inequalities are explained by the fact that, even in the public sector, Dalits are concentrated in low-end jobs. Traditional caste patterns are replicated in the entry of SCs into the public sector workforce. Table 3.3 shows the representation of Dalits in government jobs in which they benefit from reserved quotas. While SCs are represented proportionately to their share of the population at

Table 3.3 The Representation of Dalits in Government Jobs, 2006

percent

Group	SCs
A	13.0
B	14.5
C	16.4
D (excluding sweepers)	18.3
Sweepers	59.4
Average across groups A–D, including sweepers	24.3
Average across groups A–D, excluding sweepers	15.6

Source: Calculated from data of Ministry of Personnel, Public Grievances, and Pensions (2009).

Note: Data pertain to central government services as of January 1, 2006, and exclude two ministries. Group A indicates the highest level, and Group D the lowest.

each employment level within central government services, they are vastly overrepresented in the least skilled occupational categories at the lowest employment levels. In 2006, almost 60 percent of the sweepers in central government ministries were SCs, indicating that SCs are more likely to undertake ritually unclean work and manual work. If one ignores the sweepers, the average representation of Dalits in central ministries is around 15.5 percent, but, if sweepers are included, this jumps to over 24 percent. This pattern explains to a large extent why Dalits with primary education have an advantage in rural areas, where the overwhelming majority of salaried jobs are in the public sector.

As increasing numbers of qualified Dalit candidates apply in the salaried job market, especially in a context of an expanding private sector, what chances do Dalits have? Apparently, discrimination in hiring is exercised in a sophisticated manner in entry level-jobs in the private sector. Deshpande and Newman (2007) have interviewed postgraduate university students, including Dalits. Dalit students in degree programs comparable with those of their high caste counterparts show lower expectations and see themselves as disadvantaged because of their caste and family backgrounds. Because they arrive at college with weaker skills, on average, they play catch-up and often do not succeed in pulling even with more advantaged students; hence, they enter the job market with weaker English language and computing skills. In addition, they lack the social awareness and other abilities that dominate in the private sector culture.

Deshpande and Newman (2007) also find that prospective hiring managers almost universally ask questions about family backgrounds during employment interviews. Nonreservation students can offer biographies that are much closer to the upper-middle-class professional ideal. While Dalit students often perceive a hidden agenda in questions on family background, the same questions appear to nonreservation students to be innocuous or sensible inquiries from a human resources perspective. Iversen and Raghavendra (2006) find that SC workers in south Indian eating places in Bangalore and Mumbai still find it necessary to hide their identity to minimize workplace conflicts and also compete for jobs.

It is also possible that groups that are discriminated against adopt self-discriminatory behavior over time, that is, an expectation of poor outcomes given the history of poor endowments. Controlled experiments in other countries suggest that this may deepen stereotyping and that employers may simply act as "resonance boxes that reflect these differences in endowments" (Márquez et al. 2007, 8).

There are also microstudies on caste and religion in the bustling information technology industry in India. Upadhya (2007) finds that the outsourcing industry needs, in particular, English-speaking graduates who also have western social skills. These eligibility criteria manage to exclude Dalits from the pale of this growing opportunity. She cites her own study and other studies to show that, for the most part, three-quarters of the workers in jobs in information technology are from higher castes, while the remainder are in the OBC category. However, these are small samples and in no way representative of the entire information technology industry. Nonetheless, anecdotally, it is well known that Adivasis and Dalits are not represented in these jobs in proportion to their strength in the population.

Dalit Entrepreneurship and the Transition out of Casual Labor

The issue of Dalit entrepreneurship has been in the national discourse for some time. Despite impressive microlevel studies on Dalit entrepreneurship, the national data do not seem to capture a shift into self-employment. SC men are, overall, less likely to have their own enterprises, but self-employment is rare among most men in India, and the hurdles for small (often household) enterprises are well documented, including by Kishwar (2002) and, most recently, Nilekani (2008). Self-employment is more relevant in urban areas than in rural areas, where farming is still the major basis for employment and the nonfarm sector is in its infancy (see elsewhere above). It seems that, in rural areas, Dalit men have a huge disadvantage in self-employment. This could be because most rural self-employment is ancillary to agriculture, and Dalits typically do not own land, but it may also be because rural Dalit men have fewer social networks and less access to credit, markets, and raw materials relative to their urban counterparts. It is also likely that, because the national data from the NSS are no later than 2004, we are unable to catch the changes that have taken place in the last six or seven years.

Dalits are disadvantaged because they are traditionally typed into caste-based occupations, but also because they lack the social links to access credit, cheap raw materials, and markets so as to sell their produce (box 3.1). Figure 3.6 shows that Adivasis and Dalits

---

Box 3.1 Intergenerational Mobility Is Visible, but Restricted among Dalits

Ratan Chandra Jatav is among the 321 respondents interviewed by Jodhka and Gautam (2008) for their study on Dalit entrepreneurs in Panipat (Haryana) and in Saharanpur (Uttar Pradesh). He is 61 years old and a well-known businessman in Panipat. He owns two gas agencies and one petrol pump and has investments in transport and agricultural land. His net worth is about Rs 50 million. Ratan Chandra Jatav is a Dalit.

Ratan's father is illiterate and worked as a sweeper in the local municipality, in addition to selling milk. Ratan remembers the experience of discrimination in his early years, starting at school. Few people bought milk from his family, and those who did kept a distance from him when he sold milk in the city. When he was allotted a gas agency (on the recommendation of another Dalit friend), Ratan recounts that he had to sell all his wife's jewelry to raise the necessary money.

More than half the study respondents, who were engaged as small-shop owners, cited the lack of social resources as the primary reason they were unable to expand their business establishments. They also reported experiencing discrimination in starting their businesses, including in mobilizing financing, finding locations to set up their shops, or facing hostile competition in the early years of the businesses. The few who had become successful were those who had not been as disadvantaged to begin with, that is, for example, they started with initial capital accrued from government jobs or had higher education.

Why, then, do Dalits consider becoming entrepreneurs? Because they see it as a means to move out of their traditional caste-based occupations.

"It is always better to have your own business than to be a slave to others," concludes one of them. However, most of them, including Ratan, cannot avoid the traditional biases.

Ratan wraps up his interview with the following admission:

"Even now when they [non-Dalits] see me in a luxury car, they do not like it," he says.

Source: Jodhka and Gautam (2008).
Note: Names have been changed to protect privacy.

Figure 3.6 Adivasis and Dalits Have Few Social Networks in the Formal Sector

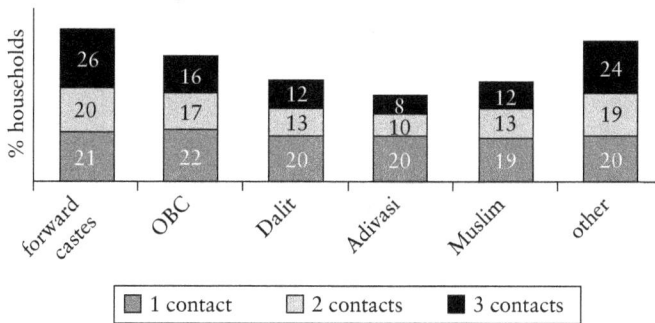

have fewer social networks than do upper castes, and the next section documents why these are central to the success of small entrepreneurs. The glass walls of Das and Dutta (2007) are a variation of the idea of glass ceilings whereby occupationally slotted castes do not leave their traditional trades or jobs. However, whereas, earlier, these were stone walls and Dalits were unable to move outside their traditional occupations, this chapter shows that there has now been a slight movement into self-employment, a movement more evident in microstudies and less evident in the aggregate data.

Self-employed occupations run the gamut from low-level subsistence activities, such as street trading, to high-end business ventures. The majority of self-employment is located in urban areas. At the national level, Dalit men in urban areas, even if they have obtained education, are less likely to be self-employed, despite microlevel evidence of thriving Dalit entrepreneurship. Only 24 percent of Dalit men with postprimary education in urban areas are engaged in nonfarm enterprises. In contrast, 32 percent of their uneducated counterparts are so engaged. This may be indicative of the type of self-employed ventures uneducated men or those with lower educational attainment undertake in urban areas. These are usually low-end informal enterprises. Table 3.4 shows that self-employed Dalit men are overwhelmingly in manual trades and are least likely to be in higher-status professional jobs or higher-earning sales jobs. Adivasi men seem to be concentrated in professional jobs, but only 8 percent are in nonfarm self-employment. As we point out in chapter 2, there may be a class of urban Adivasi men

Table 3.4 What Do Self-Employed Men Do?

percent

Employment classification	STs	SCs	OBCs	Others
Professional and technical (0, 1, 2)	60.55	28.50	42.82	37.51
Clerical (3)	0.09	0.08	0.29	0.43
Sales (4)	16.78	20.54	22.05	37.06
Service (5)	1.18	6.04	6.58	2.51
Other manual (7, 8, 9)	21.40	44.83	28.28	22.49

Source: Staff calculations based on data of the NSS, 61st round.

Note: The numbers in parentheses are the one-digit codes of the National Classification of Occupations.

who represent an elite group that has managed to break out of the traditional concentration in agriculture and manual work.

A comparison of self-employment among two minorities, Dalits and Muslims, shows that the latter have managed to skirt the primary market and set up self-employed ventures, while the former have not. Das (2009) uses a conceptual framework based on ethnic enclaves that has been developed for the labor market in the United States. According to the framework, ethnic minorities skirt discrimination in the primary labor market by building successful self-employed ventures in ethnic enclaves or ethnic labor markets. Das uses entry into self-employment among educated minority groups, Dalit and Muslim men in this case, as a proxy for minority enclaves because the NSS does not include earnings data on self-employment. Based on multinomial logistic regression, she finds that the ethnic enclave hypothesis does not hold for Dalits, who do not manage to set up self-employed ventures, but it does overwhelmingly hold for Muslims. Most insightful are the interaction effects between education level and Dalit or Muslim status. They show that, relative to other men, Dalit men with postprimary education have distinctly lower returns in the form of salaried jobs.

Previous microstudies point to the possibility that small SC entrepreneurs, especially in rural areas, are prevented from moving out of caste-based occupations into self-employed ventures. Either they are denied fair opportunities to participate in more lucrative trades, or they fail to participate in these trades out of fear of social pressure and ostracism (see, for instance, Thorat 2007). Some SCs may want to leave their traditional caste-based occupations by migrating or expanding into self-employed ventures. However, they may be prevented from doing so because of the potential loss of sub-caste networks that serve as sources of mutual insurance. Munshi and Rosenzweig (2005) use a unique panel data set from 1982 to

1999 to show that households that out-marry or migrate lose the services of subcaste networks. These networks otherwise serve as useful sources of caste loans and insurance if alternative sources of finance or insurance are unavailable.

Respondents in focus group discussions with the World Bank Moving out of Poverty study team indicated that various roadblocks may, indeed, be hampering self-employment. For instance, youth in the village of Doulatabad (Andhra Pradesh) stated as follows:

There is a lot of inequality between the low castes and high castes. People of high castes have more opportunity to earn money as they can do good farming or start any business. They can get educated and can get a job. There is a lot of distance between the two and there is no sense of unity between them.

Nowhere was the bonding within caste groups as pronounced as in the socially stratified context of Uttar Pradesh. In the village of Gokal, for instance, untouchability was common, and the higher caste Thakurs as a group did not allow the lower SC Chamars or Harijans to touch them or drink water from their wells. They also maintained a strong hold on all economic opportunities available in the village, making the lower caste laborers work on Thakur farms for a pittance and foiling all the attempts of the SCs to start small businesses. The Thakur-dominant *panchayat* (local government) ensured that all development work that came to the village, including, for example, the brick laying of village roads or the establishment of an Anganwadi center (an integrated child development service center), was focused in and around hamlets composed of Thakur families.

"There is no freedom, sir," observed a 45-year-old SC man. "Only the Thakurs are free. Neither can we do any work, drink water, nor can we do anything else."

The success story of Dharavi, the Mumbai slum that has become a hub of bustling commercial activity among traditionally stigmatized workers turned formidable entrepreneurs, is legendary. Nilekani (2008) cites Jacobson (2007) in pointing out that these "15,000 single-room factories with an annual output of US$1.47 billion" now include not only leather workers, but also furniture makers, private schools, and services such as cable television, beauty parlors, and water, electricity, and pest control for the slums. There is similar evidence also in other parts of the country (box 3.2). Using data from interviews conducted with a sample of almost 20,000 Dalit households in Uttar Pradesh, Prasad (cited in Wax 2008) finds that a majority of households send at least one member each to the city.

Box 3.2 State Support and Entrepreneurial Spirit Can Change Outcomes

A few years ago, *The Hindu* carried the story of Dalit entrepreneurs in Tirupur (Tamil Nadu) who had joined hands to revive their distressed enterprises. With support from the public sector Adi Dravidar Housing and Development Corporation, 43 ailing enterprises came together to form the Tirupur Apparel Park India Private Limited, a cluster company, with a share capital of Rs 2.8 million. The state government provided working capital of Rs 7.5 million.

"The recent developments have instilled confidence in us. Government agencies are much more supportive now," said G. P. Lenin, one of the directors of the company. "We will soon become direct exporters. This is our dream and it will hopefully come true with active Government support."

While there is no study to indicate how the initiative actually panned out, the case is indicative of ways in which entrepreneurial spirit and the creative use of state support can lead to positive outcomes.

Source: The Hindu, "Tamil Nadu: Dalit Entrepreneurs See a Ray of Hope," January 12, 2007.

The resulting remittances have led to a change in spending patterns and in social and political spaces. In 1990, about 88 percent of the families Prasad interviewed in Gaddopur, a village in Uttar Pradesh, were asked to sit separately during public dinners organized by upper castes. In contrast, in 2007, only 30 percent were asked to sit apart (Wax 2008). Jodhka (2008) and Jodhka and Gautam (2008), in their fieldwork for our report, describe the ways Dalits have circumvented the barriers and gained access to self-employment.

Despite localized changes, the space for mobility seems limited. There are signs of change, especially in urban areas, but, due to the initial conditions (for instance, their low levels of educational attainment, lack of assets, poor access to markets and social networks, and so on), Dalits remain disadvantaged relative to other groups. This shows up both in the national data, where there is a preponderance of Dalits in the ranks of the casual workforce, as well as in microlevel studies.

Despite several positive changes, caste continues to play a role in the urban economy, and for Dalit entrepreneurs it was almost always negative. Dalits lacked economic resources, but even when they had economic resources they were crippled by a lack of social resources. . . . The collective prejudice, originating from tradition, not only cripples their prospects in the market but also shapes their self-image. Caste is not simply a matter of past tradition or [a] value system incompatible with contemporary market economy but a reality that continues to be experienced as discrimination by the Dalit entrepreneurs. (Jodhka and Gautam 2008, 25–26)

In another study in an urban setting, in Pune (Maharashtra), Deshpande and Palshikar (2008) find considerable occupational mobility among Dalits. In their account, new generations of Dalits have moved to higher-paying occupations relative to their forefathers, a degree of net mobility (upward, less downward) that exceeds the mobility seen among other social groups in their sample. Yet, they find that, despite sustained mobility across generations, 77 percent of the fourth-generation SC families interviewed were still stuck in the lower-middle class (including class IV employees, semi-skilled workers) or below, compared with 52 percent of OBCs, and 11 percent of upper caste families. The authors describe the Dalits' inability to break through as "the price they have to pay for the handicap of the starting point" (Deshpande and Palshikar 2008, 66). Low levels of mobility among excluded groups are not unique to India. The Inter-American Development Bank report on Latin America also shows that intergenerational mobility is low among many excluded groups and that this is explained to a large extent by human capital deficits that have accumulated over generations (Márquez et al. 2007).

Social Networks: Does It Boil Down to Whom You Know?

The question is largely, but not solely rhetorical. Of course, it does not simply boil down to whom you know; social networks are complex; and it is difficult to define exactly how they affect the welfare of individuals and groups. Nonetheless, it is now well recognized that social networks and solidarity can help or hinder labor market and educational outcomes. Fafchamps and Minten (1998), using data on agricultural traders in Madagascar, show that social capital has a large effect on efficiency, and, after controlling for physical and human inputs, they find that more well-connected traders have significantly larger sales and gross margins than less well-connected traders. Loury (1977), in his famous study of black youth, described how they start with disadvantages in the labor market because of their lack of information on job opportunities and the parental connections that would have given them such information. Put simply, black parents are much less likely to know where the jobs are or whom to call about jobs. There is similar evidence from rural Indonesia, where Bebbington et al. (2006) find that bonding social capital can lead to elite capture. The local elites in the sample sites were able to consolidate their power through connections to the government and local private companies. O'Brien, Phillips, and Patsiorkovsky (2005, 1050) also find evidence of the restrictive nature of bonding social capital in their study of Native American, post-Soviet Russian Federation, and midwestern United States communities. They state that "the negative externalities resulting from those situations [bonding social capital relationships] threaten the very core of liberal democratic institutions." In the end, as Loury (1999) points out,

> *opportunity travels along the synapses of these social networks.*

In their fieldwork, Jodhka and Gautam (2008) found that Dalits identified lack of resources and confidence as barriers to risk-taking and to trying something new or having the courage to fail. This implicit aversion to risk is a marker of historical oppression whereby entire subcastes tend to stay in domains that are safe and known. Respondents also identified social contacts and alliances with dominant communities as central to the success of Dalit entrepreneurs.

> More than the dominant business communities, we have to work with the dominant political community of the state, the Jats. Jats matter much more than anyone else does. If they support us and do not oppose us, we can progress. (Jodhka and Gautam 2008, 24)

Adivasis and Dalits have few institutional contacts. The India Human Development Survey, in an attempt to map social networks, asked respondents across India whether they had contacts in three major types of institutions: in education, the government, or medicine (Desai et al. 2010). It found sharp differences among social groups that follow the expected status hierarchy: forward castes emerged at the top with the most contacts in these institutions, followed by OBCs, Dalits, and Adivasis (figure 3.6). Most of these differences are attributable to the educational and economic differences among the groups. The exceptions are Adivasis, who have few contacts even relative to educationally and economically equivalent forward caste Hindus. Muslims also have few contacts and, in this, are not much different from Dalits: a low standing relative to Hindus of equivalent education and economic position.

Dalits and Adivasis also tend to have lower levels of trust in local institutions. An analysis undertaken for this report looked at the correlates of women's and men's trust in several types of officials— elected leaders, government officials, community workers, and the police—in the states of Karnataka, Madhya Pradesh, and Orissa (Sharif 2008). In general, trust seems to be related to four main household and community-level factors: (1) household wealth (proxied by the ownership of durable goods); (2) caste or tribal status; (3) village, community, or government-supported groups; and (4) household location. Controlling for the location of residence, the study finds that, with some exceptions, SC and ST women are less likely than women in the general population to trust public officials. However, they are more likely than women in the general population to trust community health workers. This latter result could well be a product of better outreach of health workers among SCs and STs because of their poorer health status or because SCs and STs tend to use public systems more than other groups do. SCs overall and ST men are less likely to trust public officials. Caste and tribe markers, over time, may also increase social distance and mistrust among groups. In the 110 villages visited by the *Moving out of Poverty* team in Uttar Pradesh, mistrust across castes was evident. When asked whether people have to be alert to someone trying to take advantage of them in their village, nearly 72 percent of the 1,350 respondents interviewed for the survey agreed strongly. Qualitative data also revealed deepening social cleavages and jealousy across groups in some areas.

Growing Dalit solidarity, combined with reinforced caste-based networks, is expanding economic exchanges and helping to maintain the space of Dalits in the labor market. To circumvent their disadvantages in building networks across social groups and, especially, among higher-status individuals and groups, Dalits and, particularly, Muslims seem to be strengthening their internal bonds and using these for economic purposes. Jodhka and Gautam (2008), in their survey of Dalit entrepreneurs, found that almost all of their respondents (94 percent) claimed that they had some form of association with Dalit movements in their region or in the country. About 63 percent were involved with a local Dalit nongovernmental organization or a Dalit religious organization. This is confirmed by Munshi and Rosenzweig (2006), who use data on school enrollments, caste, and income in Mumbai over a period of 20 years to show that caste networks in the city, organized at the level of the subcaste or jati, ensure that members of lower castes send their children (boys) to schools in which the local language is spoken. The goal is to keep the boys within the network of the jati, which can help them later in job searches.

There are also examples indicating how caste networks use their ritually ordered positions to respond to new opportunities. Kishwar (2002), for instance, documents how government sweepers in New Delhi, by asserting their monopoly over cleaning and garbage collection on public land, have resisted the efforts of street vendors to self-regulate garbage disposal. Similarly, leather workers and metal workers in Uttar Pradesh have responded to new opportunities by organizing production through caste networks. During fieldwork for this report, we found that women's self-help group federations in Orissa were both caste-destroying in that they were most often multicaste groups and caste-enhancing in that they organized along caste lines. An example of the latter case is offered by a local federation in Bhadrak that decided to purchase milk only from the self-help groups among the *gopal*, the traditional cowherd caste.

Voice and Agency Have Accompanied Economic Change

> You have now a way of bringing about change, an improvement in your life conditions. That way is through political action, through appropriate laws. . . . You can make government provide for you what you are now denied: food, clothing, shelter, education. . . . Hence instead of resorting to rosary counting or prayer you should now depend on the political path; that will bring you liberation. . . . The conflict, hereafter, will not be between the British and the Indians, but between the advanced classes of India and the backward classes. No borrowed or hired person who does not belong to your class can further your welfare by the least degree. You must rid yourselves of internal divisions and organize strongly.
>
> Speech of B. R. Ambedkar (1933), quoted in Gore (1993, 213)

Dalit self-assertion has perhaps been the most potent social movement in postindependence India. In our section on labor markets, we ask: "how does the labor market behave toward Dalits?" An equally relevant question in the context of Dalit assertion is "how do Dalits behave toward the labor market and other social constraints?" The earliest movements of backward caste self-assertion that became movements for political power started in Tamil Nadu in the 1920s. After Ambedkar, the Dalit movement gathered new strength in Maharashtra and, for a period, also some militancy through the rise of the Dalit Panthers. Ambedkar organized Dalits in a mass rejection of the Hindu idiom through their conversion to Buddhism, and, later, Dalit writing acquired leadership in poetry and literature. In Maharashtra, Dalit literature became a symbol of social protest in a movement replete with the symbolism of a new, alternative caste-free world.

Social movements asserting the power of Dalits also swept through other states and acquired political significance. The southern states had already witnessed backward caste power turning into electoral power. The Republic Party of India in Maharashtra and the domination by OBCs of politics in Andhra Pradesh and Karnataka are other cases in point. This happened much later in the north. By the end of the 20th century, social movements had gathered strength in the Hindi belt as well, but only more recently have Dalit and OBC parties held power in Bihar and Uttar Pradesh. These movements have enabled the establishment of a pan-Indian bond among Dalits that no other excluded group has been able to replicate. Gupta (2000) points out that, while the old feudal elite is giving way to a new, more assertive elite that has emerged from the erstwhile oppressed castes, the metaphor within which both elites operate is based on caste.

Both Gupta (2000) and Srinivas (1966) before him focus on the horizontal solidarity among Dalits that is gradually replacing the old vertical hierarchy. As a social and political force, regardless of the process of Dalit self-assertion, this has had huge impacts on Dalit status, and this is precisely where the real difference between Adivasis and Dalits surfaces. Xaxa (2001) and Guha (2007) have argued that Dalits outperform Adivasis along a range of human development and labor market outcomes mainly on account of better voice and agency (see chapter 2).

Far-reaching changes in the Indian economy over the last two decades have also had a bearing on caste dynamics. Surinder Jodhka returned to Haryana villages where he had done his doctoral fieldwork to examine how caste dynamics had changed. He found that, in 20 years, with the exception of a small number of people in the scavenging community, Dalit families no longer engaged in traditional caste occupations.

> They go out of the village for work, and many of them have regular employment. Their dependence on local landowners for credit has also declined. They have moved away . . . from

the agrarian economy of the village and they rarely, if ever participate in the ritual life of the village, or the other caste groups on any occasion. In other words, they no longer see themselves as being a part of the social order of the caste system. This has also given them a sense of independence and political agency. (Jodhka 2008, 27)

As one respondent from a backward caste in a Haryana village told Jodhka (2008, 26), "No one (backward caste) cares for anyone simply because he thinks he is a *chaudhary* (dominant caste). *Chaudharies*, if they are, they must be in their homes. We do not care."

In a study on over 19,000 Dalit households in two blocks in the districts of Azamgarh and Bulandshahar in Uttar Pradesh, Kapur et al. (2010) document huge changes in the lifestyles and occupations of Dalits between 1990 and 2007. The changes included the near demise of the *halwaha* system, a kind of attached labor arrangement, similar to the situation Jodhka (2008) describes in Haryana villages. In addition, fewer Dalits were involved in traditionally unclean occupations, and almost 40 percent sent at least one member to work in an urban area. These findings from Uttar Pradesh, which neighbors Haryana, are wholly consistent with the findings of Jodhka (2008).

Witsoe (2008) reports similar evidence of dynamism in the caste hierarchy based on changed agrarian relations in rural Bihar. He writes that the "expanding economic status of many backward caste cultivators in the wake of the green revolution conflicted with their political marginalization, especially since the patron-client ties that had allowed their votes to be controlled by upper caste landlords were progressively weakening" (Witsoe 2008, 10).

Findings from these small-area studies need to be placed in a context of declining returns to rural landownership. Anecdotal evidence suggests that, because of the declining returns in agriculture, there has, indeed, been an inversion in the social and economic structure in many villages. Because they did not own much land, most Dalits moved out, thereby weakening traditional patron-client relationships. Thus, even though they did not gain much in absolute terms by moving out of a declining industry, they gained, in relative terms, compared with, say, upper caste groups that owned land.

Economic changes, including better opportunities and increased urbanization, have played a part in breaking down old caste norms and allowing Dalits a new space for action. Srinivas (1966) probably did not realize the extent of his clairvoyance when he identified urbanization as one of the greatest propellers of the transformation of caste. In his writings on the country-town nexus in India, sociologist Dipankar Gupta describes how Dalit aspirations to participate in political life are increasing with exposure to the urban setting. Boosted by the greater income associated with migration, low caste laborers are now seeking new social and political identities in the hierarchy of the village (Gupta and Sharma 1991). Similarly, in their study of Dalit entrepreneurs, Jodhka and Gautam (2008, 24) note as follows:

Those who had been successful in business, were invariably also attracted toward electoral politics. They found it much easier to enter into the mainstream political space. Social and cultural spaces seemed more difficult to penetrate. Democratic political process and the system of reserved quota of seats for Scheduled Castes seem to invite them to politics. Success in politics indeed helped them in their businesses. It provided them with some kind of shield in a social environment where they otherwise felt insecure and marginal.

The Dalit entrepreneurs also seemed to be aware of their move from traditional occupations to new urban occupations and the implications this was having for their caste identities and caste politics.

Along with the economic changes, a new class of young political entrepreneurs seems to be emerging in the unfolding political arena. These individuals are required to have the skills to network with the outside world of politics and development bureaucracy. At the same time, they must also link organically with different caste communities and demonstrate to these communities their leadership abilities, a step the older generation could not bring itself to take. The rise of politicians from among their own community can also aid the Dalits in the creation of symbolic identities. Witsoe (2008) records the rise of the Yadavs under the Janata Dal's rule in Bihar. In an ethnographic account of one village in central Bihar, he describes how Yadav villagers, empowered by Yadav leadership in the state, became assertive in community life. They refused to cave in to the demands of their upper caste landlords or be socially subordinated by these landlords. Similarly, the Bahujan Samaj Party, many argue, has helped Dalits establish a political identity at the national level (Pai 2007).

Dalits have benefited politically from affirmative action in the political arena. Constitutional amendments reserving seats in local governments for SCs seem to have contributed to a change in the power structure at the local level. In their study of 527 villages in four southern Indian states (Andhra Pradesh, Karnataka, Kerala, and Tamil Nadu), Besley, Pande, and Rao (2007) find that the reservations of *pradhan* (leadership) positions in village governments have been successful in enhancing targeting in government schemes—such as the allocation of Below Poverty Line cards—in favor of SC and ST households. More important, the authors indicate that reservations have helped reduce the extent of political dominance otherwise exercised by traditional village elites, including the upper castes.

Rao and Ban (2007) also look at the impact of caste-based solidarity movements on the welfare of lower castes. They use a natural experiment—the 1956 reorganization of Indian states along linguistic lines—and find that border villages matching on most other characteristics (such as language, geography, and patterns of land distribution) have different caste structures on different sides of the border. For instance, they find caste broadening to be more prevalent and Dalits to be more empowered in villages in Kerala and Tamil Nadu than in the counterpart border villages in Karnataka, perhaps because of a history of caste-based social movements in the former two states. Similarly, they report considerable differences in the incidence of landlessness (an important correlate of Dalit presence) in border villages in 2002, while, in 1951, there was no difference, highlighting the role state policies can play. They conclude that caste can be endogenous to economic and political change.

Their increased voice and self-assertion probably make Dalits both more prone to being victimized and more likely to report victimization. Crimes against Adivasis and Dalits have been common in India, and history has witnessed many grotesque acts against these groups. In recognition of this, the Scheduled Castes and Scheduled Tribes (Prevention of Atrocities) Act, 1989, was brought into force in January 30, 1990, to check and deter crimes against SCs and STs by persons belonging to other communities. This enactment has extended protection to SCs and STs in criminal law in that the penalties it prescribes are more stringent than the corresponding penalties under the Indian Penal Code and other laws. Special courts have been established in major states for the speedy hearing of cases registered exclusively under these laws. Implementation has been uneven, however, and crimes against Dalits are still common (see Narula 1999).

Globally, the literature on violence against other vulnerable groups, notably women, has shown that, if they become more empowered, these groups are also more likely to be harassed (see World Bank 2008). However, greater empowerment also means that people in these groups are more likely to report crimes and seek redress. Thus, the issues of reporting and incidence become confused, and distinguishing the two issues is difficult. In India, data on the cases filed under the Indian Penal Code and the Prevention of Atrocities Act are collected and published regularly by the National Crime Records Bureau. They show that, in 2007–08, the incidence of crimes reported against Dalits increased by almost 12 percent, but that the incidence of crimes reported against Adivasis increased by less than 1 percent (NCRB 2008). The India Human Development Survey also asked whether respondents had been victimized physically. Overall, according to this self-reporting, Dalits have been victims of crime slightly more often (8.8 percent) than forward caste Hindus (5.5 percent), or Adivasis (5.3 percent). However, the higher victimization rate among Dalits is associated mostly with the higher concentration of Dalits in Bihar, Orissa, and West Bengal, where all castes and communities report higher crime rates (Desai et al. 2010). The lower victimization rate among Adivasis shown by both the India Human Development Survey and the National Crime Records Bureau deserves additional empirical investigation (NCRB 2008).

Conclusion

This chapter documents how Dalits have fared in a time period that saw the national economy record rapid growth. Through the lens of outcomes in education, the labor market, and the political space, the chapter finds the following:

- There has been some convergence in outcomes in education, especially in postprimary education, between Dalit and non-SC/ST men. However, while the catch-up has been impressive, Dalits still lag because of their low starting points. Dalit women, in particular, do poorly, faring only marginally better than Adivasi women.
- Belief systems and the expectation of poor returns to education seem to explain why Dalit students continue to perform poorly in schools. Microstudies also suggest that there is isolation of and discrimination against Dalit students.
- Dalits are slightly more likely to participate in the labor market. However, they remain largely in casual jobs. Over time, there has been only a slight shift away from casual labor into nonfarm employment among men. More Dalit women, however, seem to be withdrawing from the labor force, perhaps on account of more education and social mobility.

- The picture that emerges on the employment options among educated Dalit men is more complex. In rural areas, higher educational attainment mostly hampers the employment opportunities among Dalits, mainly because there are few regular salaried jobs available. In urban areas, too, the combined effects of caste and education indicate that SC men have less chance (relative to other groups) of exiting casual labor and moving into regular salaried jobs if they have postprimary education. This may be a corollary of an increasing supply of educated SC men over time, leading to a system of job rationing among SCs, who cannot compete in the nonreserved salaried job market.
- Wage differentials between Dalits and others are a testimony to the continued disadvantage of Dalits in the labor market. Differences in access to occupations, or glass walls, are an important determinant of the wage gap. Recent research suggests that there is subtle caste-based stereotyping in private hiring.
- Microstudies, however, indicate cracks in the glass walls. Dalit men are gradually moving out of agricultural labor to relatively higher-paying nonfarm work and into trade and self-employment, where, however, they face other roadblocks. In addition to new economic opportunities, Dalit solidarity movements and affirmative action policies have helped Dalits claim political space. In this, they have been more successful than other excluded groups.

The words of Prasad (2008, 29) about the market generally conjure an image of how market forces are mutating the rules of purity and pollution conceived in the *Manusmriti*:

The market is more a new culture than anything else; it comes with its own set of tools, which are often caste-neutral. Compare the brooms the street sweepers or traditional sweepers use with the ones deployed in the mall. The sweeper or toilet cleaner in the mall becomes a "housekeeper" or "janitor" for a host of reasons. The broom s/he uses is a near-machine, distinct and different from the traditional broom; additionally, these workers use gloves, wear a full uniform, complete with trousers, shirt, cap and shoes. Along with a new tool which neutralizes caste, the sweeper turns into a housekeeper, looking more like a paramedic than a traditional sweeper. In one stroke, the market has liberated the broom from its caste identity, and the occupation has become caste-neutral.

Annex

Table 3A.1 Type of Employment, Rural Men

Indicator	Nonfarm self-employed		Self-employed farmers		Casual wage workers		Out of the labor force	
	(a)	(b)	(a)	(b)	(a)	(b)	(a)	(b)
age	0.013	0.013	-0.062***	-0.062***	-0.079***	-0.079***	-0.631***	-0.631***
age2	-0.000***	-0.000***	0.001***	0.001***	0.000***	0.000***	0.008***	0.008***
married2	0.051	0.052	0.218***	0.218***	0.213***	0.210***	-1.079***	-1.081***
hhsize	0.068***	0.068***	0.004	0.004	0.028***	0.027***	0.007	0.006
below_prim	-0.113**	-0.116**	-0.402***	-0.408***	-0.530***	-0.541***	-0.542***	-0.549***
prim_comp	-0.371***	-0.357***	-0.659***	-0.656***	-1.080***	-1.116***	-0.543***	-0.547***
postpri	-1.108***	-1.116***	-1.588***	-1.626***	-2.532***	-2.670***	-0.166***	-0.226***
hhhead	0.019	0.019	-0.107***	-0.108***	-0.01	-0.013	-0.780***	-0.781***
land_poss	0.141***	0.140***	0.645***	0.645***	-0.784***	-0.784***	0.339***	0.340***
north	-0.743***	-0.742***	-1.201***	-1.200***	-0.957***	-0.955***	-0.740***	-0.739***
south	0.207***	0.206***	-1.921***	-1.922***	0.234***	0.230***	-0.632***	-0.634***
east	0.091**	0.092**	-0.324***	-0.320***	0.065	0.07	-0.091*	-0.088*
NE	-0.433***	-0.433***	-0.310***	-0.311***	-0.539***	-0.536***	-0.303***	-0.301***
muslim	0.476***	0.473***	-0.192***	-0.199***	0.083*	0.061	0.179***	0.168***
otherel	-0.141**	-0.144***	-0.007	-0.007	-0.077	-0.077	0.156**	0.156**
sc	-0.196***	-0.222***	-0.443***	-0.546***	0.630***	0.405***	0.052	-0.104
st	-0.575***	-0.572***	0.065	0.061	0.666***	0.645***	-0.044	-0.057
SCprim_comp		-0.095		-0.064		0.087		-0.012
SCpostpri		-0.029		0.129*		0.481***		0.259***
_cons	1.063***	1.080***	3.343***	3.377***	4.510***	4.580***	11.306***	11.351***
Statistics								
N observations	115,390							
Pseudo R-squared	0.258							

Source: NSS data, 61st round, 2004–05.

Note: Reference: no education, central region, Hindu, non-SC/ST. Multinomial logit: type of employment, NSS round 61. Coefficients: Rural men only. Base category dependent variable: regular salaried work.

*p ≤ .05 **p ≤ .01 ***p ≤ .001.

Table 3A.2 Type of Employment, Urban Men

Indicator	Nonfarm self-employed (a)	Nonfarm self-employed (b)	Self-employed farmers (a)	Self-employed farmers (b)	Casual wage workers (a)	Casual wage workers (b)	Out of the labor force (a)	Out of the labor force (b)
age	0.047***	0.047***	-0.123***	-0.121***	-0.075***	-0.074***	-0.526***	-0.525***
age2	-0.001***	-0.001***	0.002***	0.002***	0.000***	0.000***	0.007***	0.007***
married2	0.182***	0.182***	0.380***	0.376***	0.278***	0.276***	-0.895***	-0.892***
hhsize	0.114***	0.114***	0.209***	0.209***	0.057***	0.057***	0.035***	0.035***
below_prim	-0.242***	-0.240***	-0.729***	-0.735***	-0.717***	-0.711***	-0.603***	-0.598***
prim_comp	-0.437***	-0.377***	-0.980***	-0.946***	-1.257***	-1.183***	-0.888***	-0.845***
postpri	-0.790***	-0.739***	-1.547***	-1.622***	-2.483***	-2.488***	-0.07	-0.065
hhhead	-0.349***	-0.350***	-0.013	-0.018	-0.151***	-0.153***	-0.404***	-0.402***
land_poss	0.121***	0.119***	0.440***	0.440***	-0.052	-0.049	0.156***	0.154***
north	-0.324***	-0.324***	-0.940***	-0.934***	-0.639***	-0.631***	-0.330***	-0.328***
south	-0.168***	-0.166***	-1.204***	-1.207***	0.581***	0.578***	-0.245***	-0.244***
west	-0.403***	-0.401***	-1.244***	-1.247***	0.01	0.006	-0.448***	-0.446***
NE	-0.131	-0.135	0.12	0.127	-0.17	-0.168	0.175	0.173
muslim	0.385***	0.393***	-0.485***	-0.509***	0.129***	0.120***	-0.090**	-0.090**
otherel	0.231***	0.233***	0.076	0.071	0.325***	0.323***	0.368***	0.367***
sc	-0.395***	-0.199***	-0.645***	-0.840***	0.513***	0.604***	-0.048	-0.031
st	-0.577***	-0.570***	1.077***	1.073***	0.402***	0.402***	-0.164**	-0.164**
SCprim_comp		-0.269***		-0.293		-0.310***		-0.162
SCpostpri		-0.274***		0.476**		0.034		0.003
_cons	-0.572***	-0.610***	-0.161	-0.132	2.038***	2.011***	9.096***	9.075***
Statistics								
N observations	63,664							
Pseudo R-squared	0.208							

Source: NSS data, 61st round, 2004–05.

Note: Reference: no education, central region, Hindu, non-SC/ST. Multinomial logit: type of employment, NSS round 61. Coefficients: Urban men only. Base category dependent variable: regular salaried work.

*p ≤ .05 **p ≤ .01 ***p ≤ .001.

Notes

1. Similarly, STs are also referred to as *Adivasis*. For purposes of the tables and figures presented in this chapter, we use the terms "SC" and "ST" because these are standard administrative and survey categories. In the text, we also use the terms Dalits and Adivasis (or tribals) interchangeably with SCs and STs, respectively.

2. Postprimary education is coded as any education above the primary level. It is a huge category and not useful if we wish to examine fine changes across the educational system. However, higher education is so rare among STs and among SC women that multivariate analysis does not reach useful conclusions based on such small cell sizes.

3. See, for instance, the Senthilkumar Solidarity Committee (2008) report on the suicide of Senthil, a Dalit research scholar at the University of Hyderabad.

4. See http://pmindia.nic.in/speech/content.asp?id=482.

5. STs are less beset by this demarcation because they were traditionally assigned a role outside the pale of the caste system. Because, for the most part, they own some land, they also show a higher likelihood of being active as agriculturalists.

References

Ambedkar, B. R. 2004. "Caste in India." In *Caste and Democratic Politics in India,* ed. 6. Shah, pp. 59–78. London: Anthem Press.

Banerjee, B., and J. B. Knight. 1985. "Caste Discrimination in the Indian Urban Labour Market." *Journal of Development Economics* 17 (3): 277–307.

Bebbington, A., L. Dharmawan, E. Fahmi, and S. Guggenheim. 2006. "Local Capacity, Village Governance and the Political Economy of Rural Development in Indonesia." *World Development* 34 (11): 1958–76.

Bertrand, M., R. Hanna, and S. Mullainathan. 2008. "Affirmative Action in Education: Evidence from Engineering College Admissions in India." Working Paper 13926 (April), National Bureau of Economic Research, Cambridge, MA.

Besley, T., R. Pande, and V. Rao. 2007. "Political Economy of Panchayats in South India." *Economic and Political Weekly* 42 (8): 661–66.

Das, M. B. 2006. "Do Traditional Axes of Exclusion Affect Labor Market Outcomes in India?" South Asia Social Development Discussion Paper 3, World Bank, Washington, DC.

————. 2009. "Minority Status and Labor Market Outcomes: Does India Have Minority Enclaves?" Policy Research Working Paper 4653, World Bank, Washington, DC.

Das, M. B., and S. Desai. 2003. "Why Are Educated Women Less Likely to Be Employed in India? Testing Competing Hypotheses." Social Protection Discussion Paper 0313, World Bank, Washington, DC.

Das, M. B., and P. Dutta. 2007. "Does Caste Matter for Wages in the Indian Labor Market?" Draft report, World Bank, Washington, DC.

————. 2008. "Does Caste Matter for Wages in the Indian Labor Market? Caste Pay Gaps in India." Paper presented at the Third Institute for the Study of Labor–World Bank Conference on Employment and Development, Rabat, Morocco, May 5–6.

Datcher-Loury, L., and G. C. Loury. 1986. "The Effects of Attitudes and Aspirations on the Labor Supply of Young Men." In *The Black Youth Employment Crisis*, ed. R. B. Freeman and H. J. Holzer, 377–401. Chicago: University of Chicago Press.

Desai, S. 2010. "Recasting 2011 Census: Too Little, Too Late." *Economic Times*, May 14.

Desai, S., A. Dubey, B. Joshi, M. Sen, A. Shariff, and R. Vanneman. 2010. *Human Development in India: Challenges for a Society in Transition.* New Delhi: Oxford University Press.

Desai, S., and V. Kulkarni. 2008. "Changing Educational Inequalities in India in the Context of Affirmative Action." *Demography* 45 (2): 245–70.

Desai, S., J. Noon, and R. Vanneman. 2008. "Who Gets Good Jobs? The Role of Human, Social, and Cultural Capital." Draft working paper, National Council for Applied Economic Research, New Delhi; University of Maryland, College Park, MD.

Deshpande, A., and K. S. Newman. 2007. "Where the Path Leads: The Role of Caste in Post-University Employment Expectations." *Economic and Political Weekly* 42 (41): 4133–40.

Deshpande, R., and S. Palshikar. 2008. "Patterns of Occupational Mobility: How Much Does Caste Matter?" *Economic and Political Weekly* 43 (34): 61–70.

Dubey, A., V. Iversen, A. Kalwij, B. Kebede, and A. Verschoor. 2008. "Caste Dominance and Inclusive Growth: Evidence from a Panel Data Set for India." Draft, work in progress, World Bank, Washington, DC.

Fafchamps, M., and B. Minten. 1998. "Returns to Social Capital among Traders." MSSD Discussion Paper 23, Markets and Structural Studies Division, International Food Policy Research Institute, Washington, DC.

Gacitúa-Marió, E., and M. Woolcock, eds. 2008. *Social Exclusion and Mobility in Brazil.* Washington, DC: World Bank.

Gore, M. S. 1993. *The Social Context of an Ideology: Ambedkar's Political and Social Thought.* New Delhi: Sage Publications.

Government of India. 2008. *Eleventh Five Year Plan (2007–2012)*. New Delhi: Oxford University Press.

Guha, R. 2007. "Adivasis, Naxalites and Indian Democracy." *Economic and Political Weekly* 42 (32): 3305–12.

Gupta, D. 2000. *Interrogating Caste: Understanding Hierarchy and Difference in Indian Society*. New Delhi: Penguin Books.

Gupta, D., and K. L. Sharma, eds. 1991. *Country Town Nexus: Studies in Social Transformation in Contemporary India*. Jaipur, India: Rawat.

Hoff, K., and P. Pandey. 2004. "Belief Systems and Durable Inequalities: An Experimental Investigation of Indian Caste." Policy Research Working Paper 3351, World Bank, Washington, DC.

Iversen, V., and P. S. Raghavendra. 2006. "What the Signboard Hides: Food, Caste and Employability in Small South Indian Eating Places." *Contributions to Indian Sociology* 40 (3): 311–41.

Jacobson, M. 2007. "Dharavi: Mumbai's Shadow City." *National Geographic*, May. http://ngm.nationalgeographic.com/2007/05/dharavi-mumbai-slum/jacobson-text.

Jadhav, N. 2003. *Outcaste, a Memoir: Life and Triumphs of an Untouchable Family in India*. New Delhi: Viking.

———. 2005. *Untouchables: My Family's Triumphant Journey out of the Caste System in Modern India*. New York: Simon and Schuster.

Jeffrey, C., R. Jeffery, and P. Jeffery. 2004. "Degrees without Freedom: The Impact of Formal Education on Dalit Young Men in North India." *Development and Change* 35 (5): 963–86.

Jodhka, S. 2008. "A Forgotten 'Revolution': Revisiting Agrarian Change in Haryana." Paper prepared for the study, Poverty and Social Exclusion in India, Indian Institute of Dalit Studies, New Delhi.

Jodhka, S., and S. Gautam. 2008. "In Search of a Dalit Entrepreneur: Barriers and Supports in the Life of Self-Employed Scheduled Castes." Paper prepared for the study, Poverty and Social Exclusion in India, Indian Institute of Dalit Studies, New Delhi.

Kapur, D., C. B. Prasad, L. Pritchett, and D. S. Babu. 2010. "Rethinking Inequality: Dalits in Uttar Pradesh in the Market Reform Era." *Economic and Political Weekly* 45 (35): 39–49.

Kijima, Y. 2006. "Caste and Tribe Inequality: Evidence from India, 1983–1999." *Economic Development and Cultural Change* 54 (2): 369–404.

Kishwar, M. 2002. "Working under Constant Threat: Some Setbacks and Some Steps Forward in Sewa Nagar." *Manushi* 130 (May–June).

Loury, G. C. 1977. "A Dynamic Theory of Racial and Income Differences." In *Women, Minorities, and Employment Discrimination*, ed. P. Wallace and A. LaMond, 153–88. Lexington, MA: Heath.

———. 1999. "Social Exclusion and Ethnic Groups: The Challenge to Economics." Paper prepared for the Annual World Bank Conference on Development Economics, Washington, DC, April 28–30.

Loury, G. C., T. Modood, and S. M. Teles, eds. 2005. *Ethnicity, Social Mobility, and Public Policy: Comparing the USA and UK.* Cambridge: Cambridge University Press.

Márquez, G., A. Chong, S. Duryea, J. Mazza, and H. Ñopo, eds. 2007. *Outsiders: The Changing Patterns of Exclusion in Latin America and the Caribbean.* Economic and Social Progress in Latin America 2008. Washington, DC: Inter-American Development Bank.

Ministry of Personnel, Public Grievances, and Pensions. 2009. *Annual Report 2008–2009.* New Delhi: Ministry of Personnel, Public Grievances, and Pensions.

Munshi, K., and M. Rosenzweig. 2005. "Why Is Mobility in India So Low? Social Insurance, Inequality, and Growth." Draft working paper, Center for International Development, Harvard University, Cambridge, MA.

———. 2006. "Traditional Institutions Meet the Modern World: Caste, Gender and Schooling Choice in a Globalizing Economy." *American Economic Review* 96 (4): 1225–52.

Nambissan, G. B. 2010. *"Exclusion and Discrimination in Schools: Experiences of Dalit Children."* In *Blocked by Caste: Economic Discrimination in Modern India,* ed. S. Thorat and K. S. Newman, 253–86. New York: Oxford University Press.

Narula, S. 1999. *Broken People: Caste Violence against India's "Untouchables."* New York: Human Rights Watch.

NCRB (National Crime Records Bureau). 2008. *Crime in India, 2008.* New Delhi: Ministry of Home Affairs.

Nilekani, N. 2008. *Imagining India: Ideas for the New Century.* New Delhi: Penguin Books India.

O'Brien, D. J., J. L. Phillips, and V. V. Patsiorkovsky. 2005. "Linking Indigenous Bonding and Bridging Social Capital." *Regional Studies* 39 (8): 1041–51, Regional Studies Association, Seaford, United Kingdom.

Pai, S., ed. 2007. *Political Process in Uttar Pradesh: Identity, Economic Reforms and Governance.* New Delhi: Pearson Education.

Pawar, D. 1974. *Kondwada.* Pune, India: Magowa Prakashan.

Prasad, C. B. 2008. "Markets and Manu: Economic Reforms and Its Impact on Caste in India." CASI Working Paper 08–01 (January), Center for the Advanced Study of India, University of Pennsylvania, Philadelphia.

———. 2009a. "For a New Dalit Social Contract." Livemint.com, March 16. http://www.livemint.com/articles/2009/03/15212222/For-a-new-Dalit-social-contrac.html.

———. 2009b. "Sir, the World Turned Upside Down: Radical Changes in Dalits' Occupations, Food Habits and Lifestyle Observed in Two Blocks of UP." Paper presented at the Planning Commission of India, New Delhi, November 5.

Rao, V., and R. Ban. 2007. "The Political Construction of Caste in South India." Unpublished report, World Bank, Washington, DC.

Rao, V., and M. Walton. 2004. "Culture and Public Action: Relationality, Equality of Agency, and Development." In *Culture and Public Action*, ed. V. Rao and M. Walton, 3–36. Stanford, CA: Stanford University Press.

Senthilkumar Solidarity Committee. 2008. "Caste, Higher Education and Senthil's 'Suicide.'" *Economic and Political Weekly* 43 (33): 10–12.

Shah, G., H. Mander, S. Thorat, S. Deshpande, and A. Baviskar. 2006. *Untouchability in Rural India*. New Delhi: Sage Publications.

Sharif, I. 2008. "The Determinants of Trust: Does Caste and Gender Matter?" Background paper for the study Poverty and Social Exclusion in India, Indian Institute of Dalit Studies, New Delhi.

Srinivas, M. N. 1966. *Social Change in Modern India*. New Delhi: Orient Longman.

Thapar, R. 1966. *A History of India*, vol. 1. London: Penguin Books.

Thorat, S. 2007. "Economic Exclusion and Poverty: Indian Experience of Remedies against Exclusion." Paper presented at the International Food Policy Research Institute and Asian Development Bank policy forum, "Agricultural and Rural Development for Reducing Poverty and Hunger in Asia: In Pursuit of Inclusive and Sustainable Growth," Manila, August 9–10.

Thorat, S., and K. S. Newman. 2010. *Blocked by Caste: Economic Discrimination in Modern India*. New York: Oxford University Press.

Unni, J. 2001. "Earnings and Education among Ethnic Groups in Rural India." NCAER Working Paper 79, National Council of Applied Economic Research, New Delhi.

Upadhya, C. 2007. "Employment, Exclusion and 'Merit' in the Indian IT Industry." *Economic and Political Weekly* 2 (20): 1863–68.

Wax, E. 2008. "In an Indian Village, Signs of the Loosening Grip of Caste." *Washington Post*, August 31.

Witsoe, J. 2008. "Caste, Public Institutions, and Inequality in Bihar." Unpublished working paper, World Bank, Washington, DC.

World Bank. 2008. *Whispers to Voices: Gender and Social Transformation in Bangladesh*. Washington, DC: World Bank.

Xaxa, V. 2001. "Protective Discrimination: Why Scheduled Tribes Lag behind Scheduled Castes." *Economic and Political Weekly* 36 (29): 2765–72.

Yadav, Y. 2010. "Why Caste Should Be Counted In?" *Hindu*, May 14.

Zaidi, A. 2006. "System Has Become More Pervasive: Interview with Martin Macwan, Founder of Navsarjan." *Frontline* 23 (18), September 9–22. http://www.frontlineonnet.com/fl2318/stories/20060922005101600.htm.

4

Women

A barren wife may be superseded in the eighth year; one whose children have died in the tenth; one who bears [only] daughters in the eleventh; but one who says unpleasant things [may be superseded] immediately.

The Laws of Manu IX, 81[1]

The last few decades have seen remarkable progress in the status of women and girls, and most Indian families would not now be able to identify with the anachronistic *Laws of Manu*. Yet, this chapter demonstrates that the cultural roots of gender inequality are still strong and affect a range of outcomes among women. In addition, the progress has been slower than would have been expected based on India's levels of growth in gross domestic product: it lags behind the progress in other countries at India's income level. In absolute terms, women's disadvantage stands out more in some indicators than in others: this includes women's overall survival disadvantage in childhood and in the reproductive years and women's disadvantage in labor market outcomes. In addition, educational attainment among girls lags behind that among boys. However, as in other areas, in gender inequality, too, India is highly heterogeneous. While outcomes tend to be much poorer among Adivasi, Dalit, and Muslim women than among others (in absolute terms), gender inequalities are probably smaller among the former (at least among Scheduled Castes [SCs] and Scheduled Tribes [STs]) relative to upper caste Hindus. There are also large regional variations in most of these indicators. While we use aggregate data in this chapter that can be broken down only to the state level and to social groups, yet, within these groups, there is so much variation that we are unable to capture many of the nuances.

This chapter focuses on three areas of female disadvantage. First is the survival disadvantage. Both young girls and women in their reproductive years are at elevated risk of death due to neglect or, in the case of female fetuses, at risk of being aborted. However, new evidence suggests that gender-selective abortions may be plateauing in coming years, though the evidence is inconclusive. Second, the chapter focuses on women's participation in markets. Because of data constraints, we restrict the analysis to participation in the labor market and the relationship this has to poor access to credit. Women are also much less likely than men to be employed and earn cash wages if they are employed or to own property and durable assets. Third, we focus on threats to women's physical security within and outside the home and the fact that this is correlated with poor health outcomes among women and their children. We address the issue of the voice and visibility of women within and outside the home and the extent to which this is correlated with better outcomes. The literature demonstrates that women's agency and empowerment result in huge gains not only among women, but also among families and the community (Sen 2001; Nussbaum 2000).

We draw our evidence from multiple sources of data, both quantitative and qualitative. Our quantitative analysis is based on multiple rounds of the Indian National Sample Survey (NSS), the census, two rounds of the Indian National Family Health Survey (NFHS 1998 and 2005), several rounds of the multicountry Demographic and Health Surveys, the Reproductive Child Health Survey II (RCH II 2005), and the India Human Development Survey (2005).

The Survival Disadvantage

Overall, Indian women are doing much better today than women of their mothers' generation. If they overcome their initial and peculiarly South Asian disadvantage in childhood survival, they will become healthier and more well educated than their mothers were. However, while there has been improvement in absolute terms, the gender gaps revealed by some indicators, such as infant survival, have widened. The starkest testimony to women's disadvantage is the high mortality rates and poor health outcomes among women. These outcomes are tied up with cultural mores, poor opportunities, and the inefficient supply of services. As a result, Indian women often show worse outcomes than women in neighboring Bangladesh in a number of areas. Declines in mortality rates overall have occurred more slowly in India than in Bangladesh and Nepal. India and, to a lesser extent, Nepal are the only two countries on which recent

Demographic and Health Survey data show that the survival rate is lower among infant girls than among infant boys (figure 4.1).

At the same time, there have been notable areas of progress. Declines in fertility, for instance, free women from the cycle of childbearing and child-rearing and allow them to enter into other arenas. In India, fertility rates in several states are now below replacement levels and resemble rates in developed countries. However, fertility rates in other states resemble rates in much poorer countries (figure 4.2). Contraceptive prevalence is much higher than a decade ago, and maternal mortality—while at stubbornly high levels across South Asia, except in Sri Lanka (see figure 4.5 elsewhere below)—is showing a decline that is sharper in India than in other countries.

Adverse child sex ratios in many Indian states have received considerable attention, but is there evidence of an incipient turnaround? The strong preference for sons among Indian families plays out in the neglect of daughters and, over the last few decades, in the selective abortion of female fetuses. This has led to massive outrage. Amartya Sen, in 1992, famously drew attention to the "missing women" in China and India (Sen 1992). At the core of this preference for sons seems to be a number of cultural practices, including the taboo against receiving financial help from daughters or considering daughters as old age insurance. Together with high dowry rates, this implies that daughters are perceived as a net loss in economic terms. In such a scenario, the easy availability of technology that detects the sex of the child allows families to abort female fetuses.

States in the north and west such as Delhi, Gujarat, Haryana, and Punjab show female-to-male ratios among children that are lower than the national average, suggesting a survival disadvantage among girls. Interestingly, some states, such as Gujarat, also show high rates of labor force participation by women and, consequently, higher economic independence among women, which usually deters son preference. In Haryana and Punjab, the sex ratios are so adverse that there is (now) a shortage of marriageable women, and the families of sons have to import daughters-in-law from across the country and across caste lines. Whether these trends will have longer-term consequences is yet to be determined (Kaur 2004). However, not all states fare so badly. Indicators on Andhra Pradesh, Assam, Kerala, and West Bengal are encouraging.

A study on the processes that accompany low sex ratios in those states where daughter neglect is at its worst (including Haryana, Himachal Pradesh, Madhya Pradesh, Punjab, and Rajasthan) confirms the role played by social and cultural mores.

Figure 4.1 Only in India and Nepal Is Infant Mortality Higher among Girls than among Boys

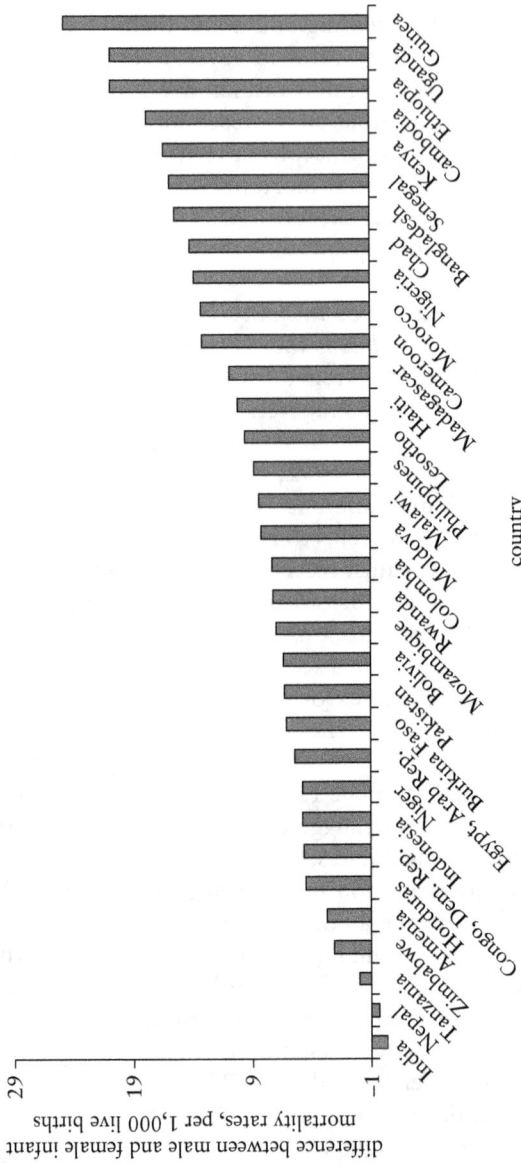

Source: Selected Demographic and Health Surveys, 2003–06.

Figure 4.2 Fertility Is Declining: Rates in Many Indian States Resemble Rates in Developed Countries

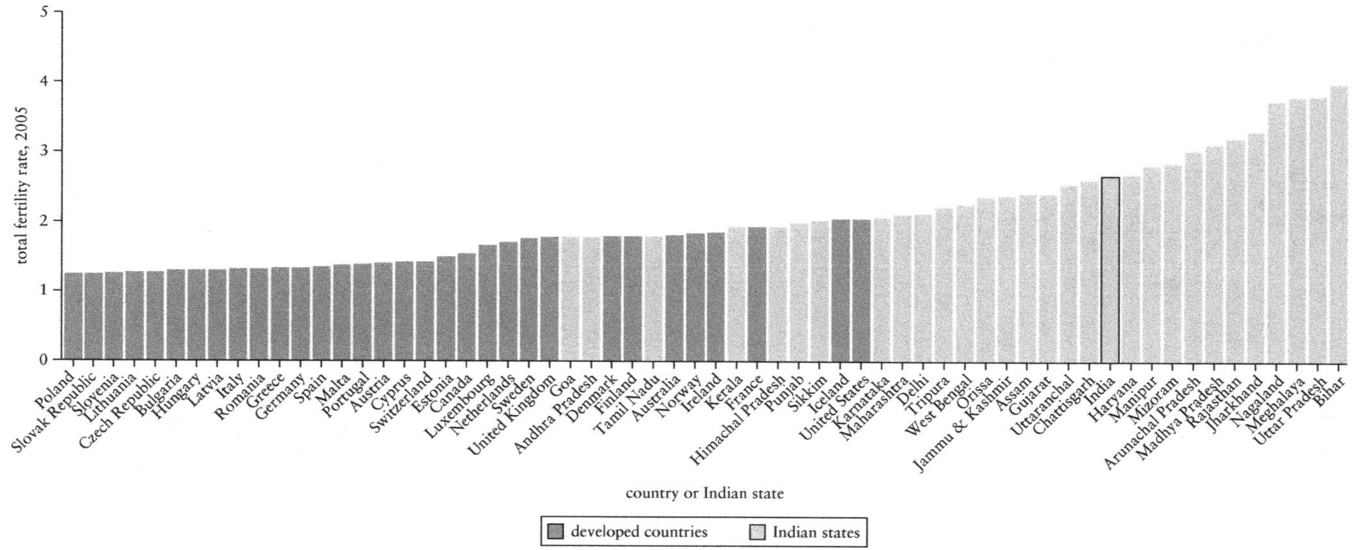

Sources: Australia: Australian Bureau of Statistics; Canada: Statistics Canada; European countries: Eurostat (data for 2008); India and states: NFHS; selected countries: Demographic and Health Surveys.

Note: The data refer to 2005 or the closest available year.

131

[The] unintended consequences of contemporary social processes (like later age of marriage and more education for girls), when combined with parental fears of the unattached sexuality of adult daughters in a context of a highly competitive and differentiated marriage market, are compounding the sense of burden represented by the birth of a daughter. She now requires many more years at home with higher investments in nutrition, health and education. Parental responsibility continues to rest on ensuring a "good" marriage, which takes her away from them, even though this does not necessarily represent the end of their responsibilities. Sons, on the other hand, embody a range of ritual and economic roles. If the current climate of economic volatility and masculine anomie makes them often fall short of expectations, nonetheless, at least one is essential for the future of the family. It is this conjuncture that is producing a falling child sex ratio. (John et al. 2008, 86)

A recent article in the *Economist* that focuses on "the worldwide war on baby girls" suggests that China and India are not the only countries with a dubious record of adverse sex ratios. It points out the following:

Other East Asian countries—[the Republic of] Korea, Singapore and [Taiwan SAR, China]—have peculiarly high numbers of male births. So, since the collapse of the Soviet Union, have former communist countries in the Caucasus and the western Balkans. Even subsets of America's population are following suit, though not the population as a whole.[2]

However, the preference for sons seems to be declining, gradually, in some countries. Das Gupta, Chung, and Shuzhuo (2009) draw comparative evidence from the Republic of Korea to show that the "masculination" of child sex ratios there had declined after the fertility preference for sons decreased, but that there was a lag between the two sets of trends. Combined with a host of policy interventions and the increased entry of women into the workforce, Korea managed to reverse the skewed child sex ratios. There is evidence of this happening in China as well, which had child sex ratios far worse than those in India. In India, too, as table 4.1 shows, the preference for sons is beginning to decline in a few states, such as Haryana and Punjab (which used to represent the worst examples of adverse sex ratios), and we may be at the cusp of a turnaround. However, it is difficult to judge given the lack of data on the situation in other parts of India.

Table 4.1 The Decline in Reported Son Preference in India, 1992–93 to 2005–06

Year of survey	India	Punjab	Haryana
1992–93	1.42	1.57	1.53
1998–99	1.35	1.36	1.46
2005–06	1.27	1.22	1.32

Source: Das Gupta, Chung, and Shuzhuo (2009), based on NFHS-3 and Retherford and Roy (2003).

What Das Gupta, Chung, and Shuzhuo (2009) call an incipient turnaround is evident in the signs of positive change that John et al. (2008) report from their careful ethnographic work in a few northern states. For instance, they find the following:

Post-2001, families in Rohtak and Fatehgharh Saheb are showing a greater acceptance of the first girl child than was true in the 1990s, even though second and third births remain harshly skewed against girl children. Also important is the fact that data on health and nutrition from Kangra, Fatehgarh Saheb, and Rohtak point towards lesser discrimination against surviving girl children. Qualitative data from these two sites also reveal a desire among mothers to ensure better futures for their daughters. (John et al. 2008, 87)

Marriage is the fulcrum around which women's lives revolve, and this has both cultural and welfare implications. Deepa Mehta's controversial film *Water* drew attention to the status of women who had married too early and were then widowed. While the film is set in the early 20th century, early marriages are still the norm in much of India. Socioreligious reform movements in India in the 19th and early 20th centuries recognized early marriage as one of the major social ills, more so because young girls would be widowed and would have to lead highly oppressive lives because widow remarriage is still not the norm in India. Pandita Ramabai's writing in 1888 holds true to a large extent even today; indeed, it was probably also true of Muslim women at the time, as it is today: "It is not easy to determine when the childhood of a Hindu girl ends and the married life begins" (Pandita Ramabai Saraswati 1888, cited in Tharu and Lalita 1993).

About 60 percent of Indian girls are married by the time they are 18, and many are married by age 15 (Desai et al. 2010). Cohabitation occurs fairly soon as well, and almost one-fourth of Indian women even in the youngest age-group (20–24) have had their first

child by the time they are 18 (PRB 2008). Globally, though the numbers have improved over the years, this puts India on a par with
Guyana and Senegal and at a level well below Vietnam, where only
4 percent of girls in the same age-group have had a child by age 18
(figure 4.3).

As with other indicators, there is considerable diversity across
states within India in the age at marriage as well. The proportion
of girls who are married by the age of 18 is quite high even in
Kerala. In Bihar, 86 percent of the girls are married by the age of
18. In Rajasthan, where the mean age at marriage is among the
lowest in the world and 79 percent of girls are married by the age
of 18, activists have been fighting against the custom of child marriage (Desai and Andrist 2010). On the notoriously auspicious day
of Akha Teej (a holy day among Hindus), which falls in the lunar
month of Vaisakha, marriages can take place without priests, and,
so, children are married off in mass ceremonies. This has brought
intense public attention to the issue, but early marriages in Rajasthan,
as in the rest of India, are the result of a complex set of factors that
hinge primarily on a pervasive culture of son preference (Singh,
Dey, and Roy 1994).

A system of village exogamy that distances married women
socially and geographically from their natal families also prevents
young women from being able to voice their needs during periods of
strain. Combined with a system of patrilocality, which entails that
married women live in the family homes of their husbands, young
brides, especially in rural areas, are isolated in the families of their
husbands. A multitude of folk songs document the isolation and lack
of power of young women, although a fair number also dwell on
everyday forms of resistance (for instance, see Tharu and Lalita
1993). Rabindranath Tagore's evocative poem describing a young
bride from a village who has been married into a city gives the flavor
of this isolation:

> No one understands why I cry,
> They wonder, they want to know the cause.
> "Nothing pleases the girl, she ought to be ashamed.
> It's always the same with girls from the villages.
> All these friends and relations to keep her company,
> But she sits in a corner and shuts her eyes."
>   Rabindranath Tagore, "Bride"[3]

While early marriage and cohabitation can place inordinate pressure on young girls, the importance assigned to these factors as
explanations for a number of poor outcomes such as high maternal

Figure 4.3 Nearly One-Fourth of Indian Women 20–24 Had Their First Child by the Age of 18

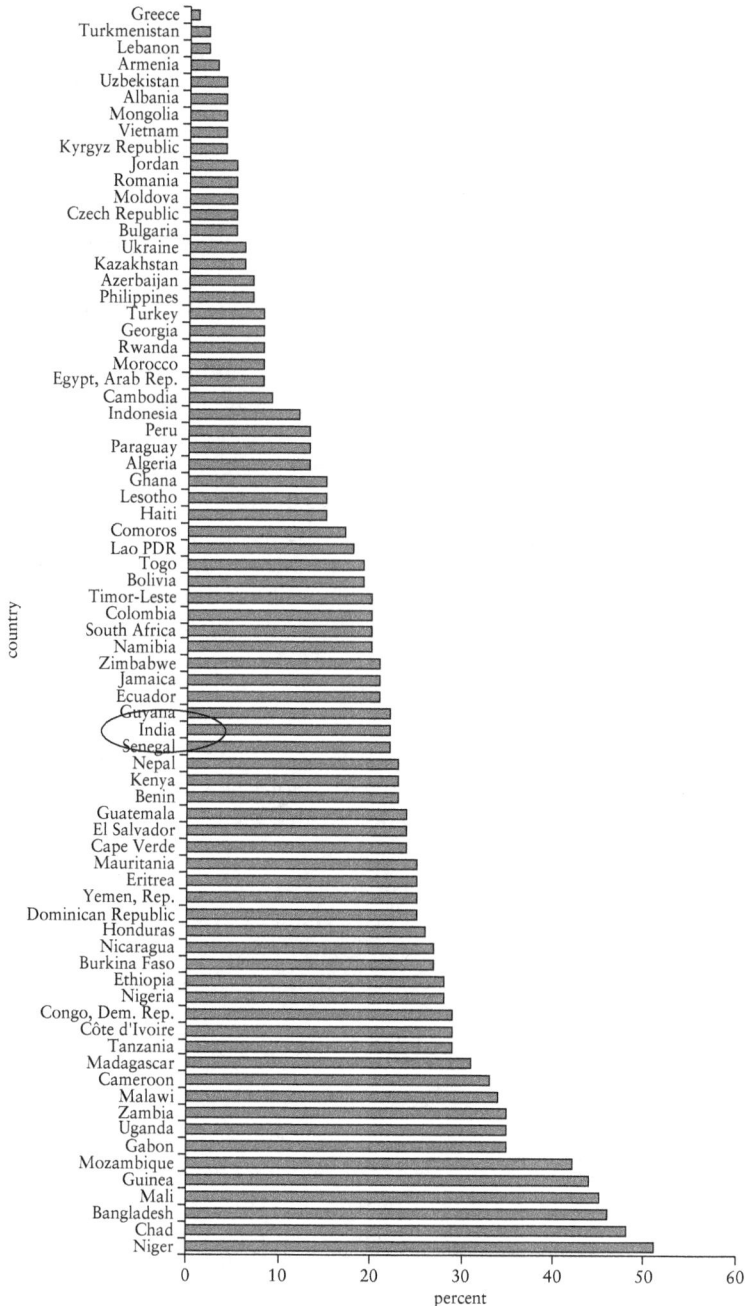

Source: PRB (2008).

mortality needs to be qualified. Thus, while better outcomes in fertility and in education among women are expected to be associated with increasing age at marriage, South Asian countries demonstrate that this need not always be the case. In Bangladesh, India, and Nepal, age at marriage has risen only slowly over the last 10 years, but fertility has declined across the board; indeed, some Indian states resemble the low-fertility countries of the Organisation for Economic Co-operation and Development (see Amin, Selim, and Waiz 2006; Basu 1993; World Bank 2008). In Bangladesh more than in India or Nepal, there has been a huge growth in secondary school enrollments, and girls now leave boys behind. Early marriage and cohabitation are probably more important in their translation into early childbirth (see figure 4.3; also see Caldwell, Reddy, and Caldwell 1983; Marimuthu 2008). However, the literature on the direct effects of early marriage and early childbirth on outcomes such as maternal and child health is inconclusive. Thus, many of the data in the United States on teenage childbearing and the associated outcomes refer to teenage mothers (overwhelmingly nonwhite) who are also poor and lack social support. In contrast, in South Asia, where early marriage and fertility are the norm and family support is more forthcoming, early marriages may not necessarily result in poor outcomes such as high levels of maternal deaths or low birthweights. Nonetheless, younger mothers do run higher mortality risks associated with first births, and there is no way to establish which way the relationship would go (for a discussion on Bangladesh, see World Bank 2008).

In Sub-Saharan Africa, a report on adolescent fertility notes that many of the problems associated with adolescent childbearing actually stem not from childbearing, but from the societal condemnation of the act in cases where the women are unmarried (Bledsoe and Cohen 1993). This leads such women to attempt abortions, with dangerous consequences. Similarly, changes in the social context, such as a rise in formal educational attainment, urbanization, and contraceptive use, could affect adolescent decisions about childbearing, as well as the societal acceptance of adolescent childbearing. The report concludes with the following observation:

> It is virtually impossible to separate the effects of young age per se on health risks from the social effects produced by the father's refusal to recognize a child. We conclude that the social context of adolescent childbearing has an effect on the outcome for the mother and the child that is as important as the physiological maturity of the mother. (Bledsoe and Cohen 1993, 3)

While a number of programs have targeted women in independent India, the focus on adolescent girls is a development of the last decade or so. The 11th Five-Year Plan for the first time placed policy emphasis on adolescent girls as a discrete group in need of special attention. A new program, the Rajiv Gandhi Scheme for Empowerment of Adolescent Girls, has been launched to provide resources to strengthen life skills among adolescent girls who are at risk of early marriage and early childbearing (see Government of India 2008, 2010).

Like many other gendered outcomes in India, marriage patterns have both economic and cultural roots. The earlier a daughter is married off, the smaller the dowry her family has to pay. Moreover, since family honor is so closely linked to women's chastity, marrying a girl off while she is young shifts the onus of her security and chastity to the husband's family. Natal families are then not expected to receive financial help from their daughters, nor do they expect their daughters to support them in old age. This also means that girls, once married and given dowries as their bequests, are no longer perceived to have a share in their ancestral property, despite legal reforms to facilitate women's inheritance (for instance, see Agarwal 1994, 1995; Kaur 2004).

The India Human Development Survey 2005 asked parents with daughters if they would consider living with the daughters in old age or receiving financial help from them. A similar question was asked as part of the World Bank Survey of Gender Norms, which was carried out in Bangladesh in 2006. At first, the Indian respondents replied the same way as the older generation of Bangladeshis: only about 9–10 percent said they would consider living with their daughters or receiving help from them (figure 4.4). However, once probed, about 24 percent of them said it was acceptable to live with daughters in old age. What is surprising is not that the proportion answering yes increased after probing, but that, *even after probing, over three-quarters of Indian parents do not see daughters as sources of old age support.* Young women, in contrast, are more accepting in terms of both receiving help from their daughters or giving help to their parents. In a survey conducted in 2005 by the Grey Global Group in India, 67 percent of the young women interviewed said they planned to take care of their parents into old age.[4]

Childbearing is entangled with cultural factors such as the early age of marriage, which, if combined with poor access to health care, are responsible for large numbers of maternal deaths. It is difficult to obtain reliable data on maternal mortality rates and the associated causes in the absence of comprehensive data on the registration of deaths and the causes of death. Measurement is additionally complicated in the Indian context given that most women give birth at home. Estimates derived from household surveys are therefore subject to

Figure 4.4 A Majority of Indian and Bangladeshi Parents Do Not Consider Daughters as Sources of Old Age Support

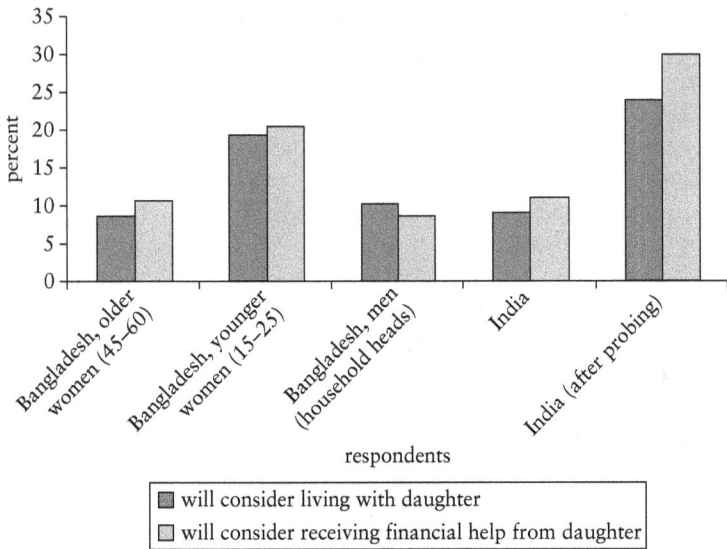

Sources: World Bank (2006); India Human Development Survey, 2005.

wide confidence intervals and long period rates (often, for 10-year periods). Based on existing data, figure 4.5 shows that Indian women face a 1 in 70 chance of dying in childbirth. This falls at the high end of the global spectrum; other comparators have much better outcomes. For instance, Chinese women face a one in 1,400 chance, and Vietnamese women, a one in 280 chance of maternal death. Within India, there is considerable variation across states, and some have performed more poorly than others over the first few years of the millennium. Assam, Bihar, Chhattisgarh, Jharkhand, Madhya Pradesh, Orissa, Rajasthan, Uttaranchal, and Uttar Pradesh together accounted for about 65 percent of all maternal deaths during 1997–2003 (Registrar General 2006). Assam also showed the slowest decline in maternal mortality rates over the first five years of the millennium, and the maternal deaths there are the highest in the country. On the other hand, worryingly enough, maternal mortality rates have increased in Haryana and Punjab over time (table 4.2). Cultural factors such as low age at marriage and general neglect of women play a role; other proximate correlates of high maternal death are the lack of care among women during pregnancy and childbirth. The government is cognizant of the slow pace of decline in maternal mortality overall, and the National Rural Health Mission has undertaken

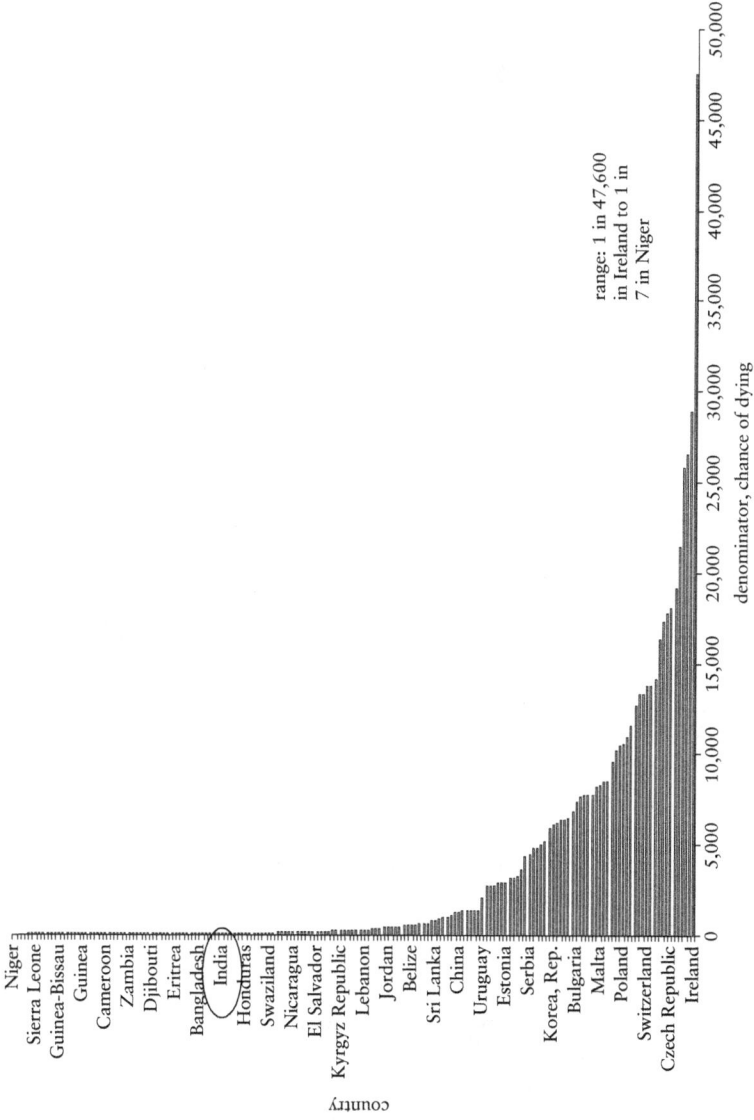

Figure 4.5 Indian Women Face a 1 in 70 Chance of Dying in Childbirth

range: 1 in 47,600
in Ireland to 1 in
7 in Niger

denominator, chance of dying

country

Source: PRB (2008).

Table 4.2 The Slow Decline in Maternal Mortality Rates, India, 2001–03 to 2004–06

rates per 100,000 live births

India and major states	a. 2001–03	b. 2004–06	Decline, a – b
All India	301	254	47
Assam	490	480	10
Bihar, Jharkhand	371	312	59
Madhya Pradesh, Chhattisgarh	379	335	44
Orissa	358	303	55
Rajasthan	445	388	57
Uttar Pradesh, Uttaranchal	517	440	77
Andhra Pradesh	195	154	41
Karnataka	228	213	15
Kerala	110	95	15
Tamil Nadu	134	111	23
Gujarat	172	160	12
Haryana	162	186	–24
Maharashtra	149	130	19
Punjab	178	192	–14
West Bengal	194	141	53
Other	235	206	29

Source: National Rural Health Mission based on Sample Registration System estimates of the Registrar General, Ministry of Home Affairs.

interventions to address the issue (Registrar General 2006). The Janani Suraksha Yojana, for instance, is a cash transfer program that creates incentives for pregnant and lactating women to access health care and take nutrition supplements (box 4.1).

Despite progress over the last decade, less than half of Indian women receive complete antenatal care, and most births take place at home. Overall, almost 60 percent of all women and 80 percent of Adivasi women give birth at home, and only a little over half of all women who gave birth in the three years before NFHS 2005 had had three or more antenatal visits. The coverage of complete antenatal care (three or more visits) expanded in 1998–2005, the most among Adivasi women and the least among OBC women (table 4.3). This is partly because Adivasi women started from a low base of 28 percent in 1998. Even now, Adivasi women have the poorest coverage, though they are in the process of catching up not so much with the national average, but with Dalit and OBC women. OBC women appear to have been left out in the drive to expand antenatal care, and, in years to come, they should be an important specific focus. Still, a large proportion of pregnant women, over three-fourths, received tetanus shots before delivery, and about two-thirds took iron supplements.

Box 4.1 Conditional Cash Transfers to Improve Survival and Development Outcomes among Women and Girls

Conditional cash transfer schemes have been implemented in India for more than 15 years.

The key centrally sponsored schemes include the following:

Indira Gandhi Matrisahyog Yojana was launched in 2009 by the Ministry of Women and Child Development. This conditional maternity benefit scheme aims to provide cash to pregnant and lactating women who have fulfilled specific conditions such as pregnancy registration, iron fortification during pregnancy, attendance at counseling sessions, birth registration, and immunization, as well as exclusive breastfeeding for newborn children.

Dhanalakshmi was launched in March 2008 by the Ministry of Women and Child Development and covers 11 blocks across seven states. The scheme provides cash transfers and insurance coverage (in certain cases) to the family of the girl child (preferably to the mother) on fulfilling certain specific conditions for the girl child, including birth registration, immunization, school enrolment, continued attendance in primary and secondary school, and marriage after the age of 18.

Janani Suraksha Yojana was launched under the National Rural Health Mission in 2005. The main objectives are to reduce maternal and neonatal mortality by promoting institutional childbirth and by making medical care available during pregnancy, childbirth, and post-birth. Women receive cash assistance if they give birth in a government health center or accredited private institution. Eligibility criteria and incentives in rural and urban areas differ across low- and high-performance states with respect to institutional delivery rates.

Balika Samriddhi Yojana was started in 1997 and covers girl children (born on or after August 15, 1997) in poor families in rural and urban areas. An eligible girl child is entitled to a postbirth grant of Rs 500 and annual scholarships for each successfully completed year of schooling as long as she is unmarried and attends school regularly until grade 9.

State-sponsored conditional cash transfer programs include the following:

Ladli was launched in Delhi and Haryana in August 2005. After the birth of their second daughter, parents are given a cash incentive for every child every year for five years. In addition to being unmarried at 18, the child must be enrolled in an early childcare center or school and be fully immunized appropriately for the age before the parents can receive the regular payments.

Devi Rupak Yojana was introduced in Haryana. If parents undergo sterilization after the first or second child, they are given a monthly pension for 20 years.

(continued next page)

Box 4.1 (continued)

Kanya Jagrit Jyoti was introduced in Punjab in 1996–97. A cash amount is invested (in the name of the beneficiary) with the Life Insurance Corporation. Between 6 to 12 years of age, the child receives a monthly scholarship. The rate of the scholarship is doubled at 12 to 18 years of age. At the end of the scheme, the beneficiary receives a lump sum, plus an accrued bonus, provided the parents continue to follow the norm of two children per family and the child passes at least matriculation. This scheme has about 8,000 beneficiaries every year.

Kanya Vidya Dhan Yojana was introduced in rural and urban areas in Uttar Pradesh. The scheme provides a cash sum to each girl in a poor family who passes the intermediate examination from the Uttar Pradesh Board.

Apni Beti Apna Dhan was introduced in Haryana in October 1994. The scheme pays a cash amount to mothers within 15 days of the birth of a girl child to meet the nutritional requirements of the child. Another sum is invested, within three months, in a savings account in the name of the newborn. Eligibility is restricted to socioeconomically disadvantaged families that have three or fewer children.

Source: World Bank (2010a).

Why is the uptake of prenatal services so low? The public health system has been concerned about the low demand for maternal health services, and cultural and behavioral factors have been implicated (see Basu 1990). Medical practitioners often cite ignorance as the reason for the poor outcomes among women (Khandare 2004). It is true that, of the women who had given birth at home, a majority felt that it was not necessary to go to a medical facility (table 4.3). However, the low demand for health care may be triggered by gaps in supply, the inability to reach a health center in time, or lack of information on whether a health center is open. For instance, women in remote areas face difficulty in reaching health facilities because of poor road access. In a series of unannounced visits to primary health centers across 19 states in 2002–03, Chaudhury et al. (2006) found that doctors were available at fewer than 40 percent. Absenteeism ranged from 30 percent in Madhya Pradesh to 71 percent in Bihar (Muralidharan 2007). In other ways, too, the poor quality of care and the lack of trust in providers may deter women from accessing care, and the opportunity costs of seeking care may be too high in forgone wages or the cost of travel.

We also examine an omitted variable—violence against women— and the extent to which this is associated with poor reproductive health outcomes. Over one-third of Indian women reported that they had experienced spousal violence at some time, and about

Table 4.3 Antenatal Care Improved in 1998–2005, but Most Women Still Do Not Find Giving Birth in Medical Facilities Necessary

percent

Indicator	SC	ST	OBC	Other	Total
% change in antenatal care 1998–2005[a]					
Three or more antenatal visits	6	12	1	11	6
First antenatal visit during					
first trimester	10	11	8	13	10
Prenatal care practitioner					
Doctor	–2	–3	–2	6	–1
Midwife, nurse	20	19	14	13	16
Other health professional	0	1	1	2	1
Home health worker	–15	–8	–18	–11	–14
Traditional assistant	2	3	1	1	2
Other	–11	–14	–9	–13	–10
No assistance	–11	–14	–9	–13	–10
Why was your last child not delivered at a medical facility?[b]					
Too costly	30	23	27	23	26
Facility not open	3	5	3	3	3
Too far, no transportation	12	17	9	11	11
Do not trust facility,					
poor-quality service	3	2	3	3	3
No female provider	1	1	1	1	1
Husband, family did not allow	6	5	5	8	6
Not necessary	69	72	74	70	72
Not customary	6	7	7	6	6

Source: Staff calculations based on NFHS 2005 data.

a. Among the 51 percent with three or more antenatal care visits in 2005.

b. Actual percentage. Among the 41 percent who had *not* received institutional delivery in 2005. The categories are not exclusive; multiple reasons were allowed.

one-fourth had experienced violence in the past year, according to NFHS 2005. A number of factors are associated with the experience of violence, and our multivariate analysis confirms the findings of previous studies showing that the education of women and their partners, the attitudes of each about violence, and the alcohol consumption among husbands are common correlates (see Kishor 2007). Violence against women is a marker of extreme inequality in gender relations; addressing the issue for its intrinsic value has important implications for human rights, but also has an instrumental value.

Globally, research shows that women who have experienced violence are more likely to experience health-related complications. Their children are also more likely to be sick and die in infancy or childhood. Heise, Pitanguy, and Germain (1994) identified violence as a public health issue, but there was little empirical evidence at the time. Since then, a number of surveys have been fielded that seek an understanding of violence and its possible impact (on Latin America and the Caribbean, for instance, see Morrison, Ellsberg, and Bott 2004). A recent multicountry World Health Organization report shows that violence against women is associated with sexually transmitted infections such as HIV/AIDS, unintended pregnancies, gynecological problems, induced abortions, and adverse pregnancy outcomes, including miscarriage, low birthweight, and fetal death (WHO 2005). There are similar findings on India (Jejeebhoy 1998; Ahmed, Koenig, and Stephenson 2006; Kishor and Gupta 2009).

Our results show a significant association between violence against women and reproductive health outcomes. Nearly 81 percent of women who have never experienced violence reported receiving antenatal care, in contrast to only 67 percent among women who had experienced violence. After controlling for a number of household and individual characteristics, including ability to reach a health center and whether the distance to a health center is a problem, we find that violence against women has a significant association with reproductive health. Table 4.4 shows that women who had given birth in the three years prior to NFHS 2005 and who had any experience of spousal violence in their lives had 18 percent lower odds of receiving any antenatal care, 13 percent lower odds of being given iron supplements, and 15 percent lower odds of receiving tetanus shots prior to childbirth compared with women who had not experienced any spousal violence. This is particularly important because the majority of women receive tetanus shots, iron supplements, and at least one antenatal visit. Who are the women who do not receive these services? It is likely that the residual among women who do not receive these services is particularly oppressed; the strong correlation with the violence variable is evidence for this conclusion.

We have also examined another important aspect of reproductive health: the likelihood of a birth that is not a live birth because of abortion, miscarriage, or still birth. Overall, about 18 percent of Indian women in NFHS 2005 had had a non-live birth of this kind, and 22 percent of these women had also experienced violence by their husbands. This bears out at the multivariate level even more (see table 4.4, model 4). After controlling for a number of characteristics such as the birth order of the child, the mother's age, her education, the husband's education, household wealth status, region, urban or rural location, religion, and caste, one finds that, *relative to women who have not experienced violence by their husbands, women who have experienced such violence are one and a half times more likely to have experienced births that were not live births.*

Table 4.4 Indian Women Who Experience Domestic Violence Also Report Poorer Reproductive Health Outcomes

Indicator	One or more antenatal visits (last pregnancy) Model 1	Given tetanus injection before birth Model 2	Given iron supplements in pregnancy Model 3	Ever had a terminated pregnancy[a] Model 4	Child stunted (last birth)[b] Model 5
Has ever been hurt by husband	0.824***	0.853**	0.872***	1.466***	1.114**
Urban area	1.076	0.792***	0.801***	0.94	1.021
Wealth quintile: second	1.141*	1.198***	1.042	0.971	0.91
Wealth quintile: middle	1.054	1.316***	1.113	1.09	0.806***
Wealth quintile: fourth	1.418***	2.076***	1.156	1.081	0.652***
Wealth quintile: wealthiest	1.916***	4.244***	1.271*	1.19	0.455***
Size of agricultural land owned by household, acres	0.992**	0.994**	0.995*	0.995	1.0
1 = SC	0.771**	0.901	0.97	0.779***	1.301***
1 = ST	1.151	0.993	1.340***	0.680***	1.045
1 = OBC	0.691***	1.007	0.761***	0.908	1.141*
Religion: Muslim	0.948	1.003	0.812**	1.008	1.038
Religion: Christian	0.728*	0.695**	0.896	0.758*	1.092
Religion: other (non-Hindu/Muslim/Christian)	0.885	0.709*	0.764*	0.629***	1.101
Mother's age at last birth: 25–34	1.187**	1.059	1.268***	1.474***	0.889**
Mother's age at last birth: 35–49	1.175	0.9	1.071	1.663***	0.797*
Partner's education level: primary	1.341***	1.436***	1.293***	1.122	1.014
Partner's education level: secondary	1.275***	1.487***	1.170**	1.199**	0.957
Partner's education level: higher	1.430*	1.731***	1.519***	1.505***	0.684***
Respondent's education level: primary	1.819***	1.691***	1.876***	1.158	0.817***
Respondent's education level: secondary	2.682***	2.793***	2.155***	0.858*	0.739***

(continued next page)

Table 4.4 (continued)

Indicator	One or more antenatal visits (last pregnancy) Model 1	Given tetanus injection before birth Model 2	Given iron supplements in pregnancy Model 3	Ever had a terminated pregnancy[a] Model 4	Child stunted (last birth)[b] Model 5
Respondent's education level: higher	5.074***	7.315***	4.372***	0.681**	0.584***
Birth order: penultimate	0.587*	0.676	0.656*	1.497	2.303***
Birth order: 3 to 5	0.348***	0.470**	0.499***	1.42	2.348***
Birth order: 6 plus	0.199***	0.281***	0.322***	1.188	2.903***
Birth interval: 8 to 24 months	1.094	1.177	1.145	0.681	0.612*
Birth interval: over 24 months	1.259	1.293	1.196	0.893	0.447***
Listens to radio at least once a week	0.926	1.112	1.163***	1.014	0.953
Watches television at least once a week	1.679***	1.467***	1.353***	1.221***	0.948
Can go to health facility alone, 2005 (yes)	1.216***	1.123*	1.234***	1.153**	1.112**
Distance to hospital presents problem (yes)	0.718***	0.573***	0.85	0.799*	0.939
Region: East	0.560***	1.929***	0.816***	1.025	0.9
Region: Northeast	0.608***	0.663***	0.746***	0.967	0.807**
Region: South	3.910***	2.242***	1.988***	0.624***	0.796***
Region: North	1.298***	1.032	0.937	0.735***	0.805***
Region: West	1.787***	1.650***	2.121***	0.683***	1.237**
Intercept	3.394***	2.874***	1.289**	0.142***	1.078
Number of observations	20,905	20,929	21,107	21,470	17,153
Pseudo R-squared	0.225	0.19	0.138	0.03	0.051

Source: Staff calculations based on NFHS 2005 data.

a. A child is stunted if height-for-age is less than −2 standard deviations of the World Health Organization's reference population parameters for the height-for-weight ratio.

b. Terminated pregnancy refers to pregnancies ending in miscarriage, stillbirth, or abortion.

*p = .05 **p = .01 ***p = .001.

Robust standard error (odds ratios reported).

The well-being of children is also conditioned by their mothers' experience of violence. That maternal characteristics have a significant effect on children's well-being is now well established. What is less well known from the empirical literature is that the children of women who have experienced violence are at greater risk of malnutrition and death. We look at stunting (deficient height-for-age) as a marker of chronic malnutrition. About 45 percent of the women who had had children in the three years preceding NFHS 2005 had children who were stunted, and the mothers of over half (51 percent) of the stunted children under the age of 3 had experienced violence. This also bears out at the multivariate level. Model 5 in table 4.4 shows that, after controlling for a host of family, maternal, paternal, and child characteristics, we find that children whose mothers have ever experienced violence at the hands of their husbands are 1.14 times more likely to be stunted than the children of mothers who have not been abused. This corroborates the analysis of Kishor and Gupta (2009) using the same data and the analysis of Jejeebhoy (1998) based on a survey in Tamil Nadu and Uttar Pradesh. After controlling for a variety of factors, the former found that mothers who had experienced violence had children who were underweight and had poorer immunization coverage. The latter found that the offspring of mothers who had experienced violence showed a higher likelihood of fetal death or death in infancy. There is similar evidence on other countries (on Nicaragua, for instance, see Åsling-Monemi et al. 2003). This indicates that violence prevention should be built more intentionally into reproductive and child health programs.

What are the likely pathways by which violence and poor outcomes are associated? Clearly, violence is an important health issue and can incapacitate women. However, women who have experienced violence are also likely to be more disempowered than others in intrahousehold relations. The psychological impact of violence or the threat of future violence is likely to make the women less able to take care of themselves and their children. It is also likely that violence is *a result of empowerment*: women who are more empowered and flout social norms are at greater risk of violence.[5] Whatever the direction of causality, it is reasonable to conclude that violence is associated with poor outcomes among women and their children, the costs of which are too high and too pervasive to ignore.

What can help protect women from violence? The evidence on whether employment protects women or confers on women greater vulnerability to violence is mixed. Thus, while some studies suggest that employment protects women, others suggest the opposite, that is, if women contribute significantly in economic terms to the household, their enhanced economic worth itself places them at greater risk of violence (see Hadi 2005; Bates et al. 2004; Kishor 2007). In our analysis of women who had experienced violence in the 12 months prior to NFHS 2005, we find that educational attainment above the secondary level and family socioeconomic status are the greatest protectors. Other correlates are region and location, which also indicate where the greatest interventions are needed. However, the husband's education matters, too, and men who have had secondary or higher education are less likely to strike their wives. However, once we control for the husband's attitude toward violence (whether or not it is acceptable to hit), the effect of secondary and higher education disappears, and, inexplicably, men who have primary education become the more likely perpetrators of violence. The husband's alcohol consumption has the largest effects on whether a woman experiences violence, but women's own attitudes matter as well. Therefore, interventions that address the attitudes of both women and men and men's drinking behavior, especially in high-risk urban areas, would likely make a big difference.

Landownership can help protect women from violence, but also has other positive effects. A study on domestic violence in India finds that, more than any other factor, the ownership of land protects women against violence and enhances the esteem and worth of women in the household and the community (Panda and Agarwal 2005). The ability of women to inherit land is limited, however, by the Hindu Succession Act 1956, which accorded rights to ancestral property only to male family members. The legislation was amended by some states in 1994 to grant daughters equal coparcenary birth rights in joint family property.[6] Deininger, Goyal, and Nagarajan (2010) compare outcomes in the inheritance of land by males and females from fathers who died before and after the amendment of the act in Karnataka and Maharashtra. They find that the amendment not only helped expand the probability of daughters owning land (a direct effect), but helped increase female empowerment within the household. A slight rise was seen in the age of marriage (a proxy for women's bargaining power within a household), but a more pronounced effect was evident in education among girls. Girls who had begun their education after the amendment came into force had attained 1.8 more years of education as of 2006 relative to those girls who had completed their education before the amendment came into force.

The ownership of property is not, of course, the same as control over property, but it is a starting point in enhancing voice. While formal property rights in South Asia do not exclude women, cultural pressures often force women to give up their inheritance. A recent piece of legislation gives women far-reaching legal protection against abuse or threats of abuse by their spouses, partners, or other males in the family, but, as in the case of other laws such as those targeted at reducing the social ills of dowries, enforcement is the key (Anderson 2003).[7] Better dissemination of information on the content and implications of laws could also significantly raise their potential impact on gender outcomes (Deininger, Goyal, and Nagarajan 2010).

Markets and Assets: Some Progress, but Continuing Disadvantage

A recent *New York Times* article reported on Indian women in the elite banking sector as follows:

> In New York and London, women remain scarce among top bankers despite decades of struggle to climb the corporate ladder. But in India's relatively young financial industry, women not only are some of the top deal makers, they are often running the show." (Timmons 2010)

The large numbers of young women in the business processing industry have also captured the public imagination with their high salaries and independent lifestyles. Clearly, women's visibility in the high-end urban labor market is much greater than it was a decade ago, but this is far from the norm. This section documents the patterns of labor force participation among women and reiterates that educated women tend, for the most part, to stay out of the labor force.

NSS data suggest that the labor force participation of women aged 15–59 has virtually stagnated, from about 36 percent in 1983 and 33 percent in 1993 to 35 percent in 2005. The stagnation is driven mainly by rural areas; urban areas have seen a 7 percent increase, from 20.3 percent in 1993 to 21.8 percent in 2005. However, the measurement of women's work is complicated, and different methods may yield different results. For instance, in a survey in urban New Delhi, Sudarshan and Bhattacharya (2009) have found participation rates that are considerably higher than those recorded by the NSS. The main reason for the difference is the inclusion by the former of all home-based piece-rate activities as work.

There is vast heterogeneity by geographical area. A recent study finds that the coefficients of variation in employment and labor participation rates among women are nearly four times the coefficients among men (World Bank 2010b). In addition to low employment and participation rates in the northeastern regions (including Tripura), Bihar and Uttar Pradesh, female employment rates are low in West Bengal and in prosperous Punjab as well. Female employment and participation rates are much higher in Andhra Pradesh, Gujarat, Karnataka, Maharashtra, and Tamil Nadu. Another analysis finds that female employment rates in West Bengal and Bangladesh are quite similar and hypothesizes that this may be caused by the low participation of women in agriculture in both areas (World Bank 2008). The largest increases in the female labor force participation rate during 1993–94 and 2004–05 were in regions that had either a low basis, such as the north and the northeast, or in regions that experienced high economic growth rates, such as the southern and western states.

The regional variation also shows up at the multivariate level. The regression results in table 4.5 show that, in comparison with the core Hindi belt states (undivided Bihar, Madhya Pradesh, and Uttar Pradesh), the labor force participation of *rural* women was lower in the eastern and northern states, but more than three times higher in the southern and western states (each statistically significant). Among urban women, the central region showed lower participation rates compared with all other regions, but the odds ratios were not as high. *So, women in the more rapidly growing regions with more liberal norms of female mobility in the west and south were much more likely to be employed than were women in the central states.*

There is also great heterogeneity in female labor force participation by caste and tribal status. The higher participation rates of SC and ST women in the labor market relative to their upper caste peers are now well documented and show up also at the multivariate level (see table 4.5). However, ST women, like their male counterparts, work mostly in agricultural self-employment and have seen hardly any change over time. Chapter 3 shows that SC women, unlike SC men, have moved out of casual labor at a much slower pace than other groups and are more likely to withdraw from the labor market over time. In comparison, women in the upper castes have always been more likely to stay out of the labor force. Their occupational profile looks quite different from that of their male counterparts as well (figure 4.6).

Framing the conundrum: education lowers the likelihood of women's participation in the labor market. Table 4.5 reports odds ratios that predict the probability of labor force participation. Two kinds of explanations have been articulated. The first is a demand-for-labor argument, which says there is a dearth of well-paying, secure jobs for educated women. Hence, educated women, who also belong to the higher socioeconomic strata, prefer to opt out of the labor force rather than accept low-status (manual) jobs. The second, a labor-supply argument, rests on cultural mores and values of status and seclusion that may cause higher-status households to prohibit women

Table 4.5 Women in Rapidly Growing Regions (West and South) Show Higher Odds of Labor Force Participation

Indicator	Rural men	Rural women	Urban men	Urban women
Age	1.933***	1.148***	2.074***	1.304***
Age squared	0.991***	0.998***	0.990***	0.997***
Married	2.792***	0.705***	3.864***	0.291***
Household size	1.004	0.966***	1.058***	0.960***
Education: ref: no education				
Education: below primary	0.917*	0.629***	1.251**	0.624***
Education: completed primary	0.498***	0.479***	1.05	0.471***
Education: postprimary	0.138***	0.323***	0.215***	0.480***
Household head (yes)	1.924***	3.006***	1.191***	3.690***
Land possessed date of survey, hectares	1	1.001*		
Region: ref: central				
North	1.067*	0.895***	1.337***	1.031
South	1.578***	3.868***	1.618***	2.571***
East	1.230***	0.680***	1.348***	1.275***
West	1.383***	3.581***	1.360***	1.718***
Northeast	0.900***	0.738***	0.859***	1.366***
Survey year: ref 1983				
Survey year 1993–94	1.019	0.885***	0.919***	0.982
Survey year 2004–05	1.068***	1.232***	0.992	1.169***
Household has child under 5		0.899***		1
Religion: ref: Hindu				
Muslim	0.986	0.412***	1.328***	0.605***
Other religion	0.968	0.787***	0.886**	1.139***
Caste: ref: non-SC/ST				
SC	1.018	1.260***	1.065	1.336***
ST	1.198***	3.146***	0.927	1.658***
Constant	0.001***	0.081***	0.000***	0.008***

Source: NSS data.
$*p = .05$ $**p = .01$ $***p = .001$

to work or demand jobs. The two arguments are mutually reinforcing. It is true that women with higher education stay out of the labor force if there is another earning member in the household or because of an income effect. However, this explanation is muddied by the fact that there are few appropriate (regular salaried) jobs.

Not only is it difficult to separate cultural factors from economic opportunities, but, often, the cultural affects the structural, and vice versa (see Das and Desai 2003; Das 2006). Thus, the extent to which women's belief systems create stereotypes and prevent women from

Figure 4.6 Occupational Structure Is Changing More among Men than among Women, and the Differences across Social Groups Are Large

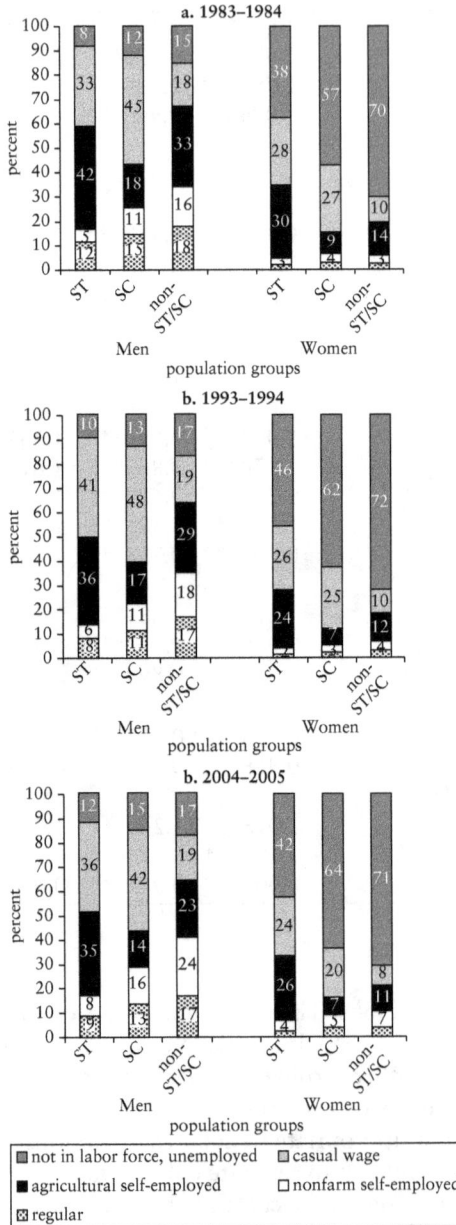

a. 1983–1984

b. 1993–1994

b. 2004–2005

Legend:
- not in labor force, unemployed
- casual wage
- agricultural self-employed
- nonfarm self-employed
- regular

Source: Staff calculations based on 2004–05 employment-unemployment schedule NSS data.

entering the labor market from a position of strength is not known. Also unknown is the manner in which hiring authorities unconsciously assign women to female occupations. In the case of Dalits, for instance, recent experiments have shown that caste stereotypes affect not only the majority community, but also minority caste groups, in this case, Dalits. In a field experiment designed to test discrimination in hiring in Lima, Peru, Moreno et al. (2004) found that women had much lower expectations of the wages they would receive relative to men. This led women to aim at wages that were 6–9 percent lower than the wages targeted by men.

Muddy waters: income effect or discouraged worker effect? The literature on women's labor force participation, particularly in the developed countries, indicates that women's employment decisions are often contingent upon the employment status and earnings of their husbands (see Cohen and Bianchi 1999). Das (2006) uses NSS data (55th round) to determine if the income or employment status of husbands affects women's employment probabilities. She finds that the education and wages of husbands do lower the probability of employment among women. Moreover, after controlling for the incomes of husbands, she finds that women's postprimary education shows a positive correlation with women's labor force participation. In fact, it takes the form of a "U," with high labor force participation by uneducated women, the lowest labor force participation among women who have completed primary education, and rising participation among women with postprimary education.

Thus, women with higher education may stay out of the labor force because of an income effect, but this conclusion is muddied by the lack of jobs that women would want to do. In the absence of regular salaried jobs, the only options available to educated women are low-status, low-paying manual work, especially in rural areas, such as work on family farms or as petty vendors, domestic servants, or day laborers. In the face of such unsuitable employment opportunities, households decide to withdraw female labor if there is another earning member (if women are household heads, they are more likely to be employed). Because educated women are usually married to educated men and are likely to have some financial resources, they remain out of the labor force instead of accepting poorly paid jobs as casual wage workers.

Women in the labor force are mostly self-employed, and only 13 percent receive any wages at all. Self-employment is more significant among non-SC/ST women compared with women belonging to the SC or ST category. The latter tend to work as casual wage workers out of necessity. While the 2004–05 numbers on women's wage work are about double the numbers in 1983 (13 relative to 6 percent), they are still extremely low. This is partly caused by the fact that women are overrepresented in unpaid work. Over the last 20 years or so, the patterns in labor market activity have remained more or less the same among all categories of workers. The greatest changes seem to have occurred among the men who are moving into nonfarm self-employment, but this is more true of non-SC/ST men than of others (figure 4.6). However, SC men also seem to be making a quiet transition out of casual wage work into nonfarm self-employment and regular salaried work. Women's participation in nonfarm self-employment has also increased, but this is more true of non-SC/ST women than of others. SC and ST women have seen small increases, though the increase is negligible among the latter. As education has expanded among SC women, the share of these women has also risen in the category of people out of the labor force.

Wages have a salutary effect on women's voice and decision making if women earn as much as their husbands do. NFHS 2005 shows that about one in five women who is currently married and who works for wages earns at least as much as her husband. Furthermore, women who earn about the same as their husbands are more likely to have a major *say in the use of the earnings of their husbands* relative to women who earn less than their husbands and women who earn more than their husbands (Kishor and Gupta 2009).

Inequalities in wages and opportunities are an additional disincentive for women to work. During the post–World War II period in the United States, the increased labor force participation of married women is explained by an increase in women's wages, which trumped the negative effect of the wages of the husbands on labor force participation. Thus, when women's wages rose, this substituted for the income effect of men's wages (Mincer 1962, cited in Blau 1998). In India by the first few years of the millennium, we had little reason to believe that anything similar was happening. The relatively flat participation of women in the workforce and the high levels of the wage differentials between women and men indicated that, unless salaried work among women expands, households would curtail the supply of educated female labor.

Our calculations based on the 61st round of the NSS 2004–05 show that women's nominal weekly wages are, on average, 71 percent of men's wages in regular salaried work and 56 percent of men's wages in casual work. The kernel density plot in figure 4.7 indicates, across the distribution, that women's wages are much lower than men's wages. Using Oaxaca-Blinder decompositions conducted with NSS data from 1999–2000, we have found that only 27.5 percent of the difference in casual wages between male and female workers could be explained by human capital and location attributes, while

Figure 4.7 Women Are Paid Less than Men across the Wage Distribution

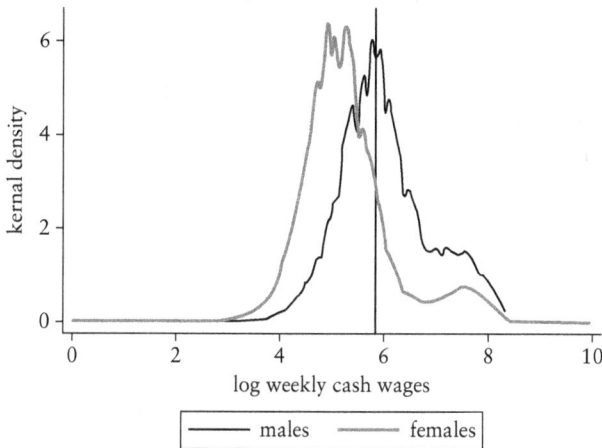

Source: Data of NSS 2004–05.

the rest were unobserved factors (Das 2006). Some of these unobserved factors may well involve discrimination. Thus, gender ideologies can spill over into hiring patterns and exclude women. Low and unequal wages and their concentration in agricultural labor and in female occupations represent added disincentives for women to work outside the home.

In a survey of 407 male and female professionals in their late 20s and early 30s in eight major cities, Teamlease (2008) found that respondents were of the opinion that men have a better chance to be successful in the workplace. However, there were regional differences. One-third of the respondents in cities in the regions in which women's participation in the labor market is higher, namely, Ahmedabad, Chennai, and Mumbai, said women have a better chance of getting ahead in the workplace. Respondents in Hyderabad, Kolkata, and New Delhi reported that there were equal opportunities for men and women to make progress in the workplace. Finally, about three-quarters of the respondents agreed that women faced constraints in advancing to senior-level positions.

Counting aspirations: Indian women clearly want to work outside their homes. One of the explanations for women's low participation in the labor market is that they would prefer not to work, given the pervasive culture of seclusion, especially in states where women's employment rates are low (see Das 2006). We find quite the reverse in women's responses to the question in the NSS on the reason women did not work outside the home. Over 89 percent of the women respondents doing only domestic work said that they did this because they were obliged. Over 56 percent said there was no other member of the household who would take on their household duties. One-third of women doing only domestic work said they would accept paid work in addition to their household duties. Clearly, household responsibilities are paramount, but the majority said they would like regular part-time jobs (figure 4.8). Those who said they wanted regular full-time work seemed to be looking for salaried work, but, among the rest, the preference was self-employment.

Credit shortfall: One of the reasons for women's low representation in nonfarm employment is the poor access of women to credit markets and financial products. About 75 percent of the women who want work, in addition to their household duties, cite tailoring and dairy as the two areas where they would like to work. Perhaps these preferences are colored by the visibility of women in these occupations, but this appears to be a proxy for nonfarm employment. Almost 60 percent of the women say finance is a major constraint, and this may, to a large extent, explain why women are so poorly represented in nonfarm employment and why their transition out of agriculture is so slow (table 4.6).

Menon and Rodgers (2009), using NSS data, look at informal and formal channels for loans accessed by men and women and find that the likelihood of engagement in self-employment in response to

Figure 4.8 The Aspirations of Women Doing Only Domestic Work

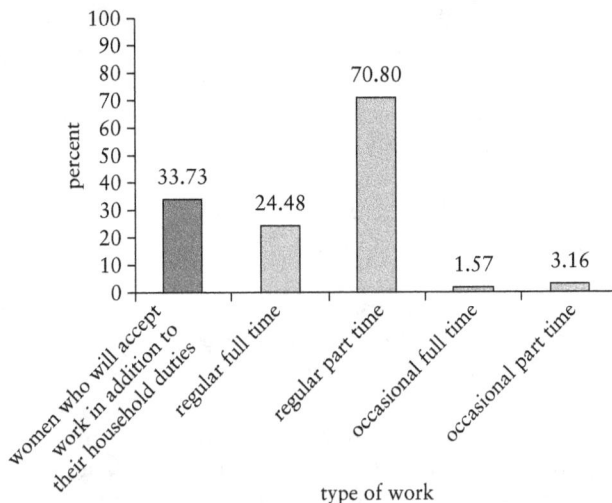

Source: Staff estimates based on NSS 61st round, 2004–05, schedule 10.0.

Table 4.6 Three in Five Women Cite a Lack of Credit
as a Reason for Not Doing the Work They Want

percent

What do you need to facilitate the work you want?	Share
Nothing	4.24
Finance and credit	58.50
Raw materials	3.68
Assured markets	7.58
Training	15.63
Accommodation	0.87
Other	9.50

Source: Staff calculations based on the NSS 61st round, 2004–05.
Note: The sample consists of women who are currently doing domestic
work, but who say they would also like to do other work.

a loan is substantially stronger among women than among men.
They suggest that women have moved toward self-employment in
the more capital-intensive areas of livestock and dairy farming. They
also find that the steady rise in the production of *bidi* (an Indian
cigarette) as a leading occupation among rural self-employed women
during the 1990s was especially pronounced among women who
had not taken out loans. The predominance of women who had not
taken loans in bidi production is consistent with the low capital
needs in this industry.

The existence of the barriers women cite in their efforts to enter
self-employment is also borne out by data on access to financial
markets. The calculations of Desai et al. (2010) from the India
Human Development Survey indicate that fewer than 20 percent of
Indian women have their names on bank accounts either individu-
ally or jointly. Similarly, NFHS 2005 data show that fewer than 40
percent of women are even aware of the credit available to them
(table 4.7). Using official data of the Reserve Bank of India, Chavan
(2008) finds that only 12 percent of all individual bank loan accounts
belonged to women in 2006. Furthermore, for every Rs 100 of bank
credit given to a man, a woman received only Rs 15. Even when
women know that credit facilities exist, they probably often cannot
negotiate the procedures or believe that they can actually obtain the
loans. Only about 10 percent of women who are aware of credit
facilities actually make the applications (table 4.7). Clearly, the
accounts of self-help groups (SHGs) do not translate into women
opening their own accounts.

Caste and religious disparities also play a role in the awareness
of and access to credit. While 29 percent of non-SC/ST/OBC women
have their names on bank accounts, only 16 percent of OBC

Table 4.7 The Poor Awareness of Women about Available
Credit Facilities

Population group	Know of loans	Applied for loans[a]
All India		
SC	38	12
ST	30	10
OBC	39	12
Other	41	7
Total	39	10
Urban		
SC	41	9
ST	37	6
OBC	49	10
Other	42	4
Total	44	7
Rural		
SC	36	14
ST	29	11
OBC	34	14
Other	40	9
Total	36	12

Source: NFHS 2005.

Note: The table refers to women's awareness and use of business loans.

a. Among those women who know about the existence of loan programs.

women, 13 percent of Dalit women, and 10 percent of Adivasi
women have their names on individual or joint bank counts (Desai
et al. 2010). Although Muslim women are more likely to be in
nonfarm self-employment, only 13 percent of them have their
names on bank accounts, and ST women lag behind all others in
the awareness of the existence of loans (table 4.7). It also appears
from the study by Chavan (2008) that caste disparities in terms of
access to banking services widened between 1997 and 2006. In
2006, Adivasi and Dalit women received only 1.3 percent of the
total credit given under small borrower accounts; this compares
with 4.8 percent in 1997.

A *rights-based alternative for poor women: the Mahatma Gandhi
National Rural Employment Guarantee Scheme* (MGNREGS),
which has adopted a rights-based approach to livelihoods, is an
example of a program that explicitly seeks to provide paid work to
poor women. The scheme mandates that at least one-third of workers should be women and makes several provisions to enhance the
participation of women (for example, the provision of crèches at
worksites for working mothers and a guarantee of equal wages
among men and women). The numbers on participation, however,

Figure 4.9 Almost Half of MGNREGS Participants Are
Women, but Some States Do Better than Others, 2010

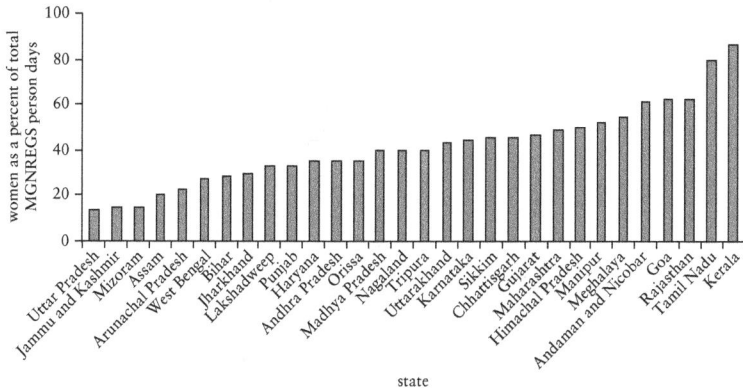

Source: Data of the Ministry of Rural Development, February 2010.

are uneven across Indian states. Women's participation in the program exceeds 50 percent only in Rajasthan (figure 4.9). While Kerala
and Tamil Nadu rank higher than Rajasthan in women's participation, the overall uptake of work through the scheme in these two
states is so low that the absolute impact of the program on women
is limited. Based on fieldwork in six northern states, Khera and
Nayak (2009) find barriers that still constrain women's participation. These include, but are not limited to, social norms concerning
working women, the lack of adequate childcare facilities (which are
only provided for window dressing), and exacting productivity
norms in some states that require harsh labor practices if women are
to earn the minimum daily wage.

Yet, overall, the scheme remains an attractive employment option
among poor women. Khera and Nayak (2009) conclude that significant benefits have already started flowing to women through the
scheme. First, the program has widened employment opportunities
in villages, thereby making it feasible for women to work despite
bearing household responsibilities. Second, the program provides
work under relatively safe and decent conditions, at fixed hours, and
at a minimum wage that is significantly higher than the wage women
otherwise receive as private laborers. Finally, the wages earned
through participation in the scheme give women the flexibility to
spend money on their own needs. Most participants end up buying
food or medicines. In the case of single women, these benefits are
even greater. (Box 4.2 offers another example of a scheme targeting
women in poor households.)

Box 4.2 Kudumbashree: Innovation for Results

Kerala's Kudumbashree Program is innovatively "reaching out to families through women and reaching out to the community through families," as its slogan announces. It has more than 3.7 million members organized in nearly 200,000 neighborhood groups and covers about half the households in the state. Since their inception (in 1998), the saving and credit groups have mobilized Rs 18 billion as thrift and have disbursed loans amounting to Rs 35 billion.

Women in poor families are organized in three-tiered community development societies. At the lowest tier are neighborhood groups of 20–45 at-risk families. These groups are federated at the ward level into an area development society and also at the municipal level into a community development society. Like other SHG models (such as in Andhra Pradesh), Kudumbashree promotes women's empowerment through savings, credit, and microenterprises linked through the three-tiered network and onward to banks under the bank-linkage program promoted by the National Bank for Agriculture and Rural Development.

The Kudumbashree experiment is unique in its conscious interface with local governments under the state government's People's Plan Campaign. Kudumbashree draws funds from various sources to ensure financial sustainability and scalability. For instance, it uses the provision in the Swarna Jayanti Shahari Rojgar Yojana, the centrally sponsored urban poverty alleviation program, to encourage microenterprises. This makes Kudumbashree a comprehensive model for local development rather than merely a microfinance-led model to enhance economic empowerment.

Sources: Nair (2008), Kumar (2008), Government of Kerala, http://www .kudumbashree.org.

Voice and Visibility in Public Spaces

No longer the passive recipients of welfare-enhancing help, women are increasingly seen, by men as well as women, as active agents of change: the dynamic promoters of social transformations that can alter the lives of *both* women and men. The nature of this shift in concentration and emphasis is sometimes missed because of the overlap between the two approaches. The active agency of women cannot, in any serious way, ignore the urgency of rectifying many inequalities that blight the well-being of women and subject them to unequal treatment; thus the agency role must be much

concerned with women's well-being also. Similarly . . . any
practical attempt at enhancing the well-being of women cannot but draw on the agency of women themselves in bringing
about such a change.

Amartya Sen, *Development as Freedom* (1999, 189–90)

The literature on women's agency and empowerment is now vast
and complex. The larger part of it focuses on intrahousehold agency
and women's ability to exercise power and thereby affect their own
and their families' well-being. A background paper for this report
shows that there is a positive association between men's earnings
and whether their wives read a newspaper regularly, do not practice
seclusion (*purdah* or *ghunghat*), and speak English, even after one
controls for a number of household and individual characteristics
(Desai, Noon, and Vanneman 2008). This section addresses the issue
of women's voice and visibility, partly in the household, but especially in the community and society as a whole.

Giribala, the protagonist of Mahasweta Devi's short story of the
same name, resists a lifetime of poverty and humiliation. Her final
act of resistance—walking away from an impossible situation—is
symbolic of the methods women can use to defy and circumvent,
while also acquiescing. No measure of decision making and empowerment can quite capture the complexity of the dialectic between
women's oppression and agency or the fact that the two can coexist.
Innumerable women protagonists of Indian literature bring this dialectic out in ways that statistical analysis cannot achieve.

*While there is a long history of anthropological work on the sub-
ject, the National Family Health Survey was among the first set of
surveys to allow for an aggregate measurement of women's voice in
the home.* A recent report based on NFHS-3 shows that, among the
decisions in which women are likely to participate, women are most
likely to participate in decisions about their own health care (62
percent), followed closely by decisions about visits to their own
families or relatives (61 percent) and decisions about purchases to
meet daily needs (60 percent). Women are least likely to participate
in decisions about large household purchases (53 percent). Age, education, and employment status are among the variables that are correlated with women's decision making in the home. For instance,
women's place in the lifecycle determines the extent to which and the
arenas within which women can wield power (Das Gupta 1995).
The multivariate analysis of the number of decisions made alone
shows that the number is higher, on average, among women with
earnings, women earning at least as much as their husbands, women
who are older, and women living in urban areas. Education and

wealth do not have a direct positive association with the number of decisions women make alone (Kishor and Gupta 2009). Also, women who have more control over their own income, mobility, and voice in decisions in the home have healthier and more better-educated children (Duflo 2003; Qian 2008; Luke and Munshi 2007; Dyson and Moore 1983; Eswaran 2002).

Voice and public action can change outcomes. Let us take the example of women's participation in MGNREGS. The states that do well on many other indicators, including overall performance in MGNREGS, do not compare with Rajasthan, which (along with Kerala and Tamil Nadu) shows a significant participation by women in the program. Rajasthan is a state otherwise known for poor indicators on gender equality, its feudal culture, and restrictions on the mobility of women. Yet, states such as Gujarat and Madhya Pradesh, in which rural poverty and tribal populations are high (both factors that should pull women into the scheme) do not do as well as Rajasthan. Why is this the case? We hypothesize that Rajasthan's performance is a function of voice and public action. The state has had a long history of struggle against the irregular payment of wages in public employment programs. In fact, the movement for equal wages among women workers has its origins in the Women's Development Program in the 1980s. The program took up the issue of women's wages in public employment schemes wherein contractors would take thumb impressions of uneducated women on receipts, but pay them lower wages than were due (see Das 2008). Subsequent movements and programs built upon the momentum of the Women's Development Program. Mazdoor Kisan Shakti Sangathan, for example, which is perhaps the most vocal and influential network today, aims to ensure that MGNREGS succeeds in Rajasthan. This network voluntarily and tenaciously monitors the program, demanding government accountability. As a result of its efforts, public officials and government institutions in Rajasthan are much more responsive and alert to problems in MGNREGS.

There are several other high-profile examples of welfare activities that are conducted hand in hand with advocacy. This is the case of Gujarat's Self Employed Women's Association, or Maharashtra's Annapurna Mahila Mahamandal, or the national Mahila Samakhya Program. Each of these provides a service of some kind, assistance with self-employment or education, for example, but also organizes women into groups to demand accountability. In addition to these more well-known examples, there are a host of small-scale movements across India that have placed issues of gender inequality and women's status in the public domain.

Legislation and policy have played a large part in giving women space and voice in the public domain. As this report was being finalized, the Women's Reservation Bill became law after years of intense lobbying. In 1993, the 73rd Constitutional Amendment reserved seats for women in local bodies. There are at least two ways in which women's representation in local and national government is important. The demonstration effect of the greater presence of women in the public domain is instructive for society as a whole and can change perceptions about women's voice. It also gives women experience and develops leadership for the next step in representation. At another level is the question of whether women's presence as decision makers changes the outcomes for other women and for gender equality. In general, well-intentioned legislation can also have good and not so good effects (box 4.3).

Do women leaders at the local level take up issues that are important to women? The evidence on India is thin, and it is mixed. For instance, women leaders in West Bengal invest more in water and road projects and less in nonformal education, while, in Rajasthan, women leaders invest more in water and less in roads (Chattopadhyay and Duflo 2004; Duflo and Topalova 2004; Bardhan, Mookherjee, and Parra Torrado 2006). In a study on 13 states, Munshi and Rosenzweig (2008) find that women representatives are better at claiming public resources for their constituencies. Yet, others find

---

Box 4.3 Legislation Can Have Unintended Consequences, Both Good and Not So Good

In a bid to eliminate the crossborder trafficking and exploitation of women, several countries have age restrictions and other safeguards requiring women to produce documentation that they will be legitimately employed and that their interests in the receiving country will be protected. However, migration policies that seek to protect women have been double-edged swords: they address genuine threats, but, in the process, also prevent women from responding to the demand for female labor in other countries. The Indian Emigration Act was amended to prevent women under age 30 from migrating as housemaids and caregivers. Nongovernmental organizations are concerned that this will lead to the illegal and undocumented migration of younger women and prevent them from accessing any benefits to which they may be entitled in the receiving country. Other countries also have age limits on women migrants, but whether this contributes to women's welfare or increases vulnerability is unclear.

Source: Manchanda (2007).

that women leaders perform no better than men leaders and that institutional factors and context matter more. In a study across 527 villages in four southern Indian states (Andhra Pradesh, Karnataka, Kerala, and Tamil Nadu), Ban and Rao (2008) find that women in reserved *gram panchayats* (local government administrative units) perform better if they have more political experience and if they live in villages less dominated by upper castes and in states where the panchayat system is more mature (for example, Kerala). Similarly, using data from a primary survey in four states (Chattisgarh, Madhya Pradesh, Orissa, and Rajasthan), Rajaraman and Gupta (2009) find that economic fundamentals matter more than the gender of the *sarpanch* (elected village leader) in making policy choices. In their sample, women sarpanches show a preference for expenditures on water, but on account of factors such as poor access to water pumps in their gram panchayats or a history of outbreaks of waterborne diseases. In this, they only reflect more closely the preferences of their electorates. (There are also numerous studies of the issue elsewhere; see box 4.4 for an example from Latin America.)

SHGs have been among the most successful empowerment programs; they have had positive effects on participants and on collective actions for communities. SHGs have built on previous programs of group formation, such as the program Development of Women and Children in Rural Areas, but their virtual saturation of the rural space can be attributed to the push undertaken based on the initial guidelines of the Reserve Bank of India, which mandated public sector banks to

---

Box 4.4 The Challenge of Giving Excluded Groups Space in Political Decision Making in Latin America

Latin America has a good track record in the area of educational quotas and quotas to increase women's participation in representative government bodies. By 2005, 11 countries had adopted such quotas. However, there are still only incipient efforts to incorporate quotas for excluded populations such as Afro-descendants and indigenous peoples. According to data from Brazil and Nicaragua, Afro-descendants are poorly represented politically. In 2003, only 27 of 594 Brazilian congressmen (roughly 5 percent) identified themselves as people of African descent, although 45 percent of Brazil's population is of African descent. In Nicaragua, there is not a single Afro-descendant in the national assembly, although Afro-descendants make up 9 percent of the country's population.

Source: Márquez et al. (2007).

lend to women's SHGs. This placed the onus equally on banks and state and district administrations. Over the years, SHGs have become platforms for women to aggregate and voice their demands and hold local institutions accountable, including the panchayats. They are also a training ground for future women leaders at the local level. Through her careful interviews in West Bengal, Sanyal (2009) shows that SHGs also provide powerful platforms from which women's groups can take collective action, in addition to the empowerment effects among members at the individual level.

A recent study in Andhra Pradesh attributes an increase in the political voice of women who are active in SHGs partly to a reduction in social divisions. A Dalit member interviewed for the study highlights the change as follows:

> The SHGs help you realize that the blood in you and me is the same. In the meetings [now] everyone sits together. There is no discrimination. This is one major change that has taken place after the establishment of SHGs in the village. (Narayan, Prennushi, and Kapoor 2009, 251)

After accounting for standard demographic predictors, educational levels, exposure to the media, and the standard of living index of households, another study found that the presence of SHGs in a community, as well as participation in group events relating to family planning, had a positive effect on the adoption of family planning in Andhra Pradesh and Tamil Nadu (Dev, James, and Sen 2002). However, the direct impact of SHGs on incomes is less clear; we have also noted the small number of women who have individual bank accounts.

One of the factors that hinder women's visibility and voice in the public domain is the threat of physical harm and the lack of security outside the home. In addition to family-based violence, the perception women and their families have of their safety and security in public places and women's fear of sexual harassment (known popularly and even reported in the media by the demeaning term "eve-teasing") pose barriers that have hitherto not been measured by national surveys in India.[8] Threats to women's security in public places also influence the ability of women to access markets and services and to claim spaces for themselves. This is where policy can make a huge difference. Making public spaces safe for women would be a major step forward in enhancing women's access to these spaces. Anecdotal evidence of the existence of pressure on local administrations in cities such as Bangalore, Hyderabad, and Pune, where the new outsourcing industry employs young women on night shifts, suggests that the governmental response to such pressure is important. Moreover, issues of security in general and women's security in particular have been taken up, for example, by India's National Association of Software and Service Companies. Backing by such influential lobbies is important in ensuring that security concerns are addressed. Yet, in rural areas, women seldom have lobbies that articulate this demand (Das 2008). Indeed, education and other, more subtle barriers continue to blunt the aspirations of women in this and other areas (box 4.5).

Box 4.5 What Do You Want to Do? Who Do You Want to Be? What Is Stopping You? The Aspirations of Young Girls in a South Delhi Slum

Shahana is a 14-year-old from Tigri, a huge slum consisting of around 3,500 shanties in south Delhi. She is among several young girls who met together for the World Bank's *Moving out of Poverty* pilot study in New Delhi. Shahana enjoys playing in the streets. She aspires to be an athlete some day. Shahana does not attend school. Instead, she says she feels sick walking in the summer heat everyday fetching pails of water.

Nine of the 11 girls interviewed for a discussion on youth aspirations in Tigri cannot read or write or dropped out of school after grade 6. Given the pressure on girls in the community to marry early and the stigma attached to women working, a majority prefer professions that are based in the home. Some in the group hope to make a living by doing minor tailoring jobs. Four of the 11 girls prefer this profession because it would allow them to earn a living while staying at home.

"Our parents would never allow us to go out and work," said Anita. "At least this way, we would be able to earn some money, if needed, even when we are married."

Another popular choice of profession is beautician. Four of the girls in the group expressed a preference for this profession. Most feel, however, that their parents are in no position to borrow money for their training.

"How can they spend money on my career when they also have to save for my sisters' and my dowry and wedding feast?" asks Shabnam.

The strain on family income was reported by most as the main reason for leaving school. A few said they left voluntarily because they had to walk two or three miles every day to the education center and had no energy left to study and do housework. The threat of physical harassment also restricts mobility and means that younger girls like Shahana, rather than older postpubescent ones, have to walk the one or two miles to fill water from community taps every day.

Source: Moving out of Poverty interviews.
Note: Names have been changed to protect privacy.

Conclusion

This chapter brings out selected aspects of female disadvantage in India. The main messages are as follows:

- Women today are doing better than their mothers' generation along a range of outcomes that include health, education, voice and visibility, and, to an extent, participation in the urban labor market.
- There are large inequalities across states in most areas of women's status.
- Poor access to reproductive health means that too many women die unnecessarily in childbirth.
- Violence against women is a strong correlate of a number of poor outcomes among women and their children.
- Despite a period of dramatic growth, female labor force participation rates virtually stagnated from 1983 to 2004–05. This is especially a problem in rural areas.
- Heterogeneity across social groups is pronounced, and Adivasi and Dalit women, in particular, are left out of nonfarm self-employment.
- Women seem stuck in farm-based employment; a major reason why they are not transitioning into nonfarm self-employment is their poor access to credit facilities.
- Over time, women's voice and agency both in the home and in public spaces have increased, but the extent to which this has impacted aggregate outcomes is unclear even at the local level.

Through examples and in the embedded discussion, this chapter also shows that, despite the deep cultural roots of many of the adverse outcomes among women, the innovative use of policy and programs can make a difference. Countries that have been more successful than India in improving outcomes among women demonstrate that national vision has helped shape policies not only that target women, but also in the relevant sectors more generally. In low-fertility countries of the Organisation for Economic Co-operation and Development, for instance, tax laws that reward employed women, while also encouraging fertility, have been central in the high levels of women's labor force participation. Sri Lanka showed us decades ago that fixing the health system with a view to lowering mortality rates had a salutatory impact on infant mortality, women's fertility, and women's status. In Bangladesh, a successfully implemented secondary school stipend program, along with growth in women's employment in the garment export industry (which requires basic literacy and numeracy), has meant that enrollments are now higher among girls than among boys. Girls enroll because, in addition to the stipend, their families perceive a return to sending their daughters to primary school. In contrast, the returns to education for girls in India come only at higher levels, that is, after the completion of secondary school. What each of these initiatives has accomplished is, first, to define an objective of gender equality or women's empowerment and, second, to determine which policy needs to be "engendered."

Notes

1. *The Laws of Manu*, trans. W. Doniger, with B. K. Smith (London: Penguin Books, 1991).

2. *Economist*. "Gendercide: The Worldwide War on Baby Girls: Technology, Declining Fertility and Ancient Prejudice Are Combining to Unbalance Societies," March 4, 2010. http://www.economist.com/node/15636231.

3. *Rabindranath Tagore: Selected Poems*, trans. W. Radice (London: Penguin Books, 1985).

4. *Bloomberg Businessweek*. "India's New Worldly Women," August 22, 2005. http://www.businessweek.com/magazine/content/05_34/b3948530.htm.

5. For a discussion of the pathways, see World Bank (2008).

6. Coparceners refers to a group of family members who acquire notional shares in joint family property, including land, to be realized upon inheritance. The amendment was extended to all states in 2005.

7. The legislation includes a comprehensive definition of domestic violence, but its critics claim that the provisions are too draconian and may be misused by women to harass men.

8. See World Bank (2008) for results on Bangladesh.

References

Agarwal, B. 1994. *A Field of One's Own: Gender and Land Rights in South Asia*. Cambridge: Cambridge University Press.

———. 1995. "Women's Legal Rights in Agricultural Land in India." *Economic and Political Weekly* 30 (12): 39–56.

Ahmed, S., M. Koenig, and R. Stephenson. 2006. "Effects of Domestic Violence on Perinatal and Early Childhood Mortality: Evidence from North India." *American Journal of Public Health* 96 (8): 1423–28.

Amin, S., N. Selim, and N. Waiz. 2006. "Causes and Consequences of Early Marriage in Bangladesh." Background report, Population Council, Dhaka, Bangladesh.

Anderson, S. 2003. "Why Dowry Payments Declined with Modernization in Europe but Are Rising in India." *Journal of Political Economy* 111 (2): 269–310.

Åsling-Monemi, K., R. Peña, M. C. Ellsberg, and L.-Å. W. Persson. 2003. "Violence against Women Increases the Risk of Infant and Child Mortality: A Case-Referent Study in Nicaragua." *Bulletin of the World Health Organization* 81 (1): 10–16. http://www.scielosp.org/pdf/bwho/v81n1/v81n1a04.pdf.

Ban, R., and V. Rao. 2008. "Tokenism or Agency? The Impact of Women's Reservations on Village Democracies in South India." *Economic Development and Cultural Change* 56 (3): 501–30.

Bardhan, P. K., D. Mookherjee, and M. Parra Torrado. 2006. "Impact of Reservations of Panchayat Pradhans on Targeting in West Bengal." Working Paper 774, *eSocialSciences.com.* http://www.esocialsciences.com/home/index.asp.

Basu, A. M. 1990. "Cultural Influences on Health Care Use: Two Regional Groups in India." *Studies in Family Planning* 21 (5): 275–86.

———. 1993. "Cultural Influences on the Timing of First Births in India: Large Differences That Add Up to Little Difference." *Population Studies* 47 (1): 85–95.

Bates, L. M., S. R. Schuler, F. Islam, and Md. K. Islam. 2004. "Socioeconomic Factors and Processes Associated with Domestic Violence in Rural Bangladesh." *International Family Planning Perspectives* 30 (4): 190–99.

Blau, F. D. 1998. "Trends in the Well-Being of American Women, 1970–1995." *Journal of Economic Literature* 36 (1): 112–65.

Bledsoe, C. H., and B. Cohen, eds. 1993. *Social Dynamics of Adolescent Fertility in Sub-Saharan Africa.* Population Dynamics of Sub-Saharan Africa. Washington, DC: National Academies Press.

Caldwell, J., P. H. Reddy, and P. Caldwell. 1983. "The Causes of Marriage Change in South India." *Population Studies* 37 (3): 343–61.

Chattopadhyay, R., and E. Duflo. 2004. "Women as Policy Makers: Evidence from a Randomized Policy Experiment in India." *Econometrica* 72 (5): 1409–43.

Chaudhury, N., J. Hammer, M. Kremer, K. Muralidharan, and F. H. Rogers. 2006. "Missing in Action: Teacher and Health Worker Absence in Developing Countries." *Journal of Economic Perspectives* 20 (1): 91–116.

Chavan, P. 2008. "Gender Inequality in Banking Services." *Economic and Political Weekly* 43 (47): 18–21.

Cohen, P. N., and S. M. Bianchi. 1999. "Marriage, Children and Women's Employment: What Do We Know?" *Monthly Labor Review* 122 (12): 22–31.

Das, M. B. 2006. "Do Traditional Axes of Exclusion Affect Labor Market Outcomes in India?" South Asia Social Development Discussion Paper 3, World Bank, Washington, DC.

———. 2008. "What Money Can't Buy: Getting Implementation Right for MDG3 in South Asia." In *Equality for Women: Where Do We Stand on Millennium Development Goal 3?* ed. M. Buvinić, A. R. Morrison, A. W. Ofosu-Amaah, and M. Sjöblom, 261–92. Washington, DC: World Bank.

Das, M. B., and S. Desai. 2003. "Why Are Educated Women Less Likely to Be Employed in India? Testing Competing Hypotheses." Social Protection Discussion Paper 0313, World Bank, Washington, DC.

Das Gupta, M. 1995. "Life Course Perspectives on Women's Autonomy and Health Outcomes." *American Anthropologist* 97 (3): 481–91.

Das Gupta, M., W. Chung, and L. Shuzhuo. 2009. "Is There an Incipient Turnaround in Asia's 'Missing Girls' Phenomenon?" Policy Research Working Paper 4846, World Bank, Washington, DC.

Deininger, K., A. Goyal, and H. Nagarajan. 2010. "Can Changes in Inheritance Legislation Improve Female Asset Ownership? Evidence from India's Hindu Succession Act." Policy Research Working Paper 5244, World Bank, Washington, DC.

Desai, S., and L. Andrist. 2010. "Gender Scripts and Age at Marriage in India." *Demography* 47 (3): 667–87.

Desai, S., A. Dubey, B. Joshi, M. Sen, A. Shariff, and R. Vanneman. 2010. *Human Development in India: Challenges for a Society in Transition.* New Delhi: Oxford University Press.

Desai, S., J. Noon, and R. Vanneman. 2008. "Who Gets Good Jobs? The Role of Human, Social and Cultural Capital." Paper prepared for the study Poverty and Social Exclusion in India, Indian Institute of Dalit Studies, New Delhi.

Dev, M., K. S. James, and B. Sen. 2002. "Causes of Fertility Decline in India and Bangladesh: Role of Community." *Economic and Political Weekly* 37 (43): 4447–54.

Duflo, E. 2003. "Grandmothers and Granddaughters: Old Age Pensions and Intrahousehold Allocation in South Africa." *World Bank Economic Review* 17 (1): 1–25.

Duflo, E., and P. Topalova. 2004. "Unappreciated Service: Performance, Perceptions and Women Leaders in India." Draft working paper (October), Department of Economics, Massachusetts Institute of Technology, Cambridge, MA.

Dyson, T., and M. Moore. 1983. "Kinship Structure, Female Autonomy, and Demographic Behavior in India." *Population and Development Review* 9 (1): 35–60.

Eswaran, M. 2002. "The Empowerment of Women, Fertility, and Child Mortality: Towards a Theoretical Analysis." *Journal of Population Economics* 15 (3): 433–54.

Government of India. 2008. *Eleventh Five Year Plan (2007–2012)*. New Delhi: Oxford University Press.

———. 2010. *Economic Survey 2009–10*. New Delhi: Oxford University Press.

Hadi, A. 2005. "Women's Productive Role and Marital Violence in Bangladesh." *Journal of Family Violence* 20 (3): 181–89.

Heise, L., J. Pitanguy, and A. Germain. 1994. "Violence against Women: The Hidden Health Burden." World Bank Discussion Paper 255, World Bank, Washington, DC.

Jejeebhoy, S. J. 1998. "Associations between Wife-Beating and Fetal and Infant Death: Impressions from a Survey in Rural India." *Studies in Family Planning* 29 (3): 300–08.

John, M. E., R. Kaur, R. Palriwala, S. Raju, and A. Sagar. 2008. *Planning Families, Planning Gender: The Adverse Child Sex Ratio in Selected Districts of Madhya Pradesh, Rajasthan, Himachal Pradesh, Haryana, and Punjab*. New Delhi: ActionAid and International Development Research Centre.

Kaur, R. 2004. "Across-Region Marriages: Poverty, Female Migration and the Sex Ratio." *Economic and Political Weekly* 39 (25): 2595–603.

Khandare, L. 2004. "Korku Adivasis in Melghat Region of Maharashtra: A Socio-economic Study; a Course Seminar." Department of Humanities and Social Sciences, Indian Institute of Technology, Mumbai. http://lalitreports. blogspot.com/2004/12/korku-adivasis-in-melghat-region-of.html.

Khera, R., and N. Nayak. 2009. "Women Workers and Perceptions of the National Rural Employment Guarantee Act." *Economic and Political Weekly* 44 (43): 49–57.

Kishor, S. 2007. "Documenting Domestic Violence in India." Presentation at "Health, Population, and Nutrition in India: Key Findings from the 2005–06 National Family Health Survey (NFHS-3)," Woodrow Wilson International Center for Scholars, Washington, DC, November 5.

Kishor, S., and K. Gupta. 2009. *Gender Equality and Women's Empowerment in India: National Family Health Survey (NFHS-3), India, 2005–06*. Mumbai: International Institute for Population Sciences; Calverton, MD: ICF Macro.

Kumar, K. G. 2008. "Empowering Women, Kudumbashree Way." *Businessline*, October 7. http://www.blonnet.com/2008/10/07/stories/ 2008100750872100.htm.

Luke, N., and K. Munshi. 2007. "Women as Agents of Change: Female Income and Mobility in Developing Countries." Working paper, Brown University, Providence, RI.

Manchanda, R. 2007. "Women: Grounded Till Thirty." *India Together*, August 21. http://www.indiatogether.org/2007/aug/wom-migrant.htm.

Marimuthu, P. 2008. "Effects of Female Age at Marriage on Birth Order and Utilization of Motherhood Services: A District Level Analysis." *Journal of Family Welfare* 54 (1): 79–84.

Márquez, G., A. Chong, S. Duryea, J. Mazza, and H. Ñopo, eds. 2007. *Outsiders: The Changing Patterns of Exclusion in Latin America and the Caribbean*. Economic and Social Progress in Latin America 2008. Washington, DC: Inter-American Development Bank.

Menon, N., and Y. van der Meulen Rodgers. 2009. "Self-Employment in Household Enterprises and Access to Credit: Gender Differences during India's Rural Banking Reform." Paper presented at the World Bank conference "Female Entrepreneurship: Constraints and Opportunities," Washington, DC, June 3.

Mincer, J. 1962. "Labor Force Participation of Married Women." In *Aspects of Labor Economics*, ed. H. G. Lewis, 63–105. Princeton, NJ: Princeton University Press.

Moreno, M., H. Nopo, J. Saavedra, and M. A. Torero. 2004. "Gender and Racial Discrimination in Hiring: A Pseudo Audit Study for Three Selected Occupations in Metropolitan Lima." IZA Discussion Paper 979 (January), Institute for the Study of Labor, Bonn.

Morrison, A., M. Ellsberg, and S. Bott. 2004. "Addressing Gender-Based Violence in the Latin American and Caribbean Region: A Critical Review of Interventions." Policy Research Working Paper 3438, World Bank, Washington, DC.

Munshi, K., and M. Rosenzweig. 2008. "The Efficacy of Parochial Politics: Caste, Commitment, and Competence in Indian Local Governments." Working Paper 964, Economic Growth Center, Yale University, Hartford, CN.

Muralidharan, K. 2007. "Teacher and Medical Worker Incentives in India." In *The Oxford Companion to Economics in India*, ed. K. Basu. New Delhi: Oxford University Press.

Nair, P. 2008. "Kudumbasree Empowering Women." *Karmakerala.com news*, January 28. http://news.karmakerala.com/2008/01/28/kudumbasree-empowering-women.

Narayan, D., G. Prennushi, and S. Kapoor. 2009. "People's Organizations and Poverty Escapes in Rural Andhra Pradesh." In *The Promise of Empowerment and Democracy in India*, ed. D. Narayan, 234–85. Vol. 3 of *Moving out of Poverty*. Washington, DC: World Bank; New York: Palgrave Macmillan.

Nussbaum, M. 2000. *Women and Human Development: The Capabilities Approach*. Cambridge: Cambridge University Press.

Panda, P., and B. Agarwal. 2005. "Marital Violence, Human Development and Women's Property Status in India." *World Development* 33 (5): 823–50.

PRB (Population Reference Bureau). 2008. "2008 World Population Data Sheet." PRB, Washington, DC. http://www.prb.org/pdf08/08WPDS_Eng.pdf.

Qian, N. 2008. "Missing Women and the Price of Tea in China: The Effect of Sex-Specific Earnings on Sex Imbalance." *Quarterly Journal of Economics* 123 (3): 1251–85.

Rajaraman, I., and M. Gupta. 2009. "Further Evidence on the Policy Impact of Randomized Political Reservation." Draft working paper, National Institute of Public Finance and Policy, New Delhi.

Registrar General. 2006. "Sample Registration System; Maternal Mortality in India, 1997–2003: Trends, Causes and Risk Factors." Working Paper 753, Registrar General, New Delhi.

Retherford, R. D., and T. K. Roy. 2003. "Factors Affecting Sex-Selective Abortion in India and 17 Major States." National Family and Health Survey Subject Report 21, International Institute for Population Sciences, Mumbai.

Sanyal, P. 2009. "From Credit to Collective Action: The Role of Microfinance in Promoting Women's Social Capital and Normative Influence." *American Sociological Review* 74 (4): 529–50.

Sen, A. 1992. "Missing Women: Social Inequality Outweighs Women's Survival Advantage in Asia and North Africa." *British Medical Journal* 304 (6827): 586–87.

———. 1999. *Development as Freedom*. New York: Alfred A. Knopf.

———. 2001. "Many Faces of Gender Inequality." *Frontline* 18 (22), October 27–November 9. http://www.hinduonnet.com/fline/fl1822/18220040.htm.

Singh, S., N. Dey, and A. Roy. 1994. "Child Marriage, Government and NGOs." *Economic and Political Weekly* 29 (23): 1377–79.

Sudarshan, R., and S. Bhattacharya. 2009. "Through the Magnifying Glass: Women's Work and Labor Force Participation in Urban Delhi." *Economic and Political Weekly* 44 (48): 59–66.

Teamlease. 2008. "Teamlease Poll, W5: Gender Difference in Bosses." Report, Synovate India, Mumbai. http://www.teamlease.com/images/reports/Gender%20difference.pdf.

Tharu, S., and K. Lalita, eds. 1993. *600 B.C. to the Early 20th Century*. Vol. 1 of *Women Writing in India: 600 B.C. to the Present*. New York: The Feminist Press.

Timmons, H. 2010. "The Female Factor: Female Bankers in India Earn Chances to Rule." *New York Times*, January 27. http://www.nytimes.com/2010/01/28/world/asia/28iht-windia.html?pagewanted=1&sudsredirect=true.

World Bank. 2006. "Survey of Gender Norms." World Bank, Dhaka, Bangladesh.

———. 2008. *Whispers to Voices: Gender and Social Transformation in Bangladesh*. Washington, DC: World Bank.

———. 2010a. "Social Protection for a Changing India." Draft report, Human Development Unit, South Asia Region, World Bank, New Delhi.

———. 2010b. *India's Employment Challenge: Creating Jobs, Helping Workers*. New Delhi: World Bank and Oxford University Press.

WHO (World Health Organization). 2005. *WHO Multi-country Study on Women's Health and Domestic Violence against Women*. Geneva: WHO.

ECO-AUDIT
Environmental Benefits Statement

The World Bank is committed to preserving endangered forests and natural resources. The Office of the Publisher has chosen to print *Poverty and Social Exclusion in India* on recycled paper with 50 percent postconsumer fiber in accordance with the recommended standards for paper usage set by the Green Press Initiative, a nonprofit program supporting publishers in using fiber that is not sourced from endangered forests. For more information, visit www.greenpressinitiative .org.

Saved:
- 7 trees
- 2 million BTUs of total energy
- 642 lbs. of CO_2 equivalent of greenhouse gases
- 3,092 gallons of waste water
- 188 lbs. of solid waste

green press
INITIATIVE

www.ingramcontent.com/pod-product-compliance
Lightning Source LLC
Chambersburg PA
CBHW070917270326
41927CB00011B/2607